Riding
in the
Backseat
with
my Brother

JUDI BLAZE

Published in the United States of America

Brilliant Books Literary
137 Forest Park Lane Thomasville
North Carolina 27360 USA

ISBN:
Paperback: 979-8-88945-351-2
Ebook: 979-8-88945-352-9

I thought we were normal. I thought all the students had been the "new kid" at some point. But I learned differently. My Gypsy Soul never left.

A faded red motel sits on the edge of a highway in a seedy area of Los Angeles. The front of the motel is wind-battered and the grounds are cluttered with cigarette butts, wrappers, and empty cans. Warm, smog-filled air and blazing sunlight stream through an open window where a curtain has fallen down. Inside, the motel is a combination living room and kitchen stacked high with cardboard boxes — some used to make walls for the makeshift bedroom in the corner.

Two toddlers, one with a drooping diaper, race around the room while a twig of a woman sits in a chair staring at nothing. Loud screams and squeals coming from the kitchenette don't stir the woman. The oldest child, Gary, climbs onto the counter and tries to reach a box of crackers, knocking down plastic cups that bounce and flip across the counter then land on the floor near Judy, the younger child. Gary grabs the box of crackers and throws them down to his little sister.

"Here, catch."

She jumps back and the crackers land on the floor. The mother, a skinny woman with paper-like skin and a pointy nose, rocks back and forth. Her sweater is wrapped tight around her. When there is a knock on the door, Judy jumps and screams while Gary crawls down from the counter and runs to the door. More knocking. Gary tries to reach the doorknob.

"Mama! Mama!" He turns to his mother and, when she doesn't move, he stands on tiptoes, barely able to reach the handle. Finally, the door opens and their Aunt Helen walks in. Her hair is combed back with a barrette holding it in place, and her neat white blouse is tucked in. Helen looks at the children and smiles, her eyes crinkling at the corners.

"Hi, Gary. Hi Judy. What's going on here, kids? How's your mama and the baby?" She bends to kiss them, her eyes darting around the cluttered and stinking room. She shuts the door with her foot. "Where's your baby brother?" Her smile changes to a look of concern when she sees their mother rocking back and forth in the chair. She sets her purse on the floor and walks over to Alice, whose eyes are focused in the distance.

Helen had seen Alice like this before. Judy walks over to her mother and stands close to Helen. "Alice? I just came over to see how you're doing with the new baby? Al thought I should check on you. Where is the . . ." She puts a hand on Alice's shoulder. Piercing baby cries rise from the corner, where sheets are piled high on a mattress on the floor. Helen walks past the unresponsive Alice toward the mattress and sees the sheets move.

"What the . . . ?"

She begins unwrapping the sheets and finally sees the wet, feces-covered baby. "Oh my god! Kids! Kids, bring me a towel, hurry! Hurry!"

The kids race toward the bathroom and return with a towel. Helen puts the towel around the baby and races to the bathroom, where she runs water and cleans the baby with the wet towel. The kids peek through the bathroom door and watch while Helen wraps a dry towel around the little body. Then she carries the baby past the kitchenette and stops in front of Alice, who is still staring.

"Alice? Why was the baby in there wrapped up? Alice?"

Gary walks close to Helen and tugs on her sleeve to get her attention. "Baby cries," he says.

Helen squeezes the baby close to her as tears well up in her eyes. The baby is now silent, sucking on his hand. Gary tugs on her sleeve again.

4

"Judy peed on the floor. In the cat's food." His furrowed eyebrows are like caterpillars against his dark skin. Helen closes her eyes, unaware of what Gary said. When she doesn't respond, he yells, "She peed, she's in *trouble*." Helen opens her eyes and touches the top of Gary's head, then goes to the closet and grabs some diapers, bottles, and baby clothes, and throws them in a garbage bag.

"Kids, I have to go now, but your daddy will be home soon. You tell him to come and see me." She kisses them and walks out with her purse, a bag in one hand and the towel-wrapped baby in the other.

The kids hear their father's truck pull up outside and run to the door, scattering the crushed crackers across the room. Al opens the door and walks in. The kids jump on his legs, laughing. He is dark-skinned, with black wavy hair framing a round, Irish face, and a spherical body to match. Cigarettes are rolled up in his shirt sleeve. Like his sister Helen, his eyes crinkle at the corners when he smiles. He tosses his lunch pail and thermos down on the counter and lunges for Gary, then Judy, hugging them.

"Hey, kids. Give your old fat daddy a kiss."

The kids giggle and kiss his cheek while he looks around the room, his eyes landing on his wife sitting and staring. After he gives each of the kids a twirl, he walks over to Alice and touches her shoulder.

"Alice. Alice?" he says, bending to kiss the top of her head. "Hey, honey, what's happening?" He shakes her shoulder and, when she doesn't respond, he goes to the bedroom area, looks at the empty mattress and pile of sheets, and walks back to her. His words come out louder than he had planned.

"Where's the baby, Alice?" When she doesn't answer he yells, "Where's the goddamned baby, Alice?" His face is red and his eyes bulge; veins stick out of his neck. Sweat begins to dot his forehead. The children stick close to Al. Gary bends to pick up the cat.

Finally, Alice blinks, turns her head, and looks up at him. "Baby's gone," she says.

Judy starts crying loudly and Gary pushes her out of the way. His eyes open wide and he takes in a deep breath before speaking. "Judy peed again on the floor." He glares at Judy.

Al shakes his head and blows air from his mouth, walking away before he turns back to Alice. He bends down and touches her hand, speaking gently. "What do you mean the baby's gone? Where's our new baby? Where's little Dougie, Alice?"

Gary goes up to his dad and taps his shoulder. "Auntie Helen took him. She wiped the poop off him, then took him. Can we have some more crackers?"

Al puts the kids in the backseat of the old Hudson and races to his sister's house — oblivious to Judy rolling down the window and sticking her face out into the wind. The tires squeal briefly as he brakes in front of Helen's house; the car is still moving slowly when he flings the door open. When it stops, he jumps out and the kids stare silently. "Stay there," he yells as he races to the door and begins pounding on it.

Embedded in a mass of avocado trees and lilacs, Helen's house faces a busy road cloaked in the unnatural quiet following rush hour. Al's thumping resonates down the street as early evening light plays with the lavender flowers.

A voice comes from behind the door. "Stop that pounding, Al, and come in. Figured you'd be here soon enough. You ever gonna get a phone?" Helen opens the door and he walks in. The house is modest, with furniture showing signs of wear. Family photos line two walls and cooking smells drift from the kitchen.

Al pushes past her and turns. "Why'd you take the baby, Sis?" Pain twists his face and his eyes sag with sorrow, making him look older than his thirty-five years.

Helen folds her arms. "She can't take care of him, Al. I went over there, the place was a mess. Piss and shit everywhere and the baby wrapped in sheets barely able to breathe." Her voice is stern and firm.

Al sits down on the couch, bends his head, and folds his hands.

"Let me get you some coffee. I'll be right back." Helen goes to the kitchen and brings him back a cup of coffee. Al continues to stare down into his hands while the news blares from the TV. Helen hands the cup of coffee to Al; he takes a sip, then looks up at Helen.

"I don't know what to do. Alice has been like this for a long time. You know that.

Hell, I have to work, I can't . . ."

Helen sits beside him on the couch. "Of course you can't. Without you working those kids would starve. It's not your fault, Al."

Al takes another sip. "I don't know . . . It *feels* like it is . . ." Tears well up in his eyes. He hurriedly wipes them away, trying to regain his composure when he sees Helen staring at him.

"It's not your fault, Al. Don't waste your time beating yourself up." After a slight pause, she says, "We have more important things to talk about." She points through her open living room window toward the car where the kids are now hanging out the window bare-assed. "Look at them. Those kids need better than that. You can't afford to take care of all of them, Al. At least let me try it with Dougie. Let me give him the chance to grow up in one place, give him some security."

This time a tear escapes and rolls down his cheek. He breathes in deeply, his face scrunching up.

Helen smiles and tries to lighten the mood. "Hell, the way you move around you would be lucky to fit all the kids in the car, let alone the cats." She laughs, but Al remains silent. After a moment of awkward silence, he seems to come to, and sits up straight. His face lightens as a thought visibly arises in his mind.

"I could quit moving, settle down. I know I've said that before, but . . ."

Helen touches his hand and pats it. "You mean well, Al. We all know you do, but settling down is not ever going to happen. You're as much an Irish Traveler as any of 'em. Hell, it's not for all travelers," she said, walking towards the window. "I just happened to be able to settle down. Let me keep Dougie. I can raise him as my own. Right here. I'm not a traveler. You know I won't move." Helen turns and heads toward the kitchen, then turns. "You think about it. I'm going to get some cookies for you to take to the kids. I've got a meat pie coming out of the oven, too."

Al takes a few deep breaths, fills his cheeks with air, then blows out. He sees the photos of his whole family before him, scattered on the walls and along the shelves, and walks over to them. All Irish Travelers, except for Helen and a handful of others.

It's not like I can't trust her, he thinks. *I can always count on her being here.*

Helen returns carrying a large cardboard box. She sets the box on the floor and walks over to Al, hugging him. Tears have streaked his dark face, and when she sees them, she begins to cry as well. Unable to talk, Helen points to the bedroom and walks toward it as Al follows. The baby is asleep on Helen's bed. On a table nearby are boxes of diapers, pajamas, and blankets. Al bends down and kisses Dougie's head, then touches his cheek with his thumb.

"Take care of my baby." He turns and leaves the room.

Helen hands him the box before he leaves the house. "There's a fruit pie in there too. Don't worry, Al. I will take care of him. You don't have to worry about that."

Two weeks later, an orange U-Haul trailer sits in front of the red motel attached to Al's dented black Hudson. Al and Alice are putting the last of the boxes inside it. Gary and Judy jump up and down in the backseat on blankets and pillows that cover a layer of boxes, laughing. Gary screams through the window, "Judy's diaper fell off!" and then breaks down into a fit of laughter.

Al closes the back of the trailer while Alice grabs her purse and sweater, then they get into the car. Al slides into the driver's seat and adjusts the mirror while the kids continue jumping up and down. "Hey! You kids settle down! If I have to stop this car, you know what will happen." Gary laughs and Judy joins in.

"You always say that. You'll dump us off like you did the cat. You wouldn't ever do that to us! Never!" Gary screams with laughter. Alice winces almost imperceptibly, and then makes a show of adjusting herself, pushing her purse under the seat and looking for her sweater. She turns to the kids with a scowl that quickly becomes a smile.

"Come on, kids. You listen to your dad and settle down. You're getting loud."

They quit laughing and look out the window as the houses of the neighborhood glide by. Gary spots his friend's house and shows Judy.

"Look! Hey, there's Martin's house. I like him. Can't we stay?"

"Nope. Got a better place to go," Al says as he lights a cigarette.

Gary looks sad, then perks up as if remembering something. He jumps up and bends over the front seat, his upper body leaning toward his dad. "Hey! Hey, Dad! What about the baby?"

"What's that?"

"You know! The baby! What about him? Is he coming with us?"

Al looks over at Alice. She looks straight ahead, her face expressionless. Al looks back at the road and then again at his wife, trying to get her attention. "Oh yeah. The baby. He's your little cousin, and when we come back, we'll go visit him." Al finally makes eye contact with Alice and nudges her with his hand. "Won't we, honey? Come and see him? As often as we want." She turns and looks at him, gives him a wan smile, then stares out the window. "You'll always be around him, kids. No matter where we go."

Al sees the grim look on Alice's face and gives her shoulder a playful nudge. He smiles and says, "Come on, smile. It's only gonna get better, right kids?" He laughs while the kids scream with excitement. Al looks in the rearview mirror and sees the happy look on his children's faces. "Hell, we're going to *Montana*!"

The kids yell, eyes bulging, "Yay! Where's Montana?" Gary asks. "It doesn't matter," Al says. "We're going to the Big Sky Country!"

Chapter 1

As I lay in my bed, my sister on the floor nearby, I can hear the insistent scratching from inside the trailer walls — probably a rat looking for warmer territory. Goosebumps formed on my ten-year-old spaghetti arms and my breath came out in clouds, dim in the early morning light. The only warm spot was in the front room where the little heater sat by the Charlie Brown Christmas tree. Christmas morning and still too early to get up, all I could do was wait and listen for sounds of the others.

He liked to move, my dad. He liked to check out the country and see if it was true that you could find a pot of gold at the end of the rainbow — and he hauled all of us along with him, no matter the season. Just because it was Christmas Day didn't mean we were going to be spared a cross-country move.

When the trailer shook, the below-zero easterly wind reached through the walls, and the sound alone made me shiver. Because my bedroom was divided from my parents' by only a thin plywood wall, I could also hear their bed shaking passionately last night. It kept me awake when all I wanted to do was sleep through the anticipation of the morning. There was no way I could get back to sleep with the excitement of the day ahead, thinking about the presents under the tree — two for each of us, plus a stocking.

I'd already checked it out. My brother Gary and I got up during the night every Christmas Eve and went through our stockings, pulling out the good stuff and shoving the apples and oranges back down to the toe, where sticky pieces of hard candy encrusted the fruit. This time, Gary, a year older than me, slept on the couch, no doubt having already tasted a few of the sweets.

Irish Traveler blood coursed the stratums of our people, including me, and put my distant and current family on the path of the wanderers. Members of my extensive family say that growing up on the road keeps your mind sharp. You learn to go with the flow, wherever that may take you. Nobody said it was easy leaving your friends behind or abandoning your belongings on the side of the road. But when I think about the brother who was given away as a baby, I realize that our worries about a bike or toy being left behind were unimportant. I grew up knowing things could change at any given time and during any situation. When Dad got itchy feet, or Mama started to hate the place we'd just moved into, it was time to climb into the Hudson and hit the road. My parents never wavered in their belief that the *grass is greener on down the road*. And I guess it was, at least for them.

When I finally heard sounds coming from the front of the trailer, I walked down the short hall and into the small room where my sister and brother sat at the base of the scraggly little tree that had been shoved into the corner of the living room. That was all that remained — that and the ratty furniture that came with the rental, and a few boxes we would pile in the backseat later, covering them with bedding for Gary's bed. Pillows or blankets would also be piled on the floor to cover the nasty hump in the middle I'd grown to hate. My road bed.

My parents stirred in the other room and I knew they were getting up. Since Gary already knew what was in his stocking, all he wanted to do was open a present. He was so excited that he jumped up and ran around, his brown, dangly arms flailing in wild circles. Linda, the baby of the family, squealed that she would tell if we sneaked a peek at a present before Mama and Dad got up. We glared at her, knowing that she would do it, too. The room echoed with our voices.

"You kids didn't open any, did you?" Mama asked as she entered the room, her pink robe twisted around her skeletal body and crisscrossed bobby pins beginning to fall out of the coils of her hair.

"Whatcha doing up so early?" Dad asked as he walked toward us, his belly spilling over the sagging waistband of his pajamas, his black hair sticking out like wings from his temples. "You packed and ready to hit the road?" We could tell by his poorly- suppressed smile and the twinkle in his eyes that he was only joking.

"Nooooo!" we all screamed. By the time the family was seated around the tree with the rattling space heater spewing warm air, we kids were like animals, clawing at gifts. Dad sat on the brown chair with cotton spilling from the armrests, while the rest of us sat on the icy floor. We dumped piles of hard candy out of our stockings — striped ribbon sweets that had become damp from the fruit now stuck to the insides of the stockings, edible even with the red fuzz coating them.

We began opening our presents before our hands got too cold. Our gifts — one toy and a pair of pajamas each — would soon be stuffed into the U-Haul and remain there until we arrived at our new location. Then it would be like Christmas all over again! I glanced at the doll staring up at me as I pulled off the bright blue bow and newspaper wrapping. Mama thought all girls liked dolls. I looked in the doll's eyes and saw a lost little girl with a hollow, distant stare. I didn't want to be plagued by something that looked at me like that.

Dad said he couldn't wait to get out of Glasgow, and we all agreed; it was past time to find a new home, one where it wasn't so bitterly cold. "Damn cold here — too cold to work, too cold to go outside and take a piss," he said.

"Al," Mama said, shushing him with her hand and making a *tsk*-ing sound with her tongue. Not that her speech was any less coarse; just last week I had watched her call a bill collector a "dumb fuck" who'd damn well better clear out before her husband got home. "If you're still here when he gets home, he'll kick the holy shit right out of you!"

"Piss up a rope" was one of her favorite sayings. Mama used Dad as a bogeyman a lot, against both hapless bill collectors and us kids. "You just wait 'till your father gets home and I tell him what you just said!"

By this time tomorrow, we'd be long gone, all five of us jammed into the car with a couple of cats, feeling the temperature rise with each mile as we headed south.

Glasgow in the winter wasn't for sissies. Dad said anyone who loitered in the Montana winter got what he deserved. But this time around, the deeper into December it got, the more I began to think we might not be moving after all, and this time I wanted to.

Dad, known to others as Al, had begun preparing for our trip the week before by pawing through stuff and discarding nonessentials, which he always did before a move. Then, the day prior, he had thrown most of the remainder into the U-Haul. But he hadn't planned the date very well — either that or he was actually unaware that moving day was Christmas.

Wherever we ended up, we would love the place at first. Soon enough, though, that would change. It usually started with Mama, who began to find reasons to hate a place even before we had completely unpacked. Then it would seep into the rest of us — that attitude, that contempt in Mama's twisted, tight-lipped frown. Of course, when we kids got older we became capable of forming our own opinions. Crossing the border into Montana the previous summer, we sang, "Montana, Montana, glory of the West . . ."

Later today, we'd all be cursing the snow and cold and the nasty, freezing trailer we left behind. Then we'd sing, "California, here we come . . ." even if we weren't sure that's where we'd end up. At this point, the precise destination didn't matter, as long as it was somewhere else. In fact, if the car broke down, that would be our destination, at least for a few months or until the car was fixed.

Once, on a cold day in a trailer not far from ours, while helping my aunt wrap presents, I asked about us as intelligently as a ten-year-old could. I wanted to know about this family of wanderers who couldn't find a permanent place to land. I was becoming aware that we picked up and left town far more often than most people and I wanted to know why. She had told me it was because we were *travelers* and that's why we moved so much — we had it in our blood. I had never heard anyone refer to us as travelers, and I had no idea what it meant. I wasn't sure there should be a name attached to the way we lived, because maybe that would make it seem just a little too weird.

People asked us all the time why we moved the way we did. Most of our friends had never heard of such a thing, and neighbors from the time I can remember questioned us regularly when we first moved to a new place. Sometimes they looked at us like we were a pack of orphans or a family of refugees. We never knew how to respond — besides Mama's *piss up a rope* — so we usually answered the way Dad would: "Because we like to see the country." I think at one time we truly believed that.

Before we took off that Christmas day, Dad agreed we could stay long enough to have Christmas dinner at his brother's house. Our Uncle Bob, Aunt Babe, and their three kids lived down the narrow lane of the tiny trailer court. It seemed they were going to hole up for the winter in Montana. Dad called Uncle Bob stupid for wanting to stay, adding that he most likely wouldn't get any work until spring and would be living off whatever he could get from welfare.

Uncle Bob's trailer was larger than ours — fourteen feet wide, at least, with a tilt- out porch that the rest of the trailer court envied. Bob and Babe also had carpeted floors instead of the slick, stained linoleum we had in our place. Their trailer was properly grounded, too, unlike ours, where an electrical shock threw me across the room one day while doing the dishes. My scream, I was told, could be heard all over the trailer court.

Even though Dad clearly itched to get going, we stomped into my uncle's house, snow falling from our boots as smells of turkey, yams, and pie greeted us. In no time at all, Dad and Uncle Bob were in a hot discussion about work and politics.

I liked watching Dad and Uncle Bob together, looking at them and their similarities: black, wavy hair and dark skin and eyes. Bob's body was much thinner than Dad's — muscles in Dad's arms rippled like a fat worm on a hill, while Bob's arms were thin and shapeless, like limp snap beans. They both had a ruddy brown look, like worn work boots, and even had the same infectious smile.

I might have been young, but I knew they were attractive because of the way women stared at them hungrily while they worked on a roof, stripped to the waist. They looked like twin blow-up dolls, except that Bob was only partly inflated.

I liked to imagine them as more than just brothers; beyond that, like partners in crime. I visualized them doing some of the things I'd only heard about. Bits and pieces of stories floated around from time to time, like them being involved in the black market.

Their father, my Grandpa Art, had taught them how to fight, talk a good talk, and survive on the streets. I also heard that Grandpa Art had put Dad and his three sisters in the Montana State Orphanage in Twin Bridges when things got too hard on the road.

Grandpa Art kept Uncle Bob, the youngest, with him and my grandmother, returning two years later to get the others. I was heartbroken when I heard the stories that came from that orphanage — how Dad suffered through the hardships with no food; how many of the nuns treated the kids like slaves.

Dad said he would never drop his kids off just because times were hard. "Family is all you have, and if you don't have that, you don't have shit."

But later I learned of my baby brother who was given away a few weeks after he was born, so I had my doubts about who he would — or wouldn't — give away.

I'd been asking Dad about his time in the orphanage for as long as I could remember, and I was always surprised at how willing he was to talk about it, especially since he hated the place. We were always morbidly thrilled to hear the stories, even if we'd heard them before.

"Grandpa Art and your grandma put us all in there, just down the road from where we used to live. I'll take you there someday. The buildings are still there," Dad said one day at lunch while spreading a thick layer of butter on his bread.

Another time, he said, "The folks kept us there for two years before picking us up.

They traveled a lot and got ran out of places, couldn't work half the time, and usually didn't have any money." He laughed as if being poor was a joke. "Some kids had it way worse than we did, though. My dad, your grandpa, was a real horse trader — a crook in some ways. It's no wonder he couldn't stay anywhere long — gave us all a bad reputation, too."

Dad said close to 400 kids in the school worked almost continuously in the vegetable gardens, the kitchens, or tending to the livestock in barns and chicken coops; they even had a shoe shop. It was the orphans' job to keep it all going and keep everything clean.

We sat in awe as he relived his days from the 1930s inside the walls of such a horrendous place. "The kids who peed the bed at night were whipped, and some were locked in a dark cloakroom for days," Dad would say. "During the night, the matrons tied their hands with ropes to keep them from playing with themselves, and sometimes they made us eat a salt shaker of salt. They thought that was the big cure for peeing at night, I guess."

Dad showed us a picture from a large, torn-up box of black and white photos he had dragged with him throughout the years. It showed him standing outside, in front of large pillars near a sign that said, "Montana State Orphans Asylum," later renamed the Montana Children's Center. He was barefoot in the snow, posing for the camera. His pants were several sizes too large and his face was as sad and vacant as a mug shot.

"Why did they do that to you guys? And how come they only kept Uncle Bob with them?" I wanted to know everything about the orphanage and Dad's sad but exciting past.

"My folks, and probably their folks, who were the true Travelers, didn't know any better, I guess; they were *real* Gypsies." Dad saw Linda and I drop our eyes. I thought Linda was going to cry as her lip quivered.

"Ah hell, it wasn't all that bad," he said. "Unless you were one of the kids who got hung from a coat hook for doing something you weren't supposed to — or if you had to shovel snow barefoot, without gloves. *Then* it could be bad."

I looked at him and wondered how he survived and how he could be so nonchalant about it. Every time I heard about the orphanage, it made me sad to think Dad had lost two years of his childhood there.

"See how good you kids have it? Now finish up, then do the dishes."

Growing up, I considered the road to be my link to adventure and joy. I recognized it as my bloodline, my twisted rope of taffy leading to far-off places. Relatives who weren't like us said it was more likely that my dad just had itchy feet, always chasing a rainbow. Dad's sister, Helen, once told me, "Your papa doesn't know any other way, and he's not willing to try to change like some of us did. 'The grass is greener' seems to be his motto." She added that he'd probably be traveling for the rest of his life. I asked her what was wrong with that, and she just rolled her eyes and walked away.

When Aunt Babe untied the apron from her wide middle, she yelled that dinner was ready. We grabbed the chairs from the circle of musical chairs where we had been playing and headed to the living room, where she had set up a table for the adults, with plates on end tables for us kids. We chose to eat on the floor near the splintered, jagged tables instead, and I had never tasted such a delicious dinner.

We wolfed it all down as if we were starving, then examined our cousins' Christmas booty. As much as I envied them, getting to stay home and have fun with their Christmas, I knew it was only a matter of time before they joined us, or moved somewhere else. My cousins were no more immune to the traveling virus than we were.

"You kids get enough to eat?" Aunt Babe asked, scooping up the dirty dishes and leftover bowls of food. I went to help her dry the dishes and saw that Mama had taken a seat in the living room and scrunched down in a soft chair, oblivious to what we were doing, staring at the toys scattered in front of her. She wasn't always so anti-social, she just had her moods.

Dad hadn't yet decided for sure where we would go — or at least he hadn't told us. "Somewhere warm," was all he'd say. One thing I learned early on was that you didn't always end up where you were told you would, because if the car broke down, a job came up, or a town caught Mama's eye, we stopped where we were. It was always a surprise — sometimes good, sometimes bad.

Mama, who could find fault with paradise, loved the road as much as Dad, even though she pretended it was all his doing, dragging her hither and yon against her will. Her excitement grew each time the move got closer, and she'd explode with nervous chatter. "Make sure you pack everything; doesn't mean you'll get to take it, but pack it anyway," she would say, grinning, childlike excitement in her eyes. But however much she loved the new place when we first unpacked, she soon grew to hate everything about it. There was too much noise, too many bugs or plumbing problems, too much or too little of something.

"I hate this place, there are bugs everywhere!" she'd scream. Her tantrums began like subtle cries, like a toddler's, then grew steadily until they were out of control. She urged us all to hate the new place as much as she did, but, as time went on, we tended more and more to find at least something positive about our new surroundings, if only a new friend.

Mama was raised in a strict, religious home with little love, lots of fighting, and no adventure. When she married Dad, a dark sailor with dimples that spun her heart, she got all the adventure she could stand. Of course, her mom and dad disowned her for marrying a common carpenter whose only claim to fame was flashing eyes and a sweet soul. Mama said her parents felt Dad was beneath her, and of course, that iced it with Dad, who told them to fuck off right to their faces.

When you're a traveler, you grow up fast in some ways, and not at all in others.

We were streetwise but almost completely ignorant of anything resembling *culture*, unless you want to count Mama's drawings and cartoon characters as a form of art. We were ignorant of many social norms most people took for granted, and we usually found ourselves on the outside looking in. But we never felt like outcasts, because we were our own best friends. Dad called us *Black Irish*. He always said you had to be two things, self-confident and streetwise, and maybe later on get a tattoo on each arm like he did. He also boasted about the tattoo across his chest, and the other one near the scar he got from a street fight while trying to protect his best friend, Jiggs. He said Jiggs helped him out of fights, no matter how many people there were. "Can't be a man if ya haven't gotten any scars," he said while I looked curiously at one of his tattoos one day.

When we left that gray Christmas afternoon, our tires crunching between cramped rows of trailers, we waved to our cousins and the few neighborhood kids brave enough to venture outdoors to play with new toys. The cold attached itself to everything, bitter white rimes of frost twisted by a snarling wind. I wasn't sorry to leave that town when sun and warmth awaited us somewhere else. Let the frozen pipes be taken care of by the next tenant; we were going where the water didn't freeze.

Once on the road, things began to look better — the sky turned a spongy blue and the ground, with its mantle of white, looked pure and inviting. We were safe inside the belly of the car, our mobile familial womb. Gary and I sat high in the backseat on boxes and blankets, and six-year old Linda sat in the front between Mama and Dad.

As Dad struggled occasionally to keep the car and trailer on the icy road, the three frightened cats yowled, jumping from the front seat to the back, strange noises coming from their throats. With hair sticking out like porcupine quills, their terrified faces matched their cries. Wherever we went, Mama always had cats. She let them run around the house, oblivious to the smell of cat piss. Some cats made the move with us, some didn't; the cats who did go often didn't make the complete trip, and were left to find another home.

When a panicked cat jumped on Dad's shoulder, sinking its claws into his meaty flesh, Dad pulled the car to the side of the road and brought it to a skidding halt. Then he took the cat out and put it on a wet school parking lot. Whitey, the now-banished cat and newest member of our family hadn't yet gotten the hang of traveling. Gary and I sucked in our breath and didn't say a word, while Linda sobbed.

Then I heard screaming coming from my mouth. "Daddy, why did you do that?"

Even though I wasn't as attached to the cat as Mama and Linda, it still frightened me to think of how easy it was to get rid of something — much like a baby brother, I assumed. Whitey crouched miserably in the parking lot. My heart pounded while I watched the cat creep through the deep snow and nestle under a small pine tree. Linda continued to blubber and tears streamed down Mama's narrow face.

"Will you all just shut up? We'll get another cat. Jesus, all of you just calm down! It's only a goddamned cat for Christ's sake." Dad had that look on his face that said he'd reached the end of his rope. Sweat spread across his forehead, accentuating deep-set wrinkles, and his mouth was set in a straight line. The two remaining cats crawled to the backseat and up onto the ledge in the back window, staring out with slanted eyes and ears flattened to their heads. They knew the score and wanted no part of that parking lot.

"You could be next," Gary said, turning to whisper to the two remaining cats.

We both placed bets as to which cat would be dumped first. Usually, it was the one with the worst disposition and the sharpest claws. However cavalier we tried to act, we were somewhat unnerved. As Linda wailed and Mama sniffled, Dad assured us all we'd get another damn cat to take its place as soon as we got a new place to live. Then he started the engine, inhaled a lungful of air, and blew it out forcefully. The whole incident ended as fast as it had started.

After fifteen minutes of uncomfortable silence, Mama — a tiny rogue of a woman — grabbed a jar of Vicks from her bag and began rubbing it on her chest, filling the car with menthol fumes. When she didn't reek of Vicks, the overpowering odor of Bengay emanated from her bony white shoulders.

"You wait 'til you kids get older; you'll see how much you need this stuff," she'd say whenever we complained about the smell. She wasn't much older than thirty-five at the time. Once a pretty little woman, Mama had let herself go, not caring much about what she wore, how her hair looked, or how medicinal she smelled. She rarely looked as good as the other road people, who didn't look that great either. But she had her fun side, and when she was in a good mood, played with us or took us skating or bike riding.

Although far from a slave to fashion, Mama liked anything red, and most of the time wore a tattered red sweater she couldn't bear to part with. When given the chance to buy something new — which wasn't very often — you could bet it would be red. She wanted to be our friend and playmate more than anything, certainly more than being our mother. Childlike, my mother swirled with Peter Pan and bounced around like her favorite child star, Shirley Temple. She respected and perhaps even envied Shirley Temple enough to want to be her. To *be* her! But since that would never happen, she wanted *me* to be her.

"Let's just take you in and get you a new hairdo," Mama said one day when I had just turned eight. She plopped me in the chair, told the beautician to curl it up good and tight with little rods, then she sat and read a magazine. When my hair was done I looked in the mirror and felt like someone's little granny. I walked out to the waiting room without saying a word. I may have only been a kid, but I knew this was not a hairdo for a young girl like me. Mama looked at me with delight seeping from her pores. She praised the beautician the whole time, counting out a handful of change she had saved up to get the disturbing act done.

Mama wanted to be like the beautiful screen stars of the day, and in her mind she was, and she danced about to prove it, her little legs kicking up a storm. She taught me how to jitterbug, and that a TV dinner meant never having to slave over a hot stove. When I grew up and had my own family, I should keep that in mind. God help her, she could only cook very simple two-dimensional foods; fried eggs with black lace hugging the edges, French toast swimming in black-flecked bacon grease, or charred meatloaf filled with chunks of bread, onions, eggs, and salt. She had never learned to cook growing up, and clearly lacked the desire to learn as an adult.

Mama liked to play games and do artwork with us. Thankfully, her artistic abilities far exceeded her talent for cooking. The colorful cartoon characters she drew or painted on whatever paper she could find were scotch-taped to the walls and each door in our house, making us laugh. If nothing else, she could tape them over the holes in the walls. That was her sunny side, creating whimsical artwork and being our playmate; the other side was filled with tantrums and wild mood swings, which only became worse as time went on.

My little sister, Linda, had hair so thick it remained matted most of the time, until Dad took thinning shears to it. When she sat in the front seat, she hurled questions from one parent to the other until Mama yelled at her to shut up. Dad told Linda about places he had lived until it was obvious that Mama's jealousy was growing out of control. She had a short fuse when it came to Linda, and no matter what happened it was usually

Linda's fault. In the meantime, Gary and I sat in the back trying to think up ways to make the trip a little more exciting.

Within hours of leaving Glasgow, Dad hollered that we had just crossed the Montana border. "I swear I can see the light of a better day ahead," he said, rolling down the window and inhaling the fresh air. "God, it feels good to get out of Montana!"

Chapter 2

We blew into Soap Lake, Washington in spitting rain and the half-light of dawn.

The light sifting through the windows of the Hudson was just enough to disclose the forms of quiet shapes in the front and back seats. The car hummed while everyone except Dad and I slept. Light danced through the windows with each passing car, and all I heard was the hypnotic hum of our tires and the sound of my father's Zippo lighter as he lit yet another cigarette, letting the smoke drift through the car like a soft fog.

When we finally stopped the car, I jumped up from the floor to look over the front seat. Dad rolled his thermos of coffee aside, opened the door to get out, and headed for the burlap bag he had tied tight to the front of the car. The canvas bag was a focal point in our travels and went with us everywhere, providing water for drinking and roadside bathing as well as for cooling and replenishing the radiator when it boiled over.

Dad tipped the bag up and let the water flow into his mouth and down his chin, wiping the drips away with the back of his hand. His short-sleeved, plaid shirt strained to keep his muscles imprisoned under the worn cotton.

Mama slumped against the car door like a rag doll, her red sweater wrapped tight around her narrow shoulders, worry lines penciled across her forehead. It had been a long night.

When Dad got back in the car, I whispered, "Daddy, what time is it? When will we get there?"

Dad flipped open the lid of his Zippo, a tinny sound in the quiet car. Glowing lights from the flame outlined his face, flashing on his drooping eyes and illuminating his curled half-smile. He looked both happy and sad at the same time, his face stretched out in all directions.

"What are you doing awake? Well, Soap Lake's just ahead, just saw the sign back there," he said. "It's five o'clock; you should be asleep. I'm pulling over soon to get a little shut-eye. I can't stay awake. Wish you were old enough to drive, I'd stick you up here. Someday."

"Are we gonna live there? I thought we were going to California." I had looked forward to seeing people we already knew and maybe some of our relatives. I liked it when relatives trailed us, and so did Dad, sometimes.

"It's like a goddamned hillbilly caravan," Dad had once said when he fixed his mirror on the cousins, aunts, and uncles who followed along with trailers stuck to the back of their cars. His voice was gruff, but he had that corner smile and a twinkle in his eyes.

"I'm gonna check it out," he said now. "We may have to stay here. We're almost out of gas. Better be a job waiting for me or we're shit out of luck, Doodle. You've lived here before; probably don't remember because you were so young. I heard that George and his family may be living around here." George was our cousin who traveled even more than we did.

What Dad said about being out of gas should have shocked my young ears, but I'd heard it before and it always seemed to work out, so I wasn't too worried. There had been more than a few times where we ended up living wherever we ran out of gas or money.

Mama muttered something, then readjusted her pillow. When she woke up she'd find herself a few hundred miles further than where she was when she fell asleep.

Soap Lake stunk. It sat in the desert of eastern Washington and had a lake filled with mineral water they advertised as being able to heal whatever needed healing. The creepy water created suds around the shore, cloud-gray, and bubbling up at the edges like Mama's eggs. Downtown, the sidewalks were dotted with drinking fountains that disgorged the precious healing water. The town had little to offer besides that — it was as though an enormous hand had plucked up this pointless collection of structures and lobbed them near the lake, like flinging pennies in a pond but forgetting to make a wish.

A sign in the middle of town shared the secret of the wondrous mineral water and how people from all over the world came here to drink it, wallow in it, and feel the water's healing powers. Soap Lake got its name from the term *Smokiam*, meaning healing waters, from the Native Americans who went there for centuries to treat themselves and their animals with the waters. But to us, it was just stinky water and a lake in which we couldn't swim.

We didn't live in Soap Lake long enough to get friendly with many other kids; in fact, I think the only friends we had were each other. Dad rented a neglected house built on a hill that spilled toward the highway and the town below. The front porch sagged, threatening to detach itself and roll down the hill if provoked, and the wallpaper hung from the living room walls in long, forlorn strips. We three kids shared a bedroom, Gary on the floor, and Linda and I on a bed comprised mainly of box springs, covered with a thick sleeping bag donated by the last tenant.

Since it was close to downtown, the house gave Mama easy access to window- shopping — as well as a good number of neighbor ladies to drink coffee with while Dad was at work. Most days, Mama gossiped with the neighbors then hurried home just before Dad arrived, feigning exhaustion from a long day of housework despite the stack of breakfast dishes in the sink that said otherwise. Not that anyone cared. We didn't discourage Mama from running around like a kid in search of adventure; we found it far better than seeing her other side, the dark side that seemed to grow more each day, where her *nervousness* made our life miserable and grew daily.

As usual, the house was prowled by a tribe of cats. Mama replaced unfortunate Whitney with a sickly-looking cat she named Tigger that had a case of ringworm, which Linda and I caught right away. Mama got enough medicine from the vet to treat all of us.

Everything was fine until later when she adopted another stray cat she found on the corner near the grocery store. It had fleas and ticks, and another round of medication was needed. Dad said if she continued to bring diseased cats home she'd better get a job to pay for the meds. We all knew that was a hollow threat since Mama hadn't been gainfully employed since she was eighteen. Mama couldn't live without her cats; in fact, sometimes I thought she wished we kids were cats. I visualized us prowling around and Mama giving us attention.

"They're my babies," she'd say when any of us grumbled about the house being overrun by cats. She gave them air kisses, too, and ticky-tacky names popular in the '50s and '60s, like Elvis or Johnny Cat, short for Johnny Cash. She talked to them in a cooing baby voice and generally treated them better than she treated us most of the time — or, at least, that's what I thought.

I began hating cats, wishing they would run away, and Gary felt the same way, talking about ways he could make them leave. Once he tied two of the cats' tails in a knot and hung them over the clothesline, something he'd no doubt learned from one of our rowdy cousins who played in the backfields shooting gophers or anything else that would pop into view.

A long clothesline ran the length of the backyard in our Soap Lake house, and Gary and I were determined to find a use for it, besides hanging wet clothes on.

"Wanna play a game?" Gary asked one day before we got enrolled in school. Mama said she wanted all of us to get used to the town before starting school and Dad agreed since Christmas break had only just ended.

I asked Gary what kind of game he had in mind; the peculiar grin on his face was too wide for it not to be something outrageous.

"Let's play cops and robbers. You be the robber." His voice still had a boyish squeak to it, matching his scrawny physique. We played until I got caught and my sentence was to be hung by the neck from the clothesline. He had learned how to make a noose from Dad and wanted to practice. He got a wobbly brown chair from the kitchen and put it under the clothesline, then fixed the noose around my neck and pushed me off the chair.

It all happened so fast, but I knew I wasn't dead when the line broke and I fell to the ground with only a red mark around my neck to show for it. When Dad got home and saw my neck, he told Gary to practice with dolls and leave me alone.

Then he said to me, "You need to learn how to play girl games and quit being a damn tomboy," as if it was my fault I got hung. I didn't know too many *girl* games, having hung out with my brother and his friends most of the time. I could climb a tree better than most of them, build forts and walk the railroad tracks looking for things to sell, but I didn't play with dolls or have too many tea parties.

I was beginning to find myself playing the familiar role of peacemaker more and more often. Discord was brewing in our family, escalating daily as we got older and grew more independent. The friction was not between Dad and Mama but between us kids and Mama. Dad often worked out of town, sometimes gone for a few days or a week at a time. When he was gone, all hell broke loose.

Mama tried to be in charge but failed horribly. The reason I say *tried* is because her attempts were futile no matter how hard she tried. How could we take her seriously as a parent when she was such a kid herself, wanting to be our friend and playmate more than our mother? When she saw that she couldn't be in charge, that's when the fighting began — and that's when I began to notice how she took things out on Linda.

"You kids just wait 'till your dad gets home," she would say with a shaky voice, tears welling up in her eyes, her lips as tight as stretched twine. Let's just say we steered clear of her when she got like that.

I began to hate it when Dad was gone because that's when the fights got worse.

The clashes between Mama and Linda were always wicked and out of control. Linda had learned defiance at a young age and could not be intimidated. She prevailed in those obscenity-laced shouting matches more often than not, driving Mama to fits of weeping, dish-throwing exasperation. Everyone said Linda was an incorrigible young girl. Dad called her *Injun* because her skin was darker than ours, and also probably because of her fierceness.

"Just go to hell!" Linda would scream when Mama tried to punish us for making a mess in the kitchen and not cleaning it up. Mama threw a fit with foot-stomping, bowl- throwing gusto. She could get herself going when she wanted to. Sometimes she would run around and slam every door in the house, even though it was Linda she wanted to slam.

As I got older, I understood more and more why Linda needed to be a tough cookie: she had to protect herself from the wicked words Mama flung at her, and more. Linda's thick, matted hair, dark skin, and short, round body gave her the appearance of a little wrestler. But inside this rock-hard wrestler was a loveable little girl with a hint of sorrow in her eyes.

Again and again, Mama would scream at Linda: "You little brat. When your dad gets home, you're gonna get spanked! I'll tell him about you calling me a bitch and trying to hit me."

When Dad did return, she always followed through on her threats — relaying information in detail, not forgetting to end her rant with a final, "And they all deserve to be punished, especially Linda."

Dad, who had barely made it through the front door with his black metal lunchbox and muddy overalls, looked at us kids, then at Mama. He never had a clue about what went on in the house when he was gone; petty fights, he most likely thought.

"I'll take care of it," he'd say. Then he'd turn to us and threaten that next time we'd get the belt. So far, though, we had never seen the belt, so we weren't too worried.

Dad never saw all of us in action, all the screaming, and the rage. He never saw the time Mama threw a bowl of salad at Gary, hitting his pinkie finger and almost breaking it. Nor did he see other objects launched across various rooms. He didn't know that when he was gone, I waited for the moment I would have to jump in and rescue someone. He didn't see the fuse in Mama light itself and go ballistic. For all of us, but especially for Dad, Mama's tirades went in one ear and out the other. I conciliated fights between them by the time I was twelve. I was pretty good at it, keeping Linda and Mama from killing — or at least hurting — each other.

Dad had no stomach for dishing out punishment to his children, whom he saw so seldom. But when he *was* home, the fights were fewer and less frequent. It wasn't that

Mama was wicked, but being put in the position of leader didn't work well for her, mainly because we didn't think of her as a rational adult who could provide guidance and an explanation of right and wrong. But in Mama's defense, when she *was* in a good mood, the world would be a whole different place. She taught us all the things a kid should know, like how to ride a bike, roller skate, and walk long distances for candy bars. Since Mama never drove — except for that one time when she took us to school and ended up running into a tree — we walked a lot.

Besides the fishing and my near-hanging experience, there was little excitement in Soap Lake during the short time we lived there. Gary and I didn't make a lot of friends, but we did learn the art of shoplifting; the little market in town made each day a bit more stimulating. While the other kids went to each other's houses or after-school events, we stalked the local market. The lady who ran the store watched every move we made, which made it a little more challenging. We weren't sure if she stared at us because of our frowsy clothes and dark skin, or just because we were kids.

"How much did you get?" I asked Gary one evening as a cold breeze reminded me that we should be getting home. Gary's hair glowed from the sunset. He was the only one in the family without dark hair, but his eyes still flashed a chestnut brown.

"One big bar," he said, holding up the large chunk of chocolate. "Would have got more but that old lady with the gray bun was looking at me weird."

"She knows we steal." I acted as if we were the only kids who ever got away with anything. "She's scared of us, though."

"What? Yeah, right."

I told Gary about my theory that she didn't want the odd new people in town coming around; especially the parents. At least that's what my cousin said. I believed that's why we got away with certain things, like stealing or walking out of class whenever we wanted to.

"You should quit stealing. *I'm* not doing it again," I said, throwing my chocolate into the lake, watching it get smothered with white bubbles and sink. Across the way, houses were lit up; reminding me we needed to hurry.

We both knew that if we ever got caught stealing we would be in big trouble and never hear the end of it. Even though we had heard it whispered that Dad had done a little ten-finger discounting himself in his day, borrowing a few tools from various work sites, he would not hear of his kids stealing. His aspiration for us was to be better than our cousins and be the first of the McAlpin clan to grow up honest and graduate from high school before getting pregnant — or getting someone else pregnant. His hope for us was to pick our fights with care and win when we fought. So far, so good — or so he thought. But since my tits were starting to look like lumps of flour in pancake batter, it gave Dad even more reason to worry that I, his daughter, could get hooked up with some high school boy.

We also learned how to make money selling things door to door while we lived in Soap Lake like the people in the stories Dad told us about. Gary and I gathered what we could find around the house, things we thought wouldn't be missed or things we had collected on our travels. Then we went around the neighborhood selling the bits of

Mama's jewelry, books, dishes, ashtrays, or whatever we could find. Amazing as it was, people would actually plunk a quarter into our palms to buy the junk! They probably threw the things away the minute we left.

The desert had a pull for Dad and he got sucked into moving there quite a few times. After living in at least six places following our stay in Soap Lake, we ended up in a dusty little town in the

Mojave Desert called Johannesburg, where the wind shrieked and covered us with dust, making Mama even more nervous. Roaming the flat land in search of adventure, finding closed mines to explore and colored bottles to collect, the desert became our playground. Once I saw how the people in the desert dressed and acted, I realized there was no way in hell people would care what *we* looked like. They didn't care that we had been in our car for five days and had worn the same clothes the entire time since Mama forgot to leave clothes out for us. It also didn't matter that our mother was nervous and shaky, or that she wore clothes that didn't match or fit. I'm sure that I thought more about her clothing issue than anyone else. I tried my best to keep her from wearing her plaid polyester pants with a bright floral top, and a cotton bandana on her head to cover the bobby pin curls. When we left after a month, Dad said we would return, and we did — several times.

Some of the towns we lived in were barely more than pit stops, a financial refueling for the next destination, making our schooling harder and making lasting relationships almost impossible. One of those destinations was a small town in Idaho, where our car broke down on the road beside a river with broad, grassy banks. Luckily, it was still warm enough for us to camp in the meadow by the river until help came. We kids felt we were on a true vacation, picnicking near the water, swimming in the gentle pools by the river's edge, just like other families on vacation. The grassy bank was more comfortable than some of the places we had lived, and much more pleasant than the car.

"What if we lived here? Right here on the meadow, no house, no stove — nothing. I could stay right here by the river forever," I said.

"Yeah, right. Until the snow fell," Gary answered, skipping rocks across the water. "When I grow up, I'm going to be a carpenter like Dad and build a house in a spot just like this so I can fish whenever I want."

"Yeah, right." Seeing how serious he was, I knew I'd have to come up with one better. I said, "Well, I'm going to be a famous dancer and live in a mansion in Hollywood." I don't think it impressed him, but as a preteen who took dance lessons when we could afford it, I felt like my dream was in the works.

On a steaming hot day in Lancaster, California, Mama and I took a walk to the store, and on the way back went on a short cut through the park. The verdant grass felt cool beneath my bare feet and palms when I stood on them.

"Wanna see me walk on my hands?" I asked Mama, bouncing around and doing a handstand before she had a chance to answer. Upside down, I saw her plaid pedal pushers and sleeveless red top with a hole around the hem. Mama watched while I walked five or six steps upside-down.

"Pretty good," she said, barely paying attention as I continued, oblivious that people were watching.

A woman walked up to us and smiled, calling me a *little acrobat*. She asked if I would like to take dance lessons down at the community center. I think my eyes might have popped out of their sockets. I looked at Mama with the saddest eyes I could, thinking *please, please, please*.

"Oh, I don't think we can afford it right now," Mama said as she began to walk away. My heart was looking for a way to leap from my chest.

"Oh, we have a scholarship program that will allow her to have her dancing paid for."

"A what?"

The woman explained to Mama where the center was, pointing in the direction just on the other side of the park, then she told us when the lessons were held. I couldn't believe my good luck, and I went early each day for fear I might miss it. When the day of the county fair arrived, four of us had been chosen to dance a simple boogie with top hats and canes. But I froze when we started. I froze, and kicked in the opposite direction than the other girls, a real deer-in-the-headlights look on my face. But Mama and Linda were only two people in the audience who knew me, so at least I wasn't that embarrassed.

Two days after our wonderful breakdown on the river, where we pretended to be a family on a real vacation, we were rescued by Dad's cousin, George, a wanderer himself, who always seemed to turn up without explanation.

"Hey, about time you got here," Dad joked.

George looked at Dad and then at our camp spot. "Hell, we've lived in worse than this," he said waving his arms.

George's flatbed truck was a mess of loose paint chipping off in a variety of colors, and the different-sized tires caused it to tilt a little. The passenger window was partially broken. When Dad yelled for us to get on the flatbed, we were assaulted instantly by a mass of splintered wood. George pulled our U-Haul up to the truck — with us sitting in the back — and drove us to his house. We had to hang on tight around the corners, which made the splinters dig in more. George wound his way up his long, crooked driveway, pulling up on the lawn in front of his house.

"Holy friggen shit," Gary yelled when he saw the house.

"Shut the fuck up," I hissed, afraid someone might hear him. But he did have a point.

The house sat in the middle of the woods with a significant amount of weeds, trees, and shrubs growing around it, blocking out any sunlight. The door hung from one hinge and crusts of ancient paint covered the front of the house. Garbage littered the surrounding area, and an emaciated cat, staring at us inertly, lay on its side barely moving its head. Smells wafted from the kitchen — not from a home-cooked meal.

"Make yourself at home. Hell, Alice, you can even cook a meal if you want."

George laughed hard until Mama gave him that look that meant she didn't find it funny. She scowled at him, her lips thin lines and her eyes piercing a hole through his skull. But deep inside I couldn't help but laugh; after all, who would want Mama to cook? That's pretty damn funny. He obviously hadn't eaten her cooking for a while or didn't care.

Dad hustled up roofing jobs while we were there, taking Gary with him to teach him the trade. Mama lounged through most days, reading movie star magazines while Linda and I explored the woods around the house. Each day we wondered how long we had to stay in the flea-ridden house. But finally, Dad came home one day, pulled a handful of bills from his pocket, and showed us that once again, he had saved the day. We could get the car fixed and be on our way.

Once again, we were fortunate to have a relative living close enough to come to our rescue. That's how we operated, even if we were on the outs with each other.

Whenever any of our family needed help, they got it. We would do the same for them even if it meant driving across the state.

Chapter 3

Dad taught us kids that there is always something you can sell if you need money bad enough. We took his words to heart and that was how our businesses began.

Gary and I ordered things from the back of comic books. We had a choice; sell stuff we had ordered from the back of the comic books — like seeds or velvet religious mottos — and earn prizes. The other option was keeping some of the money. That choice was a no-brainer. If we went for the prizes, we would most likely get screwed because we'd be long gone before they arrived. So instead, we just kept *all* the money. Gary decided it didn't matter because they would never catch us. How could they, with us being continually on the road?

Our business started up again while we were living in Richfield, Idaho — one of a thousand gritty towns that dot the west, and one of many we had called home at one time or another, if only for a while. We walked door to door with religious mottos leftover from the last town. It's easier when no one knows who you are. That's the one good thing about not being enrolled in school right away; anonymity can be useful.

Gary always insisted that I talk first when someone answered the door. So I stood there with my bird legs and spaghetti arms like an abandoned urchin, ready to make my pitch as soon as the door opened.

"Hello, we are selling religious mottos to raise money for injured animals, would you like to see them?" As I made my usual begging intro, I pictured the little Avon lady who visited Mama occasionally, pitching her voice just so, the way people do on TV ads. The ladies were usually nice enough to thumb through the stack of eight-by-ten velvet pictures depicting all kinds of religious scenes. Most of them had sayings like "Walk with God," or "Our heavenly Father."

Not being one bit religious, we didn't even know what half of them meant. "Well, look at you kids, out spreading the word of God *and* raising money for animals. I'll take this one and this one," the lady said, handing me $2.

The mottos worked better than the seeds we sold last time and much better than the junk we collected from around the house. The older I got, the more I believed that people would buy anything. It's just like Dad said, "You can sell snow to Eskimos if you try." And he could.

When I was twelve, I taught dance classes in the dirt floor garage behind our house to little desert rats who gave me a quarter for each class. Their mamas would take off for an hour for much-needed personal time, so I guess I was as much a babysitter as a dance instructor. Younger girls would line up to take my dance class, and the money went for candy from the little store.

Richfield wasn't much different from other little Idaho towns we had lived in.

There was always the Mom-and-Pop grocery with a full selection of penny candy. There was also a bar, often called the Stockman or something else equally raunchy, a barbershop with an old man cutting hair in the window, and often a handful of weird establishments that could most charitably be called *second-hand stores.*

The mountains gathered around Richfield like a good, strong grandmother's hand, but in the winter, little towns like Richfield were boring and buried in snow, and life for young girls became cramped and miserable. Like an ice-cold mountain stream, winter life in a town like Richfield numbed the mind and the senses.

Our last few moves were not as much fun as some of the others we had taken.

Being on the road took away a lot of schooling that we needed to keep up with our grades. It never seemed like an urgent thing that we study while between schools, but for me, reading books gave me what I wanted — a good way to look at the rest of the world. Dad swore he was going to settle down and quit spending money on the road, saying we would be better off if we settled down. The Hudson got more and more cramped as Gary's legs grew longer and spread out across the seat like wiggly willows. It was also becoming harder to leave our friends behind. It was one thing to be stuck in the car for days on end, but it was another to be forced to move to places we hated while saying goodbye to friends we knew we'd never see again, or at least not for a long time. As we got older, we began voicing our opinions about our living situation, because like Dad always said, "The squeaky wheel gets the grease." But for the time being, we were still getting shifted around, and the grease wasn't doing a hell of a lot of good.

Richfield was the same as I remembered it from the last time we lived there — narrow streets with run-down buildings and boarded-up houses, people who stared at anyone who walked by, and piles of black, gritty snow shoved along the edges of the streets. We had lived in the monotonous little town when we were younger.

Gary and I were in the same class, as usual, and Linda was down the hall.

Although he's a year older than I am, Mama thought it would be best if I went ahead and started school when he did since I was so shy. So, throughout our school years, we were in the same grade.

The school was an antediluvian, broken-down wooden box sitting in the middle of a large dirt parking lot. In a field across the way, gophers played in the spring, their heads popping out as if to say hi to us. A new addition to the school was being constructed on the far side of the long parking lot, which is where Dad got a job and was what kept us there to begin with. I often saw him on the roof during recess.

The school rooms smelled like thirty years' worth of old tennis shoes and stale food. We had only been in school for less than a month, but from the beginning, I could tell the teacher didn't like us. Her face scrunched up whenever she had to talk to us. She could have been a female Scrooge. Then all hell broke loose.

Gary, sitting across the narrow aisle, gave me as much support as he could, considering he liked to try to kill or maim me a good deal of the time. "Just practicing," he would say when he pulled one of his Cowboy-and-Indian tricks on me. Like many of the other teachers we had been introduced to throughout the years, Mrs. Hicks glared at us from the beginning, as if we were wild pigs plodding into her classroom. She looked us up and down with a scowl, then introduced us to the class, asking us again and again where we had come from. At first, we gave her the name of the last town we had lived in, then Gary, sick of her questions, told her we came from everywhere. All the kids laughed and Gary became popular instantly.

"We've been all around this country," he said. "We don't hang in places like this usually. So I guess you could say we're from everywhere."

Mrs. Hicks quit asking questions. Before we sat down she said, "Is that all you have to wear? It gets pretty cold here."

Gary looked at her and replied, "Dad always says it's better than wearing nothing and getting your balls frozen off." A grin spread across his face and the students howled. Gary knew what he was doing. He always had a clever comeback and made life interesting for everyone.

The teacher tried and succeeded many times in intimidating me — maybe getting even with me for Gary's outbursts. When I cried one day as she stood over me criticizing my paper, I saw the curl of her lips and think she enjoyed it. In my mind, I was thinking, "I'm gonna get even with you someday, lady." And I did.

One day, she caught Gary and me talking across the aisle and that was all she needed to get on my case. She marched over to us and glared down at me with her fleshy body pushing against my desk, the smell of sweat wafting from her. She looked as if she wanted to eat me, or sit on me.

"This is not a time to talk," she blurted, telling the other kids they could go ahead and leave for the day. I looked at the clock on the wall; she was letting them go five minutes early. I knew this was it. With all the other kids out of the room, she could have her way with the two of us. She grabbed my index finger and used it as a pointer, thumping it on the page like a crazy woman about to go out of control, the way Mama did. I was supposed to be reading, she said, breathing heavily from her oversized mouth that reeked of onions and cigarettes. I could see saliva about ready to spill out as she tried to search for words.

My finger was the size of a small lizard's tail at the time, and I cried as she continued to poke it onto the paper as if smashing bugs.

"This is what you need to be reading," she said again and again. Gary's eyes grew wide when he saw me crying. Since Dad was working on the grounds nearby, building on an addition, a light went on in Gary's head.

"Come on," Gary yelled, reaching over and grabbing my sweater while the teacher tried to hold me with her large sausage hands. But I was too quick for her. We both ran out the door, running toward the heavy door leading outside. Like maniacs, we raced across the parking lot as if our life depended on it. When we reached Dad, we were out of breath, and both of us began talking at once. I bawled and tears began running down my skinny, brown face.

"The teacher tried to break Judy's fingers," Gary said between gulps of air. "She almost broke her finger off."

I cried even louder now. Dad rushed down the ladder while I blubbered and Gary screamed his brains out. A look of confusion spread across Dad's face. Gary proceeded to tell him what happened, leaving out nothing and even exaggerating it some. Dad stared down at me with my dirt-stained face, then turned and stomped across the field toward the school without saying a word with a blank face and a set jaw, which I knew meant, "Look out teacher, you're gonna get your ass kicked now."

When we reached the classroom, Mrs. Hicks was sitting at her desk fumbling with papers. When she saw Gary and me peeking out from behind a muscular man with black hair, dark skin, and a look that said, "I might tear you limb from limb," she stood up as though to protect herself.

"What the hell do you think you're doing hurting my little girl?" Dad was short of breath, his face red as he towered over the teacher. When he got like that, there was no stopping him. Before the teacher could answer, he poked a finger at her, almost touching her chest. "If I ever hear of you touching these kids again, or treating them bad in any way, I'll have your ass fired, and besides that, I'll stick my foot up your ass."

Gary and I turned to glare at her as we walked out of the room — her face was white and her eyes doubled in size.

I later got back in sync with my age-mates when all three of us were held back for missing too much school. Sometimes we'd be out of school for weeks at a time and when we finally started again, we didn't have a clue what they were studying. Luckily, we were all relatively bright and caught on easily. Mama didn't think we needed that much schooling and begged one of us — usually me — to stay home with her so she wouldn't be alone while she was *sick*.

Days without neighbors to coffee with made Mama nervous and anxious, and she'd been getting anxious a lot lately, which is one reason she let me skip school and bake cookies while she pretended to be sick. "I just need someone to stay here and help me out with all this housework. It's hard to do it when you don't feel well."

That was kind of funny since, even when she did feel well, she wasn't much of a housekeeper. She considered washed dishes a spick-and-span house; forget the floors piled high with boxes and the cat shit or laundry far past needing to be done. Most of the time I didn't tell Dad about my days at home when I should have been in school. Linda threatened to tell him, though, because Mama never chose Linda to stay home. When she threatened that, the fights broke out. Mama's words were like barbs when directed at Linda. I noticed it more each day and began to realize why Linda fought back so often. And the fights only got worse.

Even though there was usually a shortage of food at our house, it didn't matter; Dad picked up stray men like Mama collected cats. He'd feed them, give them a shirt or a dollar, then lead them out the door. Unless it was someone he really took a liking to, or they were down-and-out, then he might invite them to live with us for a while.

Thanksgiving came while the snow mounted on the steps of our Richfield home and covered the small town. While the turkey cooked in the oven and Mama attempted to fix yams piled with brown sugar and marshmallows, Dad went to the store to get cigarettes. When he returned, there was a man with him whom I'd seen standing out on the street corner downtown. Dad said he was homeless — as if living in the car meant you *weren't* homeless.

Dad always said we may not have a pot to piss in, but as long as we had a car and each other, we had a home. The man Dad brought home took off his coat, then stood with his head down as if he was looking at the mud on his shoes. His hat hung low on his head and covered part of his face, and he kept his hands in his pants pockets as if to keep them warm.

When Dad told the man to sit down and take his hat off, I saw he was withered and had sprigs of gray hair poking out of his head, triple bags lining his eyes. He emitted a constant odor of beer and urine.

"This is . . . what did you say your name was, Buster?" Dad asked the old fellow while on his way to the kitchen to help mash the potatoes to lumps and dump canned green beans into a pot. It was fortunate for us that Dad cooked all the holiday meals.

"Roller," the man said flatly, staring at his hands like he wanted to eat them. He watched while Dad put the food on the table, his eyes darting back and forth, then back down to his scrumptious hands. Beyond that, he didn't speak throughout the entire dinner.

His hands shook when he pushed the food to his mouth with his fork, and coffee dribbled down his chin. When most of the turkey and trimmings were gone, Mama and I picked up the dirty dishes while Dad and Roller smoked cigarettes and drank coffee.

Mama was giddy; she giggled and talked about the old tramp who sat in our small dining room. I piled the remainder of the dishes into the sink while Mama talked, mostly to herself.

"Do you think he's handsome?" She smiled and I knew she was talking about Roller.

I couldn't believe my ears. *Handsome*? What was she thinking? He was older than my grandfather and a bum at that. Not that I had anything against bums; we lived all too close to the edge of that world ourselves to feel superior. Dad had taught me to respect the poor and homeless because at any time we might be in that shape (God knows we'd been close to it a few times). Besides, a bum is most likely someone's husband, brother, or son.

"They're just down on their luck," Dad had said that day when we talked about these people. But tolerance was one thing, and seeing the romantic potential in this guest was quite another. Did I want to look at one of my father's town picks, our Sunday guest? No! It was bad enough to smell him as I helped clear plates. When he left that day, I opened the doors to air the house out, regardless of the cold.

At least Roller wasn't going to be living with us as Ray did — the last guy Dad dragged in. Ray worked with Dad on a house in Bellingham, Washington, but didn't have a place to live, so Dad brought him home for dinner. Before we knew it he had moved in tools, Polaroid camera, suitcase, and all. He was younger than most of Dad's foundlings, strong and capable, and could wink and smile at the same time. Hot for his age.

I could tell Mama had a crush on Ray by the way she giggled and acted around him, always showing off her butt with tight shorts, then moaning about her aches and pains so he would give her some attention. My friends had crushes on him, too, with his large blue eyes, sandy-colored hair, and broad chest bursting out of his unbuttoned shirt.

Ray gave our house some life while he was there. He laughed a lot and when he did his eyes squinted almost shut, like the scrutinized glare of a Chihuahua. He had a way with words and read me some of the poetry he had written. Since I had an autograph book a going-away present from my last group of friends in Great Falls, Montana — he wrote poems in it for me and read what the other kids had written. He signed my book, writing: "Sometimes you act like a Devil or a doggie down the lane, no matter how you act, I love you just the same." He drew a picture of a beast that was part devil and part dog, telling me it reminded him of me, or the Oscar Meyer midget who traveled around in a little vehicle shaped like a hot dog.

Mama began to be a little *too* nice to Ray, or so I thought. No one else said anything about it. Gary liked Ray because they did artwork together, and Linda adored him for the soft way he treated her when Mama wasn't around. When Mama was around, Linda was sent out of the room. Ray laughed at the way Linda stomped out with her lower lip stuck out. I could stay as long as I laughed and giggled about Elvis, as Mama and Ray did. When Dad was gone and Ray was home, Mama batted her eyes at Ray as if she had a nervous condition called eyelid flutter. She had a fake smile, too, that she used sometimes, thinking it made her look like Debbie Reynolds. She used it a lot around him.

Two months later after Ray left our house, saying he was going back to his *old lady*, I found some of the Polaroid shots he had taken. Ray's Polaroid camera was a new technological marvel that spat out pictures on the spot, and he took plenty of them. I found a photo behind a box on Mama's dresser — a nude photo of her. I immediately thought about nights in bed listening to Mama and Ray laughing together while Dad was away working. Because it was a two-story house, I could sit in my doorway and listen to them. In the photo, she was leaning her naked body against her bedroom door frame with her arms stretched up as though searching for the hinge. On the back of the photo, there was a note: "The woman I always wanted to fuck." That gave a whole new meaning to the picture. I may have been young, but I knew the word *fuck*.

I hurried to put the picture back where I found it and never mentioned it again. Not even to Gary or Linda. I wished I had never seen it and tried to erase it from my mind. But for all I knew, Dad took that picture while Ray was gone one evening. Either way, I decided to forget it. Ray hadn't paid rent, but when he moved out, he left his Polaroid camera behind and Dad kept it, believing it was a good trade.

While on the road, we became aware that we were not the only ones who lived this lifestyle; others felt the grit of the road, too. We had lunch with families at the side of the road, and if Dad took to someone, especially a family, they might begin roaming with us.

The snow had started to fly and cover everything from the nasty lumps of mud on the side of the road to the dingy little cabins we lived in. I say cabins because they were so small we had to rent two — one for Gary and me, and one for Dad, Mama, and Linda. It was as if we were on our own. Inside the main cabin, we were warm, and smells of dinner filled the small room. Gary and I were happy this time when Dad said we were moving. Holy shit, why not?

Chapter 4

At some point, I knew my parents were not only odd in the way they did things, but they would also, most likely, not live all that long. Dad, because he assented to a life of lots of meat, desserts, butter, heavy cream, and lots of cigarettes thrown in for good measure. Pots of coffee throughout the day kept him buzzing, but he didn't drink anything stronger than that. And my mother was destined to live an unfulfilled life, most likely followed by an early death because she was often so confused and nervous. One minute her nerves were rattled and the next she was comatose in a chair, staring at the wall. In my estimation, she would not see the light of her twilight times.

So we traveled on, unknowing kids in the back of the car, as innocent as dust on a butterfly wing. The fact that our family spent so much time together in the car may have contributed to our naivety. We may have seen more of the road than most kids, but we didn't see things much further than our surroundings. I was beginning to feel that our entire family was made up of characters from a comic book. One day we were here, the next, there. It didn't matter where — some places made us happier than others, but we all stuck together as allies; on the road and off.

The main street of Alder, Montana was two blocks long with a filling station, a grocery store, a hardware store, two bars, and a schoolhouse the size of a square dance hall. It made up for lack of aesthetics with the good cafeteria food — or at least good to us, considering what Mama made. Our eating experiences made us realize more and more that Mama never learned to cook, nor did she want to.

Since there were only three other girls in my fifth-grade class, I felt like part of the team. And because there were so few girls, we all tried out for the cheerleading squad and made it. I couldn't contain my excitement when I got home to tell Mama, who was sprawled out on the couch reading a magazine. She got excited and rushed to show me cheers that the cheerleaders did in Ohio where she was raised.

"I can teach you some cheers that I learned from watching the other girls when I was in school. High school, that is. I always wanted to be a cheerleader." Mama always threw in the fact that she was in high school, even graduated. "They graduated me to get rid of me," she'd say, giggling after she said it. She may as well have said, "Unlike your dad who never finished tenth grade." Her little body sprinting about while she did her cheering made her look like a young girl. The clothes, however, made her look like a street person.

Mama lived her dreams through me. She was like a kid again, waiting for me to come home from school each day so she could pump me for information about things that were happening. With cheerleading, it was the first time I had seen her so excited about something I did. But, as excited as I was with my new venerable role as a cheerleader, it didn't take Dad long to burst my bubble and announce that we were moving, just as it didn't take long for me to pack and say goodbye to my cheerleader status. My heart ached as I told the teacher, who was puzzled as to why we would move to a town just thirty miles away. I guess she didn't know the McAlpins.

The motel we rented in the nearby town was bare-bones — a table, a couch, and two beds — but still bigger than the last place we had lived. There were even some dishes and pots left in the cupboards by the last tenant — but no food. After Dad paid rent and put gas in the car, there wasn't money left for such things as food. We knew it wouldn't be long before there would be more, but in the meantime, our growling stomachs told us we needed to do something. We scavenged through the unpacked boxes and pulled out what we hoped would make lunch.

Before Dad left for work, he said, "I'll see if I can get a draw today or tomorrow after I've worked some." His job had been planned this time and the contractor was expecting him. Dad looked hollow and worn. His naturally dark skin became ashen.

When he fell through the roof at one of his last jobs, before we left California, his arm went numb. We urged him to have a doctor take a look.

"Why? So they can tell me I need all this work done? Can't afford that. Not with the prices doctors are charging nowadays," Dad said. "You don't have to worry." He had a half-smile on his face and we weren't sure if this was good or bad. Did he really think he was healthy enough to forego a visit to the doctor? A wave of black hair caressed the top of his head, Tony Curtis style, who some said he resembled. Dad didn't pay one bit of attention when the girls whistled at him or women winked. He seemed oblivious to it all.

While Dad busied himself at work and Mama played the martyr, lying on the torn cotton bedspread reading magazines, we kids stayed home, unsure of when we were going to get enrolled in school. We prowled around the house like hungry cats.

"What the hell is there to eat?" Gary demanded digging through unpacked boxes, pulling out a half-full jar of flour and a half-full box of brown sugar that had hardened to a brick. We broke off chunks of the sugar and ate it until it was gone. Mama acted as though we were invisible while we scattered things around. She had only put a few things away; the rest sat in boxes on the counter and the floor. Some never made it from the porch. From the looks of it, she wasn't intending to put a lot away today. She was in one of her "moods."

When the brown sugar was gone, Linda began to raise hell while Gary and I made jokes about our reverberating stomachs. Linda was getting herself wound up, which we knew would only wind Mama up, and that meant fighting — something Gary and I always tried to circumvent if we could. Linda threw herself on the bed beside Mama.

"Mama, I'm hungry, too," she cried, jumping up and down. "I'm hungry. Fix something."

Mama slammed her magazine down, drew in a breath that could have filled ten balloons, then blew it out. "If you're that damn hungry you can go find something! There's nothing for me to fix. Go look in the boxes and see if there's anything. If not, you have to wait until your father comes home, that is if he brings anything. I don't know why we had to move to this beat-up shitty town anyway."

Some places Mama got tired of quicker than others. Since we were just down the road from the town we had just left, there was not a big difference in scenery, and the small motel room was a downgrade from the little cabins we had left.

"I'm hungry *now* . . ." Linda's lower lip began trembling, her face growing red, on the verge of tears. I could tell she was about to go off on a rage.

"Go away. Leave me alone." Mama's voice grew loud and bitter and when Linda started crying, Mama slapped her on the back. "Get!" she said, glaring at Linda before purposefully turning back to her magazine.

Not wanting to see a fight break out, I called Linda over to the makeshift kitchen and told her I would find us something. Gary pawed through the boxes and got what he could out of them — condiments and a partial bag of spaghetti. I boiled the noodles and when they were done we poured hot sauce, a little mustard, and ketchup on them, and by the time our *meal* was ready, we were all happy again — even Linda. We put the bowls on the table and filled them with the noodles, laughing about our lunch being world- famous spaghetti from a notoriously famous Italian recipe.

We found that as much as something could be bad, it could also be good, or at least funny. Linda ate her meal and our left-overs. She ate whenever she was anxious or sad, but she clearly was beginning to get chubby. I don't know if she did it because she wasn't sure where her next meal would come from, or if she merely ate for the comfort it brought her.

Although the ground was covered with snow and it was intensely cold, Gary and I needed to get out and explore. It didn't make sense to move to a town if you couldn't see what it had to offer. Every place — as humble or wonderful as it was — had something, and we were always determined to find it. In Dillon, Montana, we had found the butcher shop where the owner sliced meat with a stump for a hand. Dad would send us there to get sliced bologna and the whole time I would stare at the man's stump, feeling like we might be getting more than just bologna.

As much as we hated taking Linda with us on our outings — sometimes being forced to if Dad was home and saw us trying to dodge her — we didn't mind taking her this time. Leaving her home with Mama seemed a cruel joke.

Our feet crunched against the sooty snow as we walked into town to window- shop. The cold seeped through our thin coats and our lips froze. Nearing December, cold had spread like a bad disease. We zipped our coats tight and let Linda have the scarf, since she was the youngest and looked the coldest. We discovered on this first outing that the town was a conglomerate of fledgling shops filled with crocheted potholders and taverns crammed with old men. Smells of alcohol and cigarettes seeped out onto the sidewalk as we walked by. We marveled at the rows of donuts in a little bakery called *Dunk on In*. We drooled over the large chocolate cake in the window that stood at least a foot high.

Dad always said if we were ever super hungry we could go into a grocery store and look for samples. A few times, I saw him casually open a bag of cookies that we all shared while pretending to shop. But this town was small, and roaming through the grocery store munching cookies was out of the question. People here knew each other and patrons like us would surely be a focal point.

"Ya want to go inside and see if they have samples?" Gary asked.

"Why not? They can only kick us out," I said, thinking of what Dad would say.

We went inside the bakery hoping for any kind of samples. Smells of fresh bread wafted to our noses, making my mouth water. We walked through the doors with care so we wouldn't surprise the owner. The woman behind the counter was bent down, but when she straightened out, she turned and stared at us while we practically drooled on the glass case housing the donuts and swooned from the aroma of freshly baked pastries. She watched while we searched the counter for seconds, broken cookies. Then she asked why we weren't in school.

"Where do you kids come from? Haven't seen you around here, think I should know every kid in town by now, used to." She had a net over her hair and Linda couldn't quit staring at it.

"That's because we're new here," Gary said, always the spokesman. His face was serious, and his sandy-colored hair fell into his eyes, covering his bushy eyebrows.

"Well, how come you're walking around on a school day?" Her voice was like tires on gravel and when she talked there was a gurgling sound, like she was underwater. I was certain she would call the school and turn us into authorities. I felt my heart stop.

God, what would Dad think if he got home from work and found out we had been arrested? In a town this size, I imagined that every kid was accounted for.

From the corner of my eye, I saw Linda squirm, probably more from the cold than anxiety, and soon her thumb and forefinger were making an O around her eye, like a telescope — looking off into space, her escape to the unknown. This habit only got worse as she got older. If someone yelled at her, stared at her, or she knew she was in trouble, up went the makeshift telescope.

"And look at your poor little sister, nothing but a thin little jacket and scarf in this kind of weather." I just wanted to get away at this point. The baker lady made me nervous and the less she knew about us, the better. Gary, however, had a plan. He moved toward the counter and looked the lady right in the face.

"Our dad was just injured in a bad car wreck and our mom is at the hospital with him. It's bad, he may not live. We were too sad to spend the day in school, so we're just walking around. Hopefully, she'll come home soon and fix us lunch," Gary had a genuinely sad look on his face, big cow-brown eyes widened as if he might cry any minute. Linda's head snapped up at the mention of the car accident, but I grabbed her hand and squeezed it before she could speak and tell the lady we were little liars.

"Oh, you poor kids! Why didn't you say so? Come over here and sit down, I'll get you some donuts and milk. Do you like chocolate milk or white?"

God! Was she kidding? Did we like chocolate or white? Hell, we would have eaten the carton had she suggested it.

"We are open to anything," Gary said, using a term Dad used often while the bakery woman loaded us up with donuts, broken cookies, and boxes of milk. We ate everything she put in front of us and then headed home walking on a sugar high.

After three weeks, we packed up and moved back to where we'd just come from.

I never understood all the ins and outs of our travels until I was older. The nice thing about it was that many of the boxes hadn't yet been unpacked. Mama wasn't happy about moving back, but at least she didn't moan or throw a tantrum this time.

Dad found an apartment over a grocery store that fit us just fine. It had been closed for years and needed airing out because a black man had been killed there. Dad said the rednecks in the town killed him one Saturday night when they were all *drunked* up. There wasn't any blood spattering the walls or anything, it just had some bad smells. Other than that it was nice living in the middle of town, even if for a short while.

Although I didn't get my role of cheerleader back (a girl was bumped a grade and took my spot), I did get a part in the upcoming Christmas play. "I've never been in a play," I told my teacher as she looked down at the holes in my tennis shoes.

"Well, you'll be just fine. You and your brother are both talented," she said, handing me some parts to practice so I could catch up with the others. The play wasn't much and was pretty weird to boot. Basically, it was a simple march, military-style — two girls on the left of the stage and two on the right. I practiced every day, marching through our new apartment, probably shaking the lights in the store below. Mama loved having the store right below us, especially since they gave us credit. Gary and I charged candy, sometimes enough for all the kids in the neighborhood. Dad knew nothing of this, of course.

We went to a local thrift store and got the clothes we needed for our roles in the play, or at least something close to it. Gary was a Christmas soldier in the background, singing in the chorus. Mama got him pants and a shirt that looked military if you fastened the top button. We practiced marching and sang: "When the Caissons go rolling along." Why this ended up being in a Christmas program, I will never know, other than the fact that the teacher, who read the Bible to us each morning, thought it would be entertaining.

The closer the day of the program got, the more wobbly-kneed I became. Mama and Linda came to watch us but, as usual, Dad didn't plan on going; crowds bothered him.

"Come, on Dad. Come watch us," Gary pleaded, getting his costume ready.

"I have to stay here and finish packing so we can leave tomorrow. You kids go and have fun and do a good job, Doodle. You too, hon. Have fun!"

"I don't know why you can't go. It's a Christmas play! Your daughter is theatrical. You should come. We can pack later." Mama didn't expect a reply, though, and simply turned and walked off.

Dad had decided earlier that it was time to get out of this town. If we left now, he said, we could be settled into a new place by Christmas Day. He had a way of making us *want* to move. "We'll get a bigger house this time, money's better there," he said around the dinner table two weeks earlier. We were barely settled in, but I knew when Dad got the wanderlust, it was time to hit the road. Most of the time there was little or no notice, but this time there was.

Over one of Mama's dinners — a casserole of crusty hot dogs with chili poured on top and baked for several hours, and a salad of lettuce dressed with mayonnaise — Dad made us laugh and get keyed up about leaving. "You kids can even get one those fluffy little things you've been talking about."

"They're gerbils!" Linda yelled, followed by her little girl giggle. My fear of the upcoming play had disappeared, or at least while Dad tried to make us feel good about the move — one way he knew to do it was to bribe us with things he knew we wanted. It usually worked and made the move a whole lot easier.

Later that evening at the school, just before we went onstage, the gymnasium filled up and my stage fright started all over again. I saw Mama and Linda walk down the aisle and take a seat. Mama looked beautiful in her new sweater and her hair swept up at the sides. She even had lipstick on. I smiled wide at them but not sure they could see me.

The choir came on first, and when they were done singing, it was our turn to go to our designated spots on the right and left side of the stage. The lights felt hot on my skin.

We were just about to begin when Dad walked through the door of the auditorium wearing worn jeans and his torn Levi's jacket. I was so stunned I froze, staring at him — mostly because he never came to events like this, and also because he seemed in a hurry to get to the stage. He walked down the aisle with exaggerated quietness and whispered something in my teacher's ear. I saw her eyes widen, and her arms swing in the direction of the stage. Her agitation broke the spell, and I suddenly found myself running down the stairs and rushing over to them. Something was up and it wasn't good.

"Dad? What are you doing?"

By now Linda and Mama were standing there, too, and I saw Gary out of the corner of my eye heading toward us. He asked the same question and when I looked at Mama, I knew that she knew this was going to happen. Her face was blank and resigned, not excited or shocked.

"I have the trailer out front, got it loaded up early, and we need to go before the snow flies, supposed to be a good one tonight," Dad said, his thumb pointing toward the door of the auditorium, looking from one of us to the other, but mainly at the teacher who stared at him in open-mouthed consternation.

"Well, I never! I've never *heard* of anything like this!" She had overcome her shock and had regained a grim composure. As she moved to within inches of his face, Dad took an involuntary step back. The auditorium filled with whispers and shuffling. Everyone was looking at us. I wanted to crawl under the floorboards.

In a ringing voice heard by everyone in the room, the teacher declared, "If you take them right now, it will upset the whole program! There are two girls and two boys on each side of the stage, see?" She nodded toward the stage where the other kids were in place and ready to begin. "If you take Judy and Gary, you upset that. It's all been practiced with *these* two kids. Now you go sit down and give them another twenty-five minutes!"

To my utter amazement, Dad backed down. I don't think I had ever seen him back down from anything. He had never imagined such a crowd and was unnerved by everyone staring at him. He brushed us away with his hand in the direction of the stage and half-whispered, "I'll meet you at the car."

Mama and Linda went back to their seats and Gary and I climbed back up on stage where the audience looked at us like we were flies under a microscope. I stood straight, flipped my long hair over my shoulder, and waited for my part.

As soon as the program ended, after grabbing a bag of Christmas candy and before our incredulous classmates had a chance to quiz us, Gary and I elbowed our way through the crowd and out into the parking lot where the car and trailer awaited us.

That familiar orange appendage was attached to the car like a limb on a tree. We were ready to go. Mama and Linda were already settled in and the engine was idling. We weren't sure where we were going, but, of course, it would be better than here.

Chapter 5

The towns that we inhabited next were too numerous to mention. We learned not to get attached to anything — not tangible goods, people, or school projects. Friends became sore spots, at least when it came to leaving them. The older we got, the more we felt our parents were getting even with us for something; they continued to take us away instead of settling down so we could experience what our friends had; true friendship.

Was it because Linda bit her fingernails to the quick as if chewing on a dog bone? Or was it because she peed the bed too often? Could it have been because she fought with Mama too much? Could it be that we were to be travelers for the rest of our lives?

We developed a collection of addresses from our closest friends and wrote to each one of them at least once. We may not see any of them again, but we were there in spirit. We built a shell around our hearts and kept going, prepared for change. We were free but caged; caged in a car that protected us from the world and the outsiders.

The Beaverhead Mountains wrapped around the small town of Dillon, Montana like a crescent moon. The rivers veined the course for fishermen and hikers. It was one town we had lived in many times; *Big Sky Country,* Dad called it. As we pulled into town, a sea of trees adorned by robin-egg-blue sky stretched as far as the eye could see. We were back where mountaintops beckoned and air stirred nostalgia. Smells of the innocent breath of lilacs, freshly dug earth, and sweet blossoming cottonwoods crept into my nose. Mountains towered above the long valley, the sky was patrolled by hawks and an occasional eagle. It became our *sometimes* home.

The Dillon of my early youth captured something of the real rural west. Cowboys wearing ratty jeans and hats that dipped down to shield against wind and dust became part of my life. Rodeo men limped — vestiges of too many ill-tempered broncos and bulls and too many once-broken bones. There were also plenty of down-and-outers — cowboys and railroaders hanging out in front of The Moose or the Stockman's bar, either leaning against the wall or sprawled on the sidewalk. *Boomers*, we called them, vomiting where they lay.

I had seen this cast of idiosyncratic characters many times before. Everyone said to fear the Boomers, or they would surely rape and kill us. I call these the Mama myths. When drunk, the Boomers stayed wherever they dropped, often in the gutters amongst the withered leaves and cigarette butts until they slept it off or the cops hauled them away.

The same streets were our playgrounds when we were barely nine or ten running the streets.

As we drove into Dillon, I was immediately reconnected to my past by the acrid smell of railroad ties baking in the sun and the tolling of the hour from the courthouse bell. Relatives left the road to settle here. A good number of Dad's family were scattered about in small cabins in low-rent neighborhoods, some of which had been here for years. There's something magnetic about this town for my Gypsy relatives.

Dad's Uncle Bud and Aunt Belle were among those relatives, and more cousins than I can count have been here for years, some off and on like us — dating as far back as the late 1800s. A lot of them came from Scotland and Ireland and landed in Pennsylvania, eventually heading to Montana. I could never understand the attraction until I was old enough to know that the scent of a lilac bush was heaven; that the fish jumping in a clean river soothed one's soul; that the camaraderie of folks living their lives was precious. The town's only claim to fame was — and still is — Western Montana College and a kickass 4th of July rodeo.

Town and school authorities frowned on people like us who missed as much school as they attended. Despite the social disapproval, many of our clan just kept traveling. Sometimes we would caravan with other families and sometimes we traveled alone. Either way, we'd always rendezvous somewhere down the road, like mountain men after a season of trapping. Abandoning the road, I have learned, is not easy. And I wondered why.

As we cruised the town, poring over memories and reliving Dad's boyhood, he couldn't disguise his excitement. "Goddamn! It's good to be back here. Right, hon? Boy, we had some times in this town, didn't we?"

Mama mumbled something unintelligible under her breath. She may not admit it, but she loves this tumbledown town as much as he does. We kids only wished we could stay here. Gary had his head out the window, making sure he took it all in.

Driving down Main Street, bisected by railroad tracks, Dad began pointing out places across the tracks he knew as a boy — places we lived as babies and toddlers. He pointed out the historic brick and stone buildings I passed on my way to school. I walked the length of the town to get to school and, if I had money, I'd stop at the newsstand in this magnificent nineteenth-century icon to get a nickel's worth of candy while I absorbed the flavor of the place and got the evil eye from the proprietor. I felt the smoothness of the old wood and the ancient hands that had their way of shaping the curvature of the bookshelves.

I spent my money with care while studying the headlines of *The New York Times*, the *Los Angeles Times*, and the *Great Falls Tribune*:

"Gas prices sky-rocket to 25 cents a gallon!"

"Alaska becomes the 49th state!"

"Hula hoop craze sweeps the nation!"

Although I didn't understand everything I read, I wanted to be surrounded by words and candy. I knew I wanted to be a writer. Like everyone else, I wanted to write the great American novel. I wanted to be a journalist who wrote stories that would help our town, our people, and our country. And I wanted my first hula hoop.

As we continued through town, Dad suddenly spotted a sign we were all too familiar with — "House for Rent: Inquire Next-door." In the amount of time it took to find and slip into a parking place, Dad inspected, accepted, and rented the place.

After spending two nights on the floor of our uncle's house, which was filled with cigarette and pipe smoke, Dad moved us into an enormous, two-story, tacky green house next to the railroad tracks.

"Wow, this house is great!" Gary yelled when he saw the large rooms and high ceilings. The house's generous dimensions made me feel that it must have had a grand history. I imagined a massive chandelier, full-length mirrors adorned with gold leaf, and stunning teak and walnut furniture in every room.

Whatever its history, though, the house was anything but elegant now. The building was crude and split into a duplex, paint peeling in long strips from the walls, inside and out. The faint smell of mildew and ancient dirt seeped through the walls and splintered floorboards. Old, pale gray linoleum splashed with baby-shit yellow designs curled up in the corners like dried leather. The coal stove in the kitchen doubled as a cook stove, and the floor around it had been blackened by years of smoke and spilled grease.

The walls were smoke-cured and smelled like a recently-extinguished campfire. Eventually, Mama's hands turned black from filling the stove each morning and keeping it going throughout the day. That coal stove was also the source of hot water for a bath or coffee. The lifelines on Mama's palms began to branch out like road maps, the coal seeping into every pore.

If it was hard to eat Mama's meals before, it was even harder now that she had to cook on a coal stove. Mornings were cold and the deep-fried French toast she placed in front of us had grease coagulating along the edges like sap on a pine tree.

"You kids eat up now, you've got to get to school," she said, placing our food on the table. We sat around the kitchen table staring at our "breakfast" with blankets pulled around our shoulders (especially if no one had gotten up in the night to stoke the fire). Ice formed on the inside of the windows and walls, which melted and puddled on the floor when the fire got going.

Bathing in a galvanized metal tub with water heated from a coal stove is a treat when morning cold lingers and Canadian winds rattle the window panes sending gusts across the floor. After a bath in steaming water, we'd stand by the stove until we were dried off well enough to put on our school clothes. If we hung our clothes over the stove for a few minutes, we could put them on and feel the warmth all the way to school.

Neighbors gossiped that we were like wild animals, running the streets and doing what we pleased. I liked to think of it more as being free and independent. Dad always said kids only learn by being free to try things. Some of our cousins, he said, were nothing more than skirt huggers, afraid to leave their mama's side. These same overprotected kids, we found out later, typically got pregnant as teenagers, robbed gas stations or, at a minimum, dropped out of school.

Mama's complaints and nervousness grew each day. I uncharacteristically sided with her — or at least with her complaints about the coal stove, the dilapidated condition of the house, and the never-ending clatter of the trains at night. I learned that if I agreed with Mama, even if I surely didn't, it would keep peace in our house.

Linda, on the other hand, did no such thing. Consequently, most of Mama's frustration and anger — the screaming and the name-calling — fell on poor Linda. If Linda was in the room when Mama went off, and they made eye contact, a full-fledged fight ignited. When pushed, Linda pushed back hard; she knew how to throw gas on the fire. It was nothing for her to puff her chest out or throw something at Mama. Sometimes she seemed to almost beg for a fight. Mama and Linda's fights were filled with screaming and breaking glass, causing our duplex neighbors to pound on the wall. My heart froze each time this happened as I wished there was something I could do.

The morning after one particularly explosive argument, a lady down the street called to ask if our mother was O.K. I had asked myself that many times — but nonetheless answered *yes*.

I saw Linda's rage grow more and more each day, and most of the time I understood why. It benefited her because as a tough-looking new kid in school, she became a target for other students until they found out how tough she was. She never had to deal with a bully more than once.

"You better not give me shit," she would say.

Our new teacher in Dillon — a big-boned woman with wattles of skin hanging from her upper arms like a turkey's neck — theatrically opened the Bible each morning, having the class pray and listen to scripture.

"What the hell is this?" Gary asked me under his breath the first time Mrs. Peterson began a sermon. I glared at him from the next row over; we didn't have any leverage yet, and I knew we had to keep a low profile until we learned the lay of the land.

It wasn't that a Bible was foreign to us, not with a preacher for a grandpa on my mother's side, but we had never had a *teacher* do this before, and thought it all very odd. Our Grandpa Virgil used every bit of his influence with our parents to get us into his little church if we were living anywhere near him in the Southern California area. He would drive all the way to our house to pick us up and liberate us from the clutches of a heathen lifestyle. There were times we lived a couple of hours away and he would still pick us up; being anywhere in Southern California gave him the satisfaction of seeing us, the grandkids he rarely saw. He made sure we had some sense of religious experience, even though he knew once we were gone that would be the end of it, or nearly.

We only saw Virgil occasionally, but when we did he made sure that we learned about the things he was taught to make during the Depression, like donuts out of cheap pop-open biscuits and Jello out of gelatin. The short, Jewish man we called Grandpa had black hair and a powdered face to give him lighter skin and made his sermons exciting by jumping up and down. I envied his life-style and, when I was with him, I felt a sense of peace.

Once we were settled in, Dad told us that this time we would stay awhile — something we had heard plenty of times before. And, like many times before, we didn't fully believe him, even though we wanted to. But work seemed abundant now, so it seemed a pro-longed stay might actually happen.

Before we were completely moved into the dilapidated green house, Dad organized a roofing team comprised of himself, his brother, a cousin, and an uncle — all carpenters by trade, just like all the other male members of our family. Dad hit the streets first thing in the morning, *pounding on doors* — as he liked to call it — until he found work. The time was ripe for roofers since a fierce hail storm a few weeks earlier had shredded shingles from rooftops and ripped doors from their hinges. The town was like a cooling pie on a windowsill for a pack of veteran travelers. I was happy to hear that, because for once, maybe we would stay longer than a month or two.

Mama was happy when we first moved to town, remember-ing friends she had left behind last time, like old lady Georgia who stunk like pee and lived in a tiny railroad shack practically on the tracks. Her husband worked for the railroad, so they got to live for free in a two-room railroad house that sat in the middle of two sets of tracks. I imagined the trains on their way to Butte, shaking the couple out of bed dozens of times a night.

Mama bubbled around like a thin, frothy brew. Her excite-ment was our savior because then she didn't have time to fight with us. She was gone a lot, either at Georgia's house or out walking. Dad was out of town for work and we all seemed to go in our sep-arate directions. None of us seemed to know for sure where Linda went, as she was getting more and more independent and went her own way.

We were happy that Mama had her friend because it meant she didn't have to run around with us and our friends. When we didn't want to go to the movies or roller skating with her, she pouted and grew angry, trying to make us feel guilty. It worked at first. I'd often give in and go with her, giving up my own outing with a friend. She didn't like our independence or the friends we hung out with. Her anxiety grew and I was beginning to see a side of her that even *I* thought was odd. She not only wanted to be with us, but she wanted to be our age and have our friends, too.

Since my Aunt Babe lived nearby, I asked her one day what she thought was wrong with Mama, and I learned more than I bargained for. Babe said Mama was once committed to a hospital (or *nuthouse*, as she called it) because Mama had lost control and couldn't cope with life and the new baby she was carrying — a baby that would have been older than Linda. I dimly remembered something about trouble with a baby when I was not much more than a toddler. Mama had become more agitated than usual and she and Dad screamed at each other a lot. Pregnant, she sat for hours, rocking and staring at the swirly blue-and-yellow kitchen linoleum and the cluttered countertops.

Dad tried to keep everything a secret; he whispered and begged Mama not to get so loud. We never knew what was going on — not that we would have understood what was being said, anyway. The day he and Mama left, he said, "You kids get the dishes done while Mama and I are gone." Since we had never done the dishes before, we felt honored to be given the chore. But we weren't left alone. Staring at us from across the living room was a man we had never seen before — no doubt a stray Dad had picked up somewhere. The man told us to call him Fry. He stayed for two days. He had a long horse face, whiskers, and was a man of few words. Sometimes, when I talked to him, I felt his knowledge was very limited. He made us lumpy oatmeal in the morning and told us to do the dishes while he sat and stared at us or picked his fingernails.

When my parents returned, Dad had a smile on his face, but Mama looked gaunt and skinny. Her skin sagged and her shoulder bones poked out like mountains through the clouds. We were happy to see the whiskered man leave. When he walked out the door, he didn't even say goodbye.

Chapter 6

"**D**amn, it's hot," Gary blurted as we sat on the cool lawn, plucking blades of grass, putting them between our thumbs and palms, and blowing to make high-pitched screeches.

The hot summer days kept us outdoors, usually down the street playing with our cousins, Doug and Jimmy. I put a blade of grass to my mouth and blew as hard as I could. When it didn't make a sound, I threw it down.

"Ahh you can't do it? It's easy. Watch this," Dougie said. He blew, and the screech was as loud as a rooster in the early morning. When he was done, I wanted to ask him things I had always thought about.

"Dougie, how come you moved here? I thought Aunt Helen didn't like to travel like us."

Jimmy climbed the tree we were sitting under, ready to shoot birds with his slingshot. Gary sat nearby, teaching Linda how to blow a blade of grass. The shrill sound made me cover my ears.

"She just wanted us to spend the summer here and get us out of L.A. We might not stay. She thinks this is a hick town." Dougie laughed in the hoarse voice that we thought, at first, was funny; it was like the hiss from a furnace, raspy as if he worked too hard to get the words out. "She thought maybe Uncle Al would take us fishing, or something."

Between Jimmy, Doug, and us three siblings, we were like stair-steps in age; Jimmy the oldest and most annoying, Linda the youngest and most troubled. Doug seemed to be afraid of

Jimmy — and for good reason. Jimmy beat on Dougie as if he hated him.

As much as we liked Doug, there had only been a few times where we got to hang out for long periods, like this summer.

"We might start school here," I said looking at Dougie. "Too bad you can't stay."

"Yeah, probably won't though. You won't be here that long either. Mom said as soon as the weather turns, you guys will be gone." He had a point. As much as I wanted to start school here, I knew not to get my hopes up. And I knew not to tell him he was wrong.

"There's a creek right over there," I said, pointing across the meadow. The smells of tall prairie grass and cottonwoods seeped into my nose, along with an occasional fluff of cotton from the trees that tickled my nostrils. Today the gophers stood proud on their mounds, talking among each other before vanishing down their hole. "It's good swimming, too. We can trap gophers later if you want." I knew I impressed him, because where he had come from he probably never did these things.

Doug looked at me in a different light now, I could tell. In my youth, I wanted to be like Annie Oakley, so maybe this was my chance. His eyes widened as he put his hand across his eyebrows to stare out across the field after I told him about trapping gophers.

"I've done it before, sort of, the swimming in the creek I mean. I can . . ."

But before he could finish, I interrupted with a question; something that had puzzled me a lot lately. "So, I'm just curious, Dougie. If Jimmy has a different dad than you do, who is your real dad?"

Aunt Helen had told me stories about Jimmy's dad while I ate piles of pancakes at her house one day — real pancakes, not burnt ones floating in a pool of grease. She had said, "He left when Jimmy was just a newborn. Jimmy never got to know him." Helen never married again, and then let me know what she thought of men. But that made me wonder all the more, getting my detective juices flowing. If she didn't marry again, then who was Dougie's father? Where did he come from?

Surely he wasn't an orphan she picked up off the street. Or was he? Aunt Helen always changed the subject when I asked her about that. So did Dad. And, because of all that secrecy, I wanted to know even more. From the whispers and a few things I'd heard, I knew there was more to the story of Doug and where he came from.

"As soon as it jumps out, put the coffee can over it. Get the gunny sack ready. Be ready for them!" I showed Dougie how to put the can over the gophers when they crawled out of their hole to stand on the mounds. I couldn't believe I was teaching a *boy* how to bag gophers, and I bet he never built a raft before either.

"Don't ya ever do anything like this in L.A?" I asked, knowing the answer. "Hell, no." Doug watched as I got down on my hands and knees. Gary was busy chasing gophers himself and couldn't help us out. The gophers danced and strutted around, taunting us, little tails flipping from right to left.

"You little beggars," I said after missing one I tried to corner three times. Then Dougie tried and missed. "It takes a little time, but you'll get the hang of it."

Dougie laughed. "My mom says you're a tomboy."

"That's what my teachers say, too. If it means I like to climb trees and run around with you guys, I guess so." My knees were skinned, my clothes torn, my hair in a knot — and he thought I was a tomboy. Maybe I'd never look like a girl, I thought.

The more I was around Doug, the more I could see why his mom sent him here to hang out with us. His Los Angeles experiences certainly wouldn't help him here. He needed to learn some things about life — like it's O.K to get dirty.

"Would you quit worrying about that old shirt? Just take it off!" I couldn't stand it any longer one day when he worried about everything that touched his clothes. Gary and I decided we would teach him a few things, McAlpin style. Throwing him in the muddy creek was the first thing we did, making sure all of his city slicker clothes got good and muddy, even his hair.

Doug said in California they lived in a gated, high-security apartment with a combination lock, and if you forgot the combination and no one was home, you didn't get in. He said he spent a lot of his time just protecting himself from Jimmy. But instead of *protecting* himself, it seems he hid more than anything.

I figured Aunt Helen didn't know a thing about boys and continued to see her youngest son as a soft, overweight boy who shied away from things that looked different because that was his nature — until Dad told us otherwise. He said it was her fault to begin with that Doug turned out as he did, all her pampering and coddling and overprotective ways. When he told her that, she agreed to bring Doug here and let us have a crack at him, I guess; to expand his horizons and teach him the ropes. Gophers in coffee cans were just the beginning.

My Aunt Helen — who generally avoided such jobs in California — worked while they were in Dillon. She took a job waiting tables at the same restaurant she had worked at as a young woman. And, because things never changed much in this railroad town, they still served brains and eggs, and still had the late-night bums who slogged through for grub after the bars closed. Skeets Café was known for the handouts they gave to hungry Boomers; if they came to the backdoor near the kitchen, they would be handed sandwiches and leftovers. If Helen got off early, she brought home milkshakes for all of us.

Doug stayed with us while she worked, and if she had to work the graveyard shift, he spent the night, which is when we taught him how to run the streets like a pack of untamed dogs, something he never got to do in L.A. We taught him how to put quarters in the pool table, then cover the slot with a piece of plastic — a photo sleeve we tore out of Mama's wallet. When we pushed the money in, the plastic kept the quarter from going in, so we could use the quarter again and again. We also taught him how to rummage up things to sell.

I told Doug about our experience walking in downtown L.A., wondering if he had ever had such an opportunity. It was the early '60s and Dad didn't think the streets were so bad that we couldn't walk downtown alone. Gary and I had walked down one of the main streets to find a store to spend our meager allowance. We got there just in time to see the Ku Klux Klan parade down the street in bright white outfits and pointed hoods with holes cut out for their eyes. We watched the parade in awe right along with the rest of the people on the street. When we ran home that day to tell everyone about it, Dad blew his top.

"You kids stay the hell away from them. They're bad people. They're bigots and pigs and would like to see all the Coloreds dead. It's a hate group. There's always got to be a hate group."

We could play near dangerous mines and run around with knives and cherry bombs, but were not to befriend the KKK.

"Don't ever go near them. Just turn around and run the other way."

"But why?" we asked.

"Just because."

Dougie, in awe of my story, said he had never experienced that before.

Hot days brought the gophers out and, between the three of us, we ended up bagging six in one day. Not a large number, but enough to warrant taking them on a float trip down the great creek near our house.

The steady flow of water was swifter in the middle where we floated on inner tubes some days. The sweet scent of red willows bordered either side of the creek and I inhaled a lung full, reminding myself to cut a few of the lean whips to take home. Cattails swayed in the afternoon breeze like wrapped cotton — the day was perfect in every way.

With wood we had found, we put together a small raft with a hammer, nails, and a rope Gary took from Dad's worksite. When we were done, we made sure it would float before placing the squirming, gunny sack of gophers onto the slick, wet surface. We sat the bag down on the surface of the raft, then gave it a little push.

"Farewell, good gophers, and happy journey to you," I said.

"No, you say 'bon voyage,'" Gary said, giving them another push when the raft began circling near the edge of the water. We watched while the bag bobbed over the waves, floating first to one side then the other. We stared in silence while it floated out of sight. The only sound was that of the cottonwood leaves rustling with the breeze and the cry of an overhead hawk. We jumped up and down, waved, and cheered as though we had put gophers on the moon for the first time. We really did wish the best for them.

Then, suddenly, Gary threw himself in the creek, swam down and rescued the bag. I had never seen him do anything like that and was both proud and astonished. He had a heart *and* a soul! I was glad he rescued the gophers.

Once Dougie realized the gophers were saved, his face relaxed from a knot of worry to a kind smile. He asked how we were going to get them out of the gunny sack. Gary told him the string around the top was loose and he would pull it open and let the gophers free. He carried the bag to shore, loosened the top, and let them out. Gary raised his skinny arms and made fists as if he had saved the world.

While walking home, carrying tools and a few willows, Doug began asking a lot of questions about our family, about Dad. Something was bothering him; all of a sudden he was too interested in us. Granted, we thought ourselves interesting, but couldn't believe anyone else would.

"What's it like living in different towns all the time? Mom said Uncle Al's a rainbow chaser, whatever that means, and if he ever found the end of the rainbow he wouldn't know what to do with it." Doug's laugh sounded like the honk of a goose.

"It's kind of like being invisible," Gary said. "You go to a town, no one gets to know you, you move on, and when you do move on, you don't have to finish your homework!" Gary screamed with excitement.

"That's not true!" I said. "It's no different than how you grew up, Dougie. We just see more is all." *More moves and more missing friends*, I wanted to say.

He wanted to know everything about our life — I think it was the idea of not having to finish his homework that did it.

We gave him a quick synopsis of the road, meeting and leaving friends, and sleeping in the car on top of boxes and blankets. I told him how I could make the hump in the middle of the backseat floor comfortable as if it was my doll-size bedroom. We even told him about stealing, dropping cats off in strange neighborhoods, and bringing home diseased animals. Then we told him about the fights when Dad was gone and how things became crazy when we were alone with Mama. He didn't ask any more questions.

"Sometimes we sell things door to door, stuff like junk we collect here and there, or stuff we order from the back of comic books. You're supposed to send the money in, but we just leave with it," Gary said, acting as though he knew all the ropes of being a scammer.

"Wow, you guys are a blast! I've never done any of that before, and never caught gophers either!" Doug's hair had grown since he arrived, spilling over one eye like a pirate's patch, and his round and mushy, pale body — which Dad joked was bread dough — was beginning to take on some color. A lot of the neighborhood kids called him a candy ass.

"He better toughen up if he's going to start school here. This town's filled with hoods who would love nothing more than to kick his ass," Dad said."

I wanted to ask more about Dougie's father but figured this was not a good time.

Dougie remained with us through the summer while Jimmy and Aunt Helen stayed in Dillon longer than they had planned. By late August, we had all gotten to know each other pretty well. We found Doug's funny side and the emotional attachment he had toward food. We laughed at his hissing voice and his round moon face.

One day later in the summer, sitting in the shade of a tree, Jimmy — the derelict cousin we knew nothing about — told us what he had recently heard; gossip from an unknown source, as he called it. We knew he was dying to tell us by the way he teased us and giggled until we begged him for the news.

He told us that Dougie wasn't his brother, but rather he was *our* brother! We all stopped doing what we were doing and just stared. I didn't know what to do. My heart was beating out of my chest.

I felt the surge of a million questions and memories flooding through me. My first thought was about Mama. This was her child! This was our flesh and blood, the kin that Dad had talked about so solemnly —kin always takes kin in, and all that. What was that all about? Just self-serving hypocrisy? And was it really true?

Instantly I was enveloped in a wave of anger, both afraid Jimmy might be telling the truth and afraid he may not be. If Jimmy was saying this just to get to us, I would help Gary kick his ass. I continued pulling blades of grass from the area around me. Everyone talked at once, except for Linda, who was making her way across the yard toward the back door, oblivious to what we were talking about.

"Bullshit!" Gary yelled, puffing his chest out like a skinny, plucked rooster until I put a finger to my lips. No need for Mama or Linda to get in on this conversation.

That was another thing I couldn't get out of my mind — if he was our brother and Mama's third born, why did she treat him so poorly? At times after he moved in with us, she treated him worse than she treated Linda, and way worse than she ever treated Gary or me. According to Mama, Dougie couldn't do anything right, and no matter how much he tried to help out around the house, he always got shit from Mama.

"I heard my mom say that your dad should have told you guys by now," Jimmy said. "She just wanted Doug to know his brother and sisters; that's why we came here. Oh well. You can believe it or not. That's what I heard."

Doug looked from one of us to the other, taking on a scared little boy look. As shocking as the news was for us, it must have been frightening for him to know he had been given away like some discarded cardboard box. He had a secret, and I knew what it was.

"*You knew?*" I said, wishing the words wouldn't have come out as harsh as they did. "How long have you known?" I wasn't sure whether to be mad at him or not. "I *just* found out," Doug wheezed.

"He did," Jimmy interrupted. "We both just heard about it. Mom was telling someone about it and we heard."

"Jimmy's been calling me a bastard and an orphan ever since he found out. How do you think that makes me feel?" Doug had tears in his eyes. We all looked at him, then looked away.

"You're not going to cry, are you? Because if you turn into a blubbering idiot you have to leave the family," Gary said jokingly, followed by laughter from all of us.

God, we hadn't thought enough about Doug's emotions in all this. To me, he still looked like the soft little cousin who was starting to turn a golden brown; the boy who came in and out of our lives like butterflies in the spring. But if it was true, then I wanted to know more about it before talking to Dad, which I was going to do.

We bombarded Dougie with questions for the next hour while lying stomach- down on the grass. I could tell he enjoyed the attention and even seemed happy to enlighten us about his beginning on this earth, about which he said Aunt Helen had told him following all of his questions. We listened without interruption as he told us what he had heard. He said his mother, our Aunt Helen, went to the motel we were living in to see how things were going after he was born, and everything smelled like shit. Doug loved it when he could cuss around us because at home he couldn't do that.

Doug's voice shook as he continued. "You guys lived in a bad area of L.A in a rundown motel where it was dangerous to walk around. Mom — I mean Aunt Helen — just walked in and heard me screaming in the bedroom. When she went in I was covered in clothes and baby shit, so she picked me up. She tried to talk to Aunt Alice about taking me, but Alice wouldn't talk, just sat there rocking and staring at the wall. So she took me home with her where she lived with Jimmy. When she talked to Uncle Al they decided I'd be better off living with Helen. You guys were moving a lot and I guess she just wanted a new kid. So that's it," he said. "That's all I know." He was thrown away.

"She just took you? Dad wouldn't let that happen. Blood is blood . . ."

"That happened to *Dad*," Gary butted in. "In the orphanage."

I couldn't dispute that. Maybe Dad just wanted one of his kids to have a more settled life, something he couldn't offer. I wanted all of this to make sense.

When we heard the creak of the door and saw Linda walk out, we changed the subject. There was no sense in this going any further if we didn't know for sure it was true.

Weeks later, when it was understood that Doug was our brother and it was out in the open, I saw the hurt Dougie felt when Mama treated him like a stray dog. She didn't mince her words about how she felt about him.

"What are you doing, Mama?" I asked when she walked over to where we were sprawled out on the lawn.

"I have to go to the store and get something for dinner." She looked bright in her favorite pair of red pedal-pushers and a stretchy white top. Her large breasts pushed against the flimsy material, and her tight pants showed off her small, shapely body. When she saw me looking at her outfit, she smiled her fake Debbie Reynolds smile.

"Do I look like a movie star?" she asked, dancing around in a circle.

"You look like a dancer, Aunt Alice," Doug said, still unable to call her mom but obviously searching for a bone of affection. The longer he stayed, the more we realized he would *never* call her Mom — and why should he? Doug had perked up when he heard the word dinner. "What are you making?"

"What's it to you? You're always hungry. Maybe you should get a job so you can pitch in if you're going to be living with us." She clicked her tongue and scrunched up her face at Doug. "You're getting too fat anyhow."

"Mama!" I hissed. Why she couldn't accept Doug was beyond me.

"Oh, all right, damn! I'm getting TV dinners. It was going to be a surprise. But I'll surprise you anyhow with what kind I get."

She was happy we could afford TV dinners. If she had her way, we would have them every night. "You kids clean up this house while I'm gone. Do the dishes." That morning she had made us breakfast — a piece of French toast on each plate with a pool of grease puddled around it. The bread had soaked up so much grease that when we poked it, it oozed onto our plates. The edges were crunchy and, when we poured syrup on top, the syrup and grease mingled forming a pool of swirling wonder.

Linda walked away with Mama toward town, only turning to stick her tongue out at us. Mama clutched a small, brown wallet in one hand and held Linda's hand with the other. I was just glad they weren't fighting. As much as I hated them yelling at each other, I hated it more when Mama treated Linda like a stepchild.

Now Dougie was the new stepchild. It was about time our *other brother*, as he became known, was returned to the family to which he belonged. I asked Dad about Dougie; I wanted reassurance that he was not just given away out of meanness.

"I did it out of love," he said. "We were moving a lot and didn't want to have to make a baby's life miserable by packing him around." Dad said it so matter-of-factly and with such sincerity that I believed everything he said. "Besides, your Aunt Helen is a hell of a good mother. She needed a brother for Jimmy, thinking it would help him. But I can see it didn't. The kid's still a little asshole."

I continued pumping Dad for details until he finally became agitated and his mood began to slide into irritation. Eventually, he refused to talk about it any longer. He said it was done and that was that. He didn't look back and we shouldn't, either.

Dougie finally moved in with us. Helen felt he needed to get used to living with us so that, when she went back to California, he wouldn't feel abandoned — like he didn't already. We could only hope it would work out, with the way things had been going. Dad said that as long as Doug was going to live with us, we needed to teach him a few things. After all, he had been coddled by a protective mother and beat up and teased by an angry brother. Fortunately, it was a good time to take Doug and show him how to fish, hunt for garnets, and make money. The first thing we did was take him for a walk down the tracks running right through the middle of town.

There's something special about walking on the rails that carried the mighty freight trains. It smelled of creosote and oil and if we heard a train coming, there was plenty of room on each side of the tracks for us to jump off. I caressed the power of the tracks with my bare, black feet and felt the rumble of the train inside of me, like growing thunder.

As we walked, we picked up railroad spikes from the rail bed and the grounds around it. Doug had never seen the big nails and helped us gather them, not caring this time if his hands got dirty. If there was one thing we had taught him, it was that dirt is

O.K. and protects you from diseases.

"If you can't take a little dirt, then you're not a true McAlpin," Gary said.

We also taught him how to recognize edible plants, steal onions and potatoes from local gardens, and make money quickly when you had to.

"This town was named after the president of this railroad," I announced while we walked. "It's called the Union Pacific, I think. The president's name was Sidney Dillon. I read that at the museum."

Dad had told us stories about when he was a kid and had to gather coal off the tracks that had fallen from gondolas and tenders. He even sent us out to forage for coal now and then when the power was out or when it was our only source of heat.

Our hands were black by the time we had a small gunny sack full of nails. "Why are we getting these?" Dougie asked.

"Sell 'em," I said, acting like I knew everything about the business of big nails. "Somebody's going to give us money for these?" Doug asked, looking his spike over before he threw it in the bag.

"Yeah, and we can share the money."

Chapter 7

On the edge of town, where houses looked as if they could tumble with the next heavy snow, there was a second-hand shop called *Gracie's*, a local institution where we had sold things before. Dad, as a kid and as an adult, also sold things to Gracie, the owner, who knew the McAlpins well. Gracie had a voice like a raucous parrot, but a heart like a savior. She bought from anyone she felt needed money, even if it was an old Boomer selling his cowboy boots or his toothbrush for a bottle of MD2020. Gary and I sold her everything from railroad spikes to rocks and glass bottles. She would give us a nickel for each nail.

When we took Dougie inside to sell our nails, he sniffed the musty odors and squinted in awe in the dim light, looking around at the piles of mystery that filled the room. Merchandise was stacked to the ceiling and the backyard was a maze of agate and quartz rock piles, small appliances, and broken down furniture. Tables overflowed with everything from tools and dishes to used boots and hats.

We shuffled through the narrow, crowded aisles that were like tunnels to us kids. We maneuvered our way to the desk, where Gracie's smiling moon face greeted us like a happy puppet. She had eyes that danced and shined whenever she looked at someone. Her mood never seemed to change, and I wondered how she could be so happy surrounded by piles of junk and the stench of old belongings, some of which came from the local bums.

"Morning, kids! Whatcha got for me today, huh?" Gracie wore a bright red shirt and an oversized cowboy hat with snakeskin wrapped around it. Her teeth were big like horses and bright like polished ivory. We introduced Doug as our brother and I could tell he felt honored this time.

"Well, welcome Doug. Where have they been hiding you?" She laughed and exposed most of her big teeth.

When we handed her our bag, she rummaged through it with her thick, man-sized hands, counting the spikes, smiling the entire time. "Well, ya brought me a good bag of spikes, I see. Ten. That's fifty cents. How do you want it, nickels or pennies?" she asked, treating us with a familiarity she used on everyone. When she handed us some dimes and nickels, I turned to give Doug his share, but he had walked away and was staring into a case that held pocket knives, belt buckles, false teeth, and jewelry. He waved off my question about the money and I knew it didn't mean as much to him as it did to us. He couldn't take his eyes off the Davey Crockett pocket knives.

"Wow, those knives are great. I'd give anything to have a knife..."

"Maybe you could trade her something for it," I said.

"No. Mom would never let me have one of those." He acted as if we had asked him to take a rattlesnake home.

"But Dad will," I said. While Doug stared into the cases, Gary and I walked over to the table holding Army shirts and combat boots. I asked Gary if he would pitch in his share of money so we could buy Doug the knife. Gary balked, saying he needed the money for candy. He tried to ignore me until I promised him that the money from the next batch of spikes would all go to him. I followed him until he caved. Then, without his knowledge, we bought the knife for Doug, planning to give it to him on his upcoming birthday. We left and all Dougie could talk about was the knife that he would get one day when he found something to trade for it.

It didn't take long for Doug to start hating Mama even more. She made him iron her clothes and, while he did, she made fun of the way he ironed. I could tell Dad loved Dougie and maybe that is what made Mama so mean. Maybe she was jealous of the relationship they were developing. Whatever it was, Doug grew to hate living with us and told Dad he wanted to leave. Then he told us.

The warm, sticky air took on the sweet smell of cottonwoods in late summer. I looked over at Dougie, who had grown solemn. Summer had toughened him up, at least physically. His gut was almost gone and the overall bread dough appearance now took on some shape and color. But I could tell he was an emotional wreck. Who wouldn't be after finding out your parents didn't want you enough to keep you?

Doug took a deep breath, blowing out through his mouth. "I'm gonna leave in a few days. Summer's over and I want to start school in California. Already talked to my mom about it, or rather my aunt." He still had that squeaky laugh.

I was stunned. I wanted this other brother to live with us. "Oh crap. I thought you were going to stay with us! Just because we move a lot doesn't mean we always will.

With you here, maybe we'll settle down," I said, knowing it would be a cold day in hell when that happened. I pulled my hair to the side, trying to get a cool breeze across my neck. My mind reeled with questions. Why would he want to leave the family he finally discovered?

Doug looked serious and said, "Hey, I'm not your cousin, I'm your brother. I guess I could if I wanted to." He pushed his hair to one side, showing off his large, round eyes shaded by bushy eyebrows, just like mine. "Yeah, I can if I want."

"Well, why don't you, then?" Gary asked.

"Because your mom — I mean my mom —" Doug laughed, "doesn't seem to like me much. I think she hates me."

"She's just that way, Dougie. She has to *like* you, you're her son," I said. But as much as I tried to convince him to stay, I knew how horrible it had been for him to spend time at our house. Mama never let up on him and tormented him whenever she got the chance, which was often.

We spent a good deal of time at Helen's house that summer before she left, eating pots of soup that steamed on her stove almost daily and mounds of potato salad. In the morning, there were stacks of pancakes, fluffy and tasting of vanilla. She gave them to us without asking if we had eaten. I figured maybe at one point in time she had tasted my mother's cooking. I saw how gently Helen treated Doug and could see why he accepted Helen over Mama. He saw the same side of Mama that Linda saw — only he had an out and Linda didn't.

Within two weeks, on a bright late-summer morning, as clouds formed at the base of the Beaverhead Mountains, we stood next to the car that Aunt Helen was loading with Doug's belongings. It seemed she wasn't really sick and maybe just wanted Dougie to take another crack at liking our family. While the grownups talked, all of us kids — except for Jimmy, who now hated us — gathered in a knot behind the car. We told Linda about the present we were going to give Doug and even let her wrap it and sign the hand-made card.

When we handed it to him, Doug said, "What? What's this?" He looked down at the wrapping that consisted of last week's funny papers. He laughed, probably thinking we wrapped it that way as a joke, not realizing it was all we had.

"A present, dummy," Gary said. Doug started to unwrap it. "It's not poison oak, is it?" he asked, not waiting for an answer. When he looked down at the Davy Crockett knife he had coveted, his mouth opened but words wouldn't come. He looked toward his mother and hurriedly rewrapped the knife.

"I can't keep this," he said, nodding toward Helen. "She'll kill me."

"Sure you can," Gary said, grabbing it and opening it, pulling out the shining blade. "Hell, I'd keep it. But if you don't . . ."

"He's keeping it," I said. "Hide it. Find something to put it in so Jimmy doesn't find it." I looked him in the eye. "It's so you'll remember us and the fun we had gathering those Goddamn nails."

Doug's look told us everything. His eyes turned down and I knew he was holding back tears. His lower lip quivered and he sniffed, then came over and hugged each one of us. When he was called to the car, he stuck the knife in his shoe and thanked us before walking away. I waved and wished it would have worked out, him staying with us. I had grown attached to him. Little did we know it would be many, many years before we would see him again.

Doug and Helen went back to California while we stayed and watched summer slide into fall and the leaves turn from gold to brown. Each night brought a hard frost and fresh snow crept down the mountains, crawling at a slow pace, but, nevertheless, flanking our town. It was only a matter of time before the grounds would be covered in white and stay that way for months.

∗∗∗

There was not much to be happy about living across the narrow street from the tracks, especially for Mama. Loud and obnoxious boxcars smashing metal against metal wasn't exactly a lullaby. The vociferous pounding of metal cars always woke us up with the forceful clanging. If a friend spent the night I could be sure she'd have nightmares at some time during the night. She would kick and scream each time the sound erupted. In the morning, she had no idea what her night had been like. I felt somewhat like a voyeur looking into her mind while her nightmares chased her, and I did not even attempt to wake her.

Hardships, I learned to realize, made us tougher and much more flexible with change, unlike most of our friends. We were independent, free to do dangerous things that many parents wouldn't allow their kids to do. We could make a meal out of noodles and ketchup and think it was the most gourmet thing we'd ever tasted as we laughed about the expensive china from which we ate — which was really Melmac, burnt a little around the edges.

Mama was beginning to find fault in everything around her and we all knew that meant it wouldn't be long before we were told to pack up. Her layers of vexation caked like coats of paint on a canvas. When she started, she'd plead with us to take her seriously and feel her pain — or at least agree with her about our living environment. If we didn't, her face tightened, her lips turned to cracks, and soon she would scream and run to the bedroom, slamming the door behind her. Or she would take it out on someone, usually Linda, threatening to give her away or put her in a girl's home if she didn't behave. Threatening to give her away had a whole new meaning for me now.

As I have said, Dad didn't know the depth of these fights. He was at work and missed out on the chaos that took place while he was gone. Linda retaliated with hate, bitter words, and behavior that even I couldn't understand. The more Mama shamed Linda with her biting words and concealed emotions (I say concealed because deep down I know Mama loved Linda), the more radical Linda became.

In Hamilton, Montana, a bar, a magazine stand, and cigar shop stood in the middle of town where old-timers and barflies hung out, shooting the breeze or playing cards. The large, gray stone building had a window ledge that jutted out about three feet; a perfect seat for Linda to perch on. While cruising the drag one day after school with my high school friend, Helen, she slowed the car and pointed.

"Oh my God! Isn't that Linda hanging out in front of the bar like a prostitute?" Helen squealed, laughing, waiting for a response.

I looked across the street at the window ledge and saw Linda with her arms wrapped around her knees like a bird on a nest. She was almost twelve, but had the hardened look of an older girl, at least in her expressions. Her dark hair matched her skin and hung in long, thick ropes to her sides. Her profile highlighted her chiseled face and high cheekbones, and even though — or maybe *because* — it was 1964, people walked by, staring with horrified looks on their faces.

"Yell at her or something, for Christ's sake. She's just embarrassing herself," Helen said. She sped off without waiting for me to say anything. In the rearview mirror, I saw Linda sitting there, looking like she didn't have a friend in the world. My heart went out to her, but as much as I knew I should do or say something, I didn't say a word.

A week later when I got home from school, Dad sat sorting through his personal cardboard boxes that never totally got unpacked, something he always did when he got the wanderlust. The boxes — filled with various rocks, jars of garnets and sapphires, bones, buttons, shells, a gold pan, silver cigarette lighters from when he was in the Navy, and an assortment of pocket knives — were too full and needed to be lightened, he said. At one time there were two old silver dollars in a case that I coveted, but he spent them a while back when we were hard up. One of his friends, a man with a hole in his nose, gave us silver dollars whenever we saw him, which wasn't often. If we didn't spend them right away, they would have to go to the family for food.

His treasure boxes drew me in. As a young girl, I would sit on the floor in front of him while he sorted, dazzled by his collections. Now, as a teenager, they still drew me in.

I helped him separate and sort, begging for a few things, until we had made three boxes into two, leaving out what didn't fit. It was his way of lightening the load. As a prospector at heart, he had all the tools and plenty of rocks.

"What are you going to do with the stuff you don't take?" My knees were sore and black from sitting on the splintery wooden floor. When he didn't answer, I asked, "So I guess we're moving, huh?" Everything indicated we were; the sorting, the whispering that went on between my parents.

"I'll give the stuff to the boys at the gas station. And no, it doesn't mean we're moving right away. Takes money to move," Dad said, not looking up from his sorting. Dad's health was getting worse and he had gained weight in the past year. Small heart attacks, as he called them, came and went. Since there was never money for a doctor, we all just sloughed it off, but they were only getting worse. "People have too much junk, gotta clear it out sometimes."

Considering everything we owned fit in a U-Haul, I didn't feel we were a family noted for conspicuous consumption.

This time, though, I didn't want to talk about moving. I wanted to stay and have high school friends forever.

Dad saw my expression. "You'll get new friends, always do. Hell, you're probably one of the prettiest girls in school."

Clearly he couldn't believe that, I thought. He turned back to his sorting — a little emotion went a long way with him.

When Aunt Helen jokingly mocked Dad one day for being a wanderer — or Gypsy — during a break in a hot pinochle game, Dad laughed it off as smoke drifted from his mouth.

"Why, you *can't* settle down, can you?" She said it teasingly, but I could tell it bothered Dad. "Pretty soon you're going to be too old for this life. And don't tell me about how we were raised like that and came out all right, because I already know.

Besides, the kids are getting older now and need some stability. You know how the other kids got looked at when they lived here," she said, speaking of our cousins.

Aunt Helen had sway, and her words were like a command. I liked her deep- rooted power, and at this time, women didn't have a lot of power. As I sat on the floor in the corner watching the game, running for fresh pots of coffee when necessary, I saw how meek and withdrawn Mama was next to her. I didn't want to be the meek woman. I wanted to be strong like Aunt Helen.

"Hell, you're no different than we are," Dad said with a knowing smile and a half- curled lip. But it spiked my curiosity; I was about to start high school and wanted to know if this *stigma* I had heard about was going to follow me down the halls of Beaverhead High.

The adults in our family gossiped a lot and I heard things I don't think were meant for my ears, like whispers when I was younger about my parents giving away a baby. I used to wonder if I had just imagined hearing these things, or if they came from dreams.

On the outskirts of Dillon, there was a sapphire mine that Dad claimed as his. Since he owned other mines here and there around the country and is a rock fanatic, I considered it to be true. It made me feel rich knowing we had all these mines that produced rocks that I heard were worth a lot of money.

Dad pored over his rocks for hours at a time and even bought a rock saw and a polishing wheel with money he'd earned from selling rocks. He was determined to make money, no matter how much we suffered while he tried. The rolling hills and small creek near the mine were like a paradise, full of wildflowers and cottonwoods. Some days when Dad went to dig we went with him; it was as if we had become a part of that land. We picked garnets off the ground — like gifts offered to us by the great Mother Earth. Dad told us to take only the bigger garnets and we could sort them for black spots when we got home. He took a Folgers coffee can and put plastic over it with a light inside so we could grade the stones, separating the good from the bad. Later he took the garnets to Butte to sell. If we were hard up, he'd go the same day.

***

Our Scottish-Irish relatives spilled out across California, from the sprawling big city of L.A. to the Mexican border. The roads were filled with people just like us, belongings stacked on top of the cars, kids eating bologna rolled with cheese, or cold hot dogs and crackers. The dirt was everywhere, but even more so on the faces of the migrant workers and their families who worked in the valleys picking fruit. Dad said they were good people who just got a bum rap.

A good portion of our relatives eventually settled, got married to regular people, had kids, and took whatever jobs were available. We, on the other hand, lived all over Los Angeles before following the black rope out in search of another home, another state. From West Covina and Santa Monica to Whittier and Costa Mesa, Oroville to Pulga — and many, many more — we saw everything from the down-and-out in East L.A. to the plush Tujunga Canyon homes where my Grandpa Virgil, Mama's dad, lived with his new wife, Wilma.

Wilma wasn't as old as Grandpa and refused to let us call her Grandma. She was skeletal, with a bony, pale face and thin lips painted across her face in a straight line, like the way I draw my stick people. She was friendly enough in her own cold, eye-slanting way, but it was obvious she didn't like being around a bunch of kids, especially dirty little dark kids who hadn't yet learned grace.

Since Mama's mother, my Grandmother Ida, was such a bitch, Grandpa resorted to marrying Wilma. He had spent eighteen years in hell married to the wet blanket know- it-all known as my grandmother. They lived in Ohio when the kids were little, then moved to Los Angeles, where Mama graduated from high school — an event she considers the highlight of her life.

Grandpa Virgil and Grandmother Ida went to two different churches the whole time they were married. She believed in the taut teachings of the Catholic Church and he chose the Church of Christ. Mama said when she was in high school they fought all the time. Her mother would throw forks or knives at Grandpa Virgil from across the table while Mama and her sister Betty looked on. Soon, Grandpa started staying in his shop making religious artistic experiments, like a large-mouth carving that shot out flames like spewing lies — or perhaps sins?

I would later learn that the most unemotional, unkind woman in our family was Grandmother Ida, the woman who raised my mother and was, in essence, responsible for her weirdness.

Grandpa Virgil, unlike my grandmother, asked us questions about places we had lived since he last saw us. We tried to remember them all, but couldn't. Dad said we should get a map and put a star on every town we could remember living in, and he'd put stars on the ones we forgot. Grandpa was most interested in Montana, "the Big Sky Country," and the rivers that were said to hold more trout than any other state. He'd read that when you caught them, the rainbow shimmered across the fishes' backs in the afternoon light like diamonds in the sun. He'd seen it in pictures.

Gary and I told Grandpa stories about the deer and elk meat we ate that came right from family members who shot, gutted, and made into steaks or hamburgers. When Dad cooked it with homemade gravy, we said it was one of the best things about Montana.

Grandpa listened to us as if we were telling him the best story he had ever heard — which was more than most people did when we told them of our road stories. Most people looked at us wide-eyed, like we were making up stories as no one else could. Sometimes we talked about the summer evenings when we sat out on an August night, when the mosquitos weren't too thick and we listened to crickets and frogs.

Grandpa would get so excited; I knew he lived vicariously through us and enjoyed our visits, no matter how he may have felt about our nomadic lifestyle. He'd sit in awe, his Jewish nose standing out from his dark, lightly powdered face. Mama said Grandpa Virgil liked to powder his face because he was so dark and didn't want people to know he was Jewish. He had all the features of a fine Jewish man, though — black hair and eyes like round chunks of coal. When he laughed, it was always a belly laugh.

Since Grandpa Virgil only saw us on occasion, he didn't want to complain about my dad traipsing us all around the country. Instead, he wanted to teach us how to take care of ourselves, the way he took care of himself during the Depression.

"Judy, you're too skinny. You too, Gary." He always chuckled. He even laughed at the things we kids would agonize over, and we tried to see how it was funny. He made us laugh each time we saw him. He liked us all and I could tell that he thought of Linda as extra special. He winked at her and smiled, and I think he knew that she was the child who got the brunt of things. He enjoyed us and we had always wished his wife, Wilma, would feel the same way about us.

Linda's weight, even as a kid, would fluctuate. During her pre-teen years, when I wished I had more than a swelling of tits, she got round like a wrestler. Grandpa liked that she had a passion for food because he wanted to feed her — and there was no doubt she wanted to be fed.

"Let's eat. You like dates? I have lots of dates." He would pull out bags of the sweetest, moistest dates I had ever tasted. They melted in my mouth, unlike the sugar- coated dates I'd had before. From then on, I thought of him as the *date grandpa*. Grandpa

Virgil was a saint when it came to plying us with sweets. One of his lessons for hard times, which he learned from the Depression era, was how to make donuts with little money and no trouble. He took rolls of premade biscuits from the refrigerator — the kind you pop open on the edge of the counter — then let us poke the centers out with the top of a small aspirin bottle, creating small donuts. Then he'd throw them into boiling grease. When they were browned just right, Grandpa drained them and rolled them in cinnamon and sugar. That was our favorite treat when we visited — that and the fresh-squeezed orange juice he made every morning from the trees out back.

He retired from Boing Company young, so for the majority of my childhood, he was a preacher. It was all he wanted to do with his spare time, but Dad said it was pretty much a waste of time. Just a few inches over five feet tall, Grandpa Virgil kept the good church people awake with his enthusiastic sermon; jumping up and down like he was on a pogo stick. If we had to attend, Gary and I would sit in the back and watch, trying not to laugh too loud.

We hadn't seen him in years before he died at the age of seventy-five, and we didn't attend his funeral. I always regretted that.

Dad said the whole Los Angeles area looked different than it did when he was a kid. It all ran together, spreading out like tree roots. "I worked the streets for pennies back then, playing marbles, and later boxing. Kids today don't do that, they'd rather mooch off their parents."

Except for us kids, I wanted to say.

After staying with cousins in West Covina and Whittier for a couple of weeks while Dad worked odd jobs, he eventually got a call to build a new school in Montebello — a job that would *last a while*. To be closer to his job, we moved again, this time ending up on Dad's ex-wife's doorstep to stay until he got his first paycheck. His former wife, June, a tall woman as big around as Mama and Dad put together, had been pretty once, but she sure wasn't when we were kids. Time had sugarcoated her and surrounded her with a mean veneer. I tried to picture Dad and her together but somehow couldn't.

June's house sat on a corner with straw for grass and a yard filled with toys, litter, and debris. Garbage, kids, and dogs were scattered from one end of the lot to the other and the whole area reeked of dead animals. Inside, the smells weren't much better; the whiffs that emanated from that woman's kitchen almost made me sick. It was a cross between vomit and rotting duck. She clucked when she talked and used the toilet with the door open, making all kinds of sounds that I didn't want to hear.

When no one was around, June told me stories about how she and Dad had sex in the backseat of a friend's car when they first met and that's how she got pregnant with their first son, Danny. She said they would do it on the beach and she would get sand up her ass. Too much information! I don't know why she insisted on telling a young girl about her sex life with my dad, but she did, almost salivating as she talked. Now she was so fat that I couldn't imagine how they could screw at all. My cousins always said fat women needed to be rolled in flour in search of the wet spot. There was no doubt our education consisted of a lot more than schoolwork.

June and Dad were married when they were only seventeen, and had three kids right off the bat. My half brothers and sisters looked somewhat like us, especially Danny, the oldest, with thick Elvis lips and flashing brown eyes. He and Gary were almost identical, except in size. Danny was almost six feet tall. June's youngest daughter, June Bug, had been conceived after Dad had already left the family and met Mama in Long Beach. Mama had an appetite for a man in a uniform, and that was Dad when he was younger. But some relatives said June was already pregnant when Dad left to run off to Las Vegas with Mama to get married. And since Gary and June Bug are just a few months apart, it's possible. Of course, at my age, it was something I knew nothing about.

Surprisingly, though, there was just a small amount of animosity between June and Dad. She and Mama seemed to get along great, and since we were now living there, that was a plus. June liked to talk and Mama liked gossip, so they were a good match. It wasn't the first time we had to stay with her. When we were all babies we did for a while, I just don't remember it, but heard about it.

Between all of us, we filled the house with dirty diapers and continuous screaming and fighting from the toddlers. Mama had to be taken to a local hospital, and in my mind I remember being told — maybe from Dad — that she needed a "rest." Once Mama was taken away, June told Dad that Mama was nuttier than a fruitcake and needed to stay in the hospital until she could see a shrink.

"Ya picked ya a good one didn't you, Al?" she said, her words joking their way out of her mouth.

Dad turned up his lip and didn't say a word. I squatted in the living room, hardly old enough to know what was going on, but I remember some of the conversation.

"I like her, don't get me wrong, but she's nuttier than a fruit cake."

"She's just tired, June. Nothin wrong with her. Just needs a rest."

"Well, she's getting one now — right in the loony bin." She laughed. Neither one of them knew I was sitting right there taking it in.

When Mama returned from her stay in the *hospital*, she became withdrawn and stayed in her bedroom most of the time, staring at the wall or out the window. Dad told us to stay out of her way and let her rest. He said we needed to settle down so she could have a permanent place and get well. I heard that again and again throughout my life. But why would he want to do that to Mama? She liked the road as much as anyone and hated almost every place.

Aunt Helen stopped by, giving Dad yet another lecture about the road. "She needs a permanent place, Al. Get rid of the road, man. You're living like our Dad did. Do you want to do to your kids what they did to us? Huh?"

Aunt Helen had a point. She used this argument more times than I can remember, and Dad shook his head and tried to agree with her every time. But — like someone addicted to drugs, food, or alcohol — our family was addicted to the road; the lure of the long black line that led to new and old places alike. It gets in your blood, and even I could see that. Gary and I made it as fun as we could.

When Dad got paid and Mama seemed normal again, we prepared to move to Arizona instead of getting our own place in L.A. Dad said the job wasn't what he wanted it to be and that there was a better job waiting for him down the road. The land in Arizona, he said, stretched further than the eye could see with cactus, dusty red earth, giant bugs, and intense heat. People were dry and cracked. The earth was thirsty, but water rarely quenched that thirst.

Dad said there was good prospecting to be done and gold to be found. We all yelled and whooped, not because we *loved* the place we were going, but because Dad had a way of making us *think* we liked where we were doing, even if we didn't know a thing about it. He reeled us in with spine-tingling, captivating words that promised a permanent home and staying there to grow a garden and get old.

Dad said we had enough money to move and proved it by flashing four hundred dollars at us. He laughed when our eyes opened wide and we exaggerated the excitement of the bills. With that money, we could rent a U-Haul and a house when we got there.

Somehow, Dad once again made it possible for us to leave and move wherever he wanted. The excitement and lure of the road hit us all.

"You kids get packed up. We need to get there, get a place, and find a job. Hot as hell there and it's only gonna get hotter," Dad said.

We hurried and tossed our things into cardboard boxes from June's basement, then the next day loaded the boxes into the U-Haul.

Arizona was a good place — we had been there before. But not yet.

Chapter 8

We never made it to Arizona but ended up in Bellingham, Washington instead, where I was a gawky, bony girl with teeth like a beaver, round eyes, and hair that had been cut with a bowl. As homely as I was, two fourth grade boys still thought I was hot. Roy and Eddie Carson were brothers — Eddie was short and squatty with freckles and a turned-up nose, and Roy was skinny as a goat with wisps of thin hair and buck teeth.

They both liked me, but it was Roy who was in love with me. He spent hours at our house trying to get me to like him, but I found him a little creepy. When I told him one day that I didn't like him as a boyfriend, he ran out of our house crying.

Mama came running into my bedroom, asking, "What did you do to him? He's outside drinking out of a mud puddle."

I ran to the window and, sure enough, there he was on the ground over an oil- slimed puddle, crying his eyes out, taking gulps of dirty water. I realized then that girls — no matter how young — had some jurisdiction over the men in their lives. I felt quite beautiful and wanted until I was shot down by a visit from my grandfather, Dad's father days later.

I had just gotten my sixth-grade school pictures taken. We didn't always get to buy the pictures, but this time we had enough money to afford the extravagance of class photos. Dad worked a lot. We rented a two-story pink house right across from the school. When the teacher handed out the envelopes containing our photos, I couldn't wait to rip mine open. But when I looked at the pictures, my heart stopped. Staring up at me was a plain girl with lopsided ponytails, big teeth, bangs cut at an uncertain angle, and a vacant look. Hot tears began to form as I stared at that photo — I looked like a cheap plastic doll that had been played with too much.

Because there weren't any relatives in the area to give the photos to, we were stuck with them, and Mama made it a point to plant them all over the house — "Wall decoration," she'd say, tacking them next to her drawings of cartoon characters. I had to look at those pictures for years, but eventually tore up most of them.

When my paternal grandfather, Arthur, arrived one morning, I was still in bed but heard the loud knock on the door and the even louder greeting from Dad. It was early and rain tapped at the windows, muffling words from the other room, but I picked up some of the conversation.

"Just left Montana. Sick of that damn snow," Grandpa Art said. "Not sure where I'll end up, but I'm just here for a visit." His wife, my Grandma McAlpin, died at the age of forty of a heart attack, so we never got to know her, except for the short time she lived with us in California. She had been in a wheelchair — I had no idea why. For some reason she had a romantic interest in all holidays, especially Easter, and sent us cards every year that Mama kept in a box with our photos.

While I listened from the bedroom, I couldn't help but think how this man, my grandfather, made my dad's life miserable; cheating him out of things, using Dad's name for his own purpose. He roamed around alone and usually hunkered down for periods with one relative or another. Because he ripped my dad off so many times, Dad didn't like him being around for more than a day or two.

"What? You'd rather have this than snow?" Dad asked while the rain hammered the roof.

Grandpa Art was a little man with a muddy face, red hair, brown eyes, and rounded Irish features. His voice was gritty, like tires on gravel. He had a mean streak, and I could tell he didn't much like kids. He would look at us, then turn away, rarely saying anything. Either that or he flipped out his false teeth in an attempt to scare us. He had trailed us to Bellingham by way of Salmon, Idaho, with a few pit stops in between. He said he was thinking of settling down. I learned that's what all our Traveler relatives said. Maybe they even meant it, but for most of the family, it just didn't happen.

I listened from the bedroom while the two of them continued talking. Then Grandpa Art let out a loud whoop and laughed hysterically. I sat up so I could better hear what was going on.

"Goddamn! That is just about the ugliest photo I've ever seen, why, hell she's just. . ." He stammered, then chuckled while Dad whispered, saying something I couldn't hear — probably explaining that it was a bad school picture, maybe I had a bad hair day, maybe they caught me off guard, who knew.

I heard Dad say, "You know how they are, those damn photographers!" The haircut he gave me didn't help either.

The words stung me like a wasp. I felt something growing inside my throat, strangling me, blocking off my air. I was destined to be ugly and not fit for others to look at. I couldn't come out of my room and stayed right there on the top bunk all day, pretending to be sick while I read and reread *National Velvet* and *Tom Sawyer*.

Thankfully, Grandpa Art only stayed two days — just long enough to torment me with his false teeth and nasty attitude. He didn't scare me like he did when I was little, just pissed me off. I told Mama one day, "If he pisses me off again I'm going to tell him to fuck himself." She shushed me, then told me to quit cussing.

Why? I wondered. Everyone else in the family cussed a blue streak.

Grandpa Art longed to make me cry like I used to. But now that I didn't, he gave up and started in on Linda.

Dad and Grandpa Art would eventually fight if they were around each other for too long. They both had outrageous Irish tempers, pushing each other's buttons like telephone operators. Dad thought his father was a thief and a liar and would say as much if provoked.

"That old bastard would steal money from an orphanage," he'd say after an argument. I always wondered if it wasn't more than an idle insult.

Dad started out in life with Grandpa's name, Arthur, and some relatives still called him Art. But when Dad started getting Grandpa's bills and repossession notices, he changed his name to Albert. It was just another thing for the family to talk about. They liked to talk about each other, sometimes embroidering on real events, sometimes making things up out of whole cloth. But when they ran into each other, they were long lost buds.

***

As I got older, my confidence grew. I didn't care if kids liked me or not, because I knew I wouldn't be staying in the town long anyhow. I could always meet new friends wherever we went, right? Yeah, that's what Dad said. If there was a disparaging side to our travels, it would be that we learned at a young age that we didn't *have* to *finish* things. No one told us it was O.K. to leave things unfinished; it's just what we learned through our travels. I could have mounting homework assignments, but once I heard the word *move*, I breathed a sigh of relief, threw the assignments in the garbage, and took on the attitude of *let's not finish anything*. That attitude didn't help me much through high school, and it sure didn't help Gary, who dropped out of school in his junior year. Our stabs at money-making schemes were also left unfinished when it came time to move.

Linda became more and more troubled as time went on. She was insecure and would still put her thumb and index finger together to form a circle around her eye — her little telescope. She'd look through it when she got rattled or tried to avoid a lecture or Mama screaming at her. That finger telescope went up to her eye whenever things were chaotic or she was embarrassed. Sometimes I felt great empathy for her. She loved nature and spent hours alone in the woods or the desert, depending on where we lived.

Sometimes I felt regret about not wanting to drag her along with us.

Mama had become our sidekick. No matter what we did, she wanted to do it with us. Movies, roller skating, bike riding, it didn't matter. But the older we got, the more we didn't want to do all the kid stuff with Mama. We wanted to do things with our friends. Gary and I had reached a point where it embarrassed us to have her hanging around, trying to fit in. Her tiny body wasn't much bigger around than mine, but her clothes were too creepy — plaid pants and a floral shirt, even when I asked her to put on something that matched. She'd laugh. "Why? This is how I like to dress." How could I argue with that?

Mama loved having our friends around but began getting jealous when we ignored her for them. She wanted to be accepted so much that she joined in no matter what we did. Then she would scream at Linda if she tried to interrupt our play.

"Goddamn, Mama, give her a break. She just wants to play," I'd say, acting as though I was the mother, which became the case more and more often as time went on.

The '60s came alive for us; the road was more exciting than ever and the music took over my body. I had listened to music all my life — country and rock and roll from Mama; classical, opera, and blues from Dad. But now there was something more compelling about it. It was *my* music. I was coming into myself.

I loved Grace Slick and Surrealistic Pillow. I wanted to be the White Rabbit, and it was the first thing I learned on the guitar I bought with money I'd saved up from working a part-time job at the local library. I also grew my hair out to my butt, made love beads, and grew to like cigarettes.

Dad's political conversations and rants grew, but he knew better than to try to discuss politics or world affairs with Mama, whose interest centered on Elvis, soap operas, the peccadilloes of movie stars, and local or family gossip. So instead he would corner me when he wanted to talk government.

Most people remember every detail of where they were and what they were doing when the announcement of Kennedy's death was broadcast across the nation. I remember every fragment about where I was and what I was doing because it was such a traumatic day for me. I was in class stewing about the watch I had received two weeks earlier from Dad for my birthday and had lost sometime during the day. I worried myself into what could have been cardiac arrest had I been older. I didn't know how to tell Dad that I wasn't mature enough to take care of a nice watch. I rehearsed a few different ways to say it. Then, when the news of Kennedy's death hit the airwaves, I forgot all about my predicament. And when I did finally tell Dad, he waved it off. "I'm sure you'll take better care of the next one you get."

I had never seen Dad cry, but that night when he walked in from work; tears were rolling down his face. He put his thermos and lunch pail down on the counter as if it weighed a hundred pounds. He wiped his face. None of us said a word; we knew what had happened and we knew it was a grim time for our country.

"The best president this country will ever see is gone," he said, throwing himself down in his chair — the overstuffed one with the cotton sticking out of holes. "The Goddamn country's gone to hell in a hand basket." He pulled a cigarette from the pack, lit it, and blew smoke from his mouth with a big sigh.

"You'll never see another president like Kennedy because there won't be another.

He was a good man," Dad said when incumbent Lyndon Johnson took over the presidency after Kennedy was killed. I always thought Kennedy's Navy background and war hero reputation had a lot to do with Dad's opinion.

In light of the upcoming presidential election, Dad bought a tiny black and white TV so he could watch the debates, one of the first times they were ever televised. It was said Johnson was going to win by a landslide and Dad wanted to see it for himself. Gary and I didn't care about the debates, which were incomprehensible and boring to us, but since we seldom owned a TV, we didn't care what he watched, as long as we got to watch it occasionally — anything, even the commercials, sounded good to us.

We knew that we wouldn't have the TV for long because most likely it would be left behind or given away the next time we moved. So we made the most of it while we could. "We can always get another," Dad would say whenever we had to leave it behind. And we would, eventually. Nothing tangible had a significant amount of importance to us. There was no wiggle room when it came to coveting anything. Dad's collections were an incongruity; he saved the best and left the worst. There just wasn't enough room to haul it all.

We combed through everything and hand-picked with care because leaving things behind was inevitable. When I was a kid, it would be my favorite toys or roller skates that got safely packed, but as I got older, those things would get discarded. Later, I wanted to take my friends, and eventually my boyfriends, because it was becoming obvious we were Gypsies and the hurt of not being able to stay in school with our friends was becoming unbearable.

With our new TV, we watched reports of the Russians putting a man into space, a development that disturbed my dad, who lectured me about the U.S. falling dangerously behind a mortal enemy.

"Pretty soon those Communists will come here and take over. You watch and see," Dad said. Like many others at the time, Dad was afraid the *Commies* would, as Khrushchev had said, dance on our graves. World War II had ended — and prematurely, as it seemed to Dad. He expected we'd have to finish the job with the Soviet Union sooner or later.

Chapter 9

Light flooded the car from Las Vegas's glow and glitter. Large hotel and casino signs, like the *Flamingo* and *Circus Circus,* flashed in luminous colors, brilliant against a coal-black sky. Even though we weren't on the Las Vegas strip, I felt its energy. All of us kids stared in wonder, even though we had been here many times before. The blinking lights announcing *showgirls, gambling,* and other such things mesmerized me as we drove down the strip. I wanted to be a part of that glitter and told myself I would come here again when I was older to dance in the shows.

***

The car became cramped and miserable. Words like daggers shot between us and when Dad wasn't in the car, Mama and Linda almost killed each other. I once again felt like the conciliator, trying to keep them from actually harming each other. Each trip now seemed like it took twice as long as it did before. Gary's legs stretched the length of the seat and I was becoming too big to fit on the floor where my bed had kept me cozy for so many nights.

It wouldn't have taken so long to get to California had the tired, old Hudson not broken down. We ended up on the outskirts of Las Vegas and stayed in a dilapidated motel the first night. Urine, smoke, and sweat enveloped the room and pounding on the other side of the walls kept us up all night. The walls were military green with yellowish tinges to the windows. We all slept in one room, except Gary, who preferred to sleep out in the car, saying it was better than sleeping on the slimy carpet. He had a point. I think I saw small white things embedded in the puckers of the rug.

The motel was close to the garage that was supposedly fixing our car, and the price of the motel was cheap. But by the third night, with money being tight, we all ended up sleeping in the car, Gary and I huddled in the backseat. As I tried to settle in and make the most of it, I heard Mama complaining about being out of Vicks with no drugstores around, and Dad grumbling about the garage.

"The fuckin' guy has to get the part from the wrecking yard. Hell, I could have had that part and had it put on that piece of shit car in an hour. Then you could get some Vicks. Those dumb bastards. Excuse my language kids."

Gary and I would often roll our eyes in wonder of how we had made it from point A to point B. But we always seemed to do it. It was the luck of the Irish, Dad said.

Mama could not shut up about her Vicks, because she wasn't going to get it any time soon. Dad hadn't slept much in the past two days and his sagging face and puffy eyes made him look grouchy and old. He still had the same good looks that drew women's attention, but there was a distinctly sickly look to him now. His dark hair was getting a little salt at the temples, and his ailing body and weight gain had started to take a toll on him. Regardless of how exhausted he was, he never let on about his heart or the pains. But as much as he tried, he couldn't completely leave us in the dark about his health because we had seen him in the hospital following his first heart attack when he was thirty-eight. When we asked about it, he said not to worry; he was as strong as he had ever been — just needed to change his diet. But it was hard to do while on the road.

Like a pack of Gypsies, we scouted out the few little shops nearby while we waited for the car to be fixed — it was either that or sit in the car all day in the oppressive Vegas heat. It was only late spring, but much warmer than where we had been. Our last few trips had taken us through several towns in Idaho, Montana, Washington, and Northern California. Some of the towns were too far away from the schools, so we hadn't attended.

Dad spotted a pawn shop and told us we could all go in if we *acted civilized.* I was beginning to wonder why he said that because he never meant it. Besides, his version of civilized and someone else's was most likely very different.

"Don't act like a bunch of horses' asses. And don't beg for stuff," he said, adding that he was going to hock the jade jewelry he'd made. He still carried around specimens he'd extracted from the mine he owned in the Sierras. With the money, he could pay for the repair and have enough left for gas and food. Because — as pissed as he was about the garage taking so long — he was now pissed that we had used all the money while waiting for the repair.

We had all grown fond of pawn shops. There was something about the gnarly smell of dirt and leather and the money that exchanged hands that gave me a sense of familiarity; that reminded me of the old pawn shop in Dillon where we taught Dougie how to make money from things he found. This shop, like all the others, was filled with musty-smelling tools, clocks, TVs, and radios. Shelves were stacked almost to the ceiling with everything from toasters to fishing gear. The walls — yellow with the cigarette smoke we had become accustomed to — smelled of mold and tickled my nose.

Mama chose to stay at the car while we looked around, saying Dad would get going on one of his jags and wouldn't shut up until the man got sick of hearing him. When we left her, she had her bare feet sticking out the window while she leaned back and read a magazine.

Looking around the dusty old shop, I found a small, red plastic transistor radio that nearly made my heart stop. It sat on a shelf between an old brown AM radio and a phonograph. I lusted for it immediately. In school, the girls my age carried them around, stuck to their ears or pushed in their coat pockets. I begged Dad to pay the $5 for this beautiful red wonder, but he shook his head without saying a word. He had a look that said *"No, and don't ask again."* Sometimes even my sad eyes didn't work.

The gaunt proprietor, with eyes as sharp and shiny as the silver in the showcases, watched our exchange of words in silence.

Sensing my yearning and Dad's vulnerability, he offered it to Dad for one dollar, "as a treat for your little girl." Glaring at the proprietor, Dad sighed and nodded his head to indicate he'd take it. My eyes widened when the owner gave Dad the money for the jewelry, keeping $1 for himself.

"You have to share it with your brother," Dad said. I was ecstatic — now I could listen to all the Bobby Vinton and Beatles songs I wanted to.

As soon as I got out the door, I flipped the radio on and found a station that was playing "Jail House Rock." I turned it up while we walked back toward the garage and the car. I felt my feet floating across the pavement, as though I could dance all day. I had my first transistor radio and I was fucking proud of it.

Mama sat stoically in the front seat, by now wilted with her limp movie magazine sprawled across her. When I opened the door, her legs fell out. She sat up and fanned herself, and when she heard Elvis on my radio, her little eyes became as round as walnuts. Elvis cured whatever ailed Mama. She owned most of his records and played them on an old phonograph   the one thing that never got left behind. She'd sing right along with him then grab me to dance. We'd do the jitterbug;—something she did well and did often when she was young. She taught me how to slide between her legs and spin around when her hand went over my head. Before she met Dad, she said she went to dance clubs in Long Beach and danced the night away with the sailors. Learning to jitterbug was one of her gifts to me.

Between the classical music and the Roy Orbison songs Dad liked and Mama's beloved Elvis and Hank Williams tunes, there was always music in our house. And if there wasn't, and Mama was in a good mood, she'd yodel and we kids would join in, sounding like a bunch of howling hound dogs. I could never get the hang of yodeling. But Mama came from a long line of yodelers. Her father, Virgil, and her uncles — four dark Jewish men — all yodeled together. Dad said yodeling wasn't really music and he thought it was strange that grown men would do such a thing.

"Sounds like a bunch of dying dogs," he'd say.

The *Five hamburgers for $1!* sign across the street beckoned to us once again. We had been eating cold weenies and crackers in the car, and Dad figured it was time for a change; for something more nourishing. We sat at a table with a speaker box through which we ordered thin burgers and foamy milk. Who the hell cared how greasy the burgers were — hamburgers on the road were the best! Especially after tolerating Mama's burgers, which she made with lots of bread and onions fried into the meat. She would cook them so black there was never a question they were done. So this was a treat, regardless of size.

I could tell the road and being stuck in this town was getting to Mama. She had the look of her latest cat — all worn out, gaunt, and indolent, as though life had given her a bum role. The black circles beneath her eyes made her look more tired than usual. It made her eyes seem more sunken than they were, like tiny marbles pushed into clay. Her face was so thin her eyelids looked blue. We all looked a little worn down.

The legs that shot out of my baggy orange shorts were stork-like and covered with purple bruises, rusty scrapes, and dirt. My hair was greasy and pulled back in a tight ponytail, causing my ears to stick out. Gary wore frayed cutoffs that hung below his knees and red tennis shoes with holes in the toes. Linda looked like a refugee parrot in her bright yellow stretch pants and pink top. She was barefoot — somewhere along the way she'd lost her sandals. Mama said it was good we were all so colorful because we could always find each other in a crowd.

"The heat getting to you, Mama?" I asked, stirring the bubbles in my milk. We hadn't bathed since making the car our home, following our departure from the motel, and we looked and smelled it. We always kept out a change of clothes while on the road, but this trip was taking longer than planned and we'd already gone through the few clean clothes we had. Linda's hair hadn't been brushed for days. It was so thick and knotted that it could not be subdued without a heavy session with Dad's beloved thinning shears.

Mama sighed before speaking. "I'm just going to be glad to get there. My feet and back hurt, and I have a cold."

Mama always had something wrong with her and complained about it to anyone who would listen. I think she made herself sick so she would have something to talk about. Some people called her a hypochondriac. She cried wolf so often that when she actually was sick, no one paid much attention.

When we got back from lunch, we found out the part for the car had come in, and in a couple of hours, we would be back on the road.

When we departed this time, everyone was in a good mood. The car was fixed, we had some money, and things were looking up. We all looked forward to getting somewhere, renting a house — regardless of how long we would be there — and unloading everything out of the U-Haul. We went from Vegas straight to L.A.

"Are we still going to see Grandma?" Linda asked, hopping up and down in her chair like a wind-up doll. Since we were going to be living in California, Dad said we could stop for a visit, something we rarely did. Mama perked up at the mention of a visit with her mother, while Dad, who made little effort to conceal his dislike of the woman, muttered something under his breath.

Ignoring Dad, Mama stared meaningfully at each of us in turn and said, "Yes we are, and you kids better behave! Grandma gets nervous around kids, so be good."

Nervous was not the word for Grandma. The only thing good about going there was the cookies. That stiff and wordless woman showed no emotion; she was the kind of grandmother you only read about in fairy tales.

After breakfast at a quaint truck stop and casino, Mama took Linda to the bathroom to clean her up. While she was gone, Dad said if it was up to him we'd never lay eyes on *that woman* again, meaning my Grandmother Ida. He told us we were better off not having a grandmother at all than to have one like her, even if she was the only grandmother we had now.

We sat scarfing up the remains of breakfast, dazzled by the machines that flaunted big winnings. The whistles and brilliant lights of the slot machines across the room caught our attention.

A man with no neck began jumping up and down in front of his machine like a toad on hot coals. Gary leaped out of his chair and ran over to see, almost as excited as the winner. When he got back he asked Dad if he could play one of them.

"What? You mean throw your money away, don't you?" Dad chuckled. He always warned us about gambling, letting us know how it had ruined many lives. "Maybe you should just take the money and throw it out in the road." Even though he was making a joke of it, I could tell he was serious.

"Come on. Just a dime," Gary begged. He was almost fifteen years old and felt the testosterone flowing through his body; the ego and the youthful belief that he was already grown up. But he could twist Dad around his finger in a way none of the rest of us could. They bonded as men, and the older Gary got, the more the bonding grew.

"Those machines are for suckers, Buddy. You might as well throw your money in the toilet as to put it in one of those one-armed bandits. Why do you think there are so many down-and-out people in Nevada? It's because they're addicted. They lose their Goddamn money and hock their car for more. It's as addictive as dope."

"*Please*," Gary begged, putting his hands together as if praying. His eyes were like shiny pennies and his sun-bleached hair brushed his eyebrows, falling to one side. The combination of his wide grin and lugubrious eyes was too much to resist, and Dad handed him three dimes and said, "Go ahead and lose your money. Be my guest." He had that smirk on his face, and before I could ask him for dimes, he said, "That's it, that's all I have."

Gary almost tripped running for the machine nearest our table. When Linda got back from the bathroom, we followed close behind. "You have to share," I yelled. But there was no response. Gary put the first dime to his mouth, kissed it, and rubbed it between his thumb and finger before dropping it into the slot. He was — as usual — theatrical about the ordeal and we all laughed, not caring whether he won or lost, just happy to watch the hypnotic flash of the machine.

"Let me kiss it, too," Linda squealed. Gary ignored her as he dropped the first two dimes in the slot. Lucky sevens and fruit spun around like windup tops, then stopped.

Nothing happened, even though Linda and I were screaming as if he'd won. He hit the machine with the side of his fist then looked around to see if anyone was watching.

He finally dropped the third dime in while we watched the mesmerizing roll of the colorful cherries and lucky sevens. Then, all of a sudden, coins began to clatter into the tin tray below. The sound was like hail in a metal bucket. We all jumped up and down and flung our arms while dimes clattered into the tray. I felt all the eyes in the restaurant on us. Our squeals brought Mama and Dad over. Mama screamed and Dad just nodded his head and walked back to the table. Gary walked away with more than $5. Split three ways, not so bad. No one said a word.

Chapter 10

Crossing the border to California felt good. Dad's spirits lifted when the soft blue skies and *Welcome to California* sign greeted us. Work would be plentiful right now, he said, and we would rent a nice house this time, with a yard for the cats and the German shepherd that rested on the floorboard near my feet — where my bed used to be. The fellow at the garage said he had to get rid of the dog and if we took it he would give Dad $25 off the car bill. So, Buddy became our cats' nemesis and took over a good portion of the backseat.

Days in the car were beginning to get to everyone. Gary and I bickered about how little space we had and how one of us was getting cheated out of our side of the car. The boxes below us sagged, the blankets on top of them wadded up in balls and layered with cookie crumbs and empty hamburger wrappers.

"Throw that shit out the window," Dad yelled when he saw how littered the backseat was.

Words started fights, and more than once Dad stopped the car and threatened to drop us off if we didn't stop. He reminded us that we still had a ways to go, as well as a stop in outer L.A. to see Grandma Ida.

The closer we got to the city, the more intense the traffic became. Dad merged into the flow of traffic and managed to finagle the trailer through the cars. Between warm city smells, honking horns, and the general commotion of people sprinkled on sidewalks here and there — or huddled together waiting for a bus — life was good and all of this commotion proved it. The energy in the car grew to a level of excitement. California meant fresh avocados and oranges picked right off the trees, sunshine, and warmth, and meeting new kids to hang out with on a Saturday night. And, if we went to visit Grandpa Virgil's house in the canyon, he would gather oranges from his yard and make fresh- squeezed juice or miniature donuts.

We were now in the bowels of the greater Los Angeles area where all the towns seemed to run together. Dad pointed out areas where he had lived as a boy and some we where we had lived as babies.

"Look, look, that's where we lived when Gary was in diapers and you were just born," Mama said. The motel she pointed to was in a rundown area of Montebello. Dad had taken a long and permanent leave of absence from the Navy, and they were madly in love and didn't care where they lived. Later, I learned Dad left the Navy about the same time he left his wife, June. Mama was pregnant (as was June), so Mama and Dad hitched off to Vegas and got married. That motel made me think of Dougie. Could that be like the motel where they gave him away?

We never talked about Doug much after that. It was as if he walked into our lives, then walked out again. No one wrote him and since we rarely had a phone, there were no calls. I thought of him, though. And when Gary and I talked about him, we called him *the other brother*. No one thought of looking him up while we were in Los Angeles; it was as if he quit existing once he moved back to California to continue his life with Aunt Helen. "How far to Grandma's?" Linda asked, squirming with impatience. Since she was the youngest and hadn't seen Grandma Ida as much as we had, she didn't know what to expect. She'd soon learn that this grandmother was not like the kind you read about in books. This was the kind of grandmother you might expect your demon doll to have.

Following Linda's stream of questions, all of the laughter in the car stopped and Mama became serious — if not a little nervous and agitated — moving around in her seat as if she couldn't get comfortable. She only saw her mother every few years and only heard from her once a year at Christmas when Mama received a card with $10 in it.

Grandma forgot about inflation, I guess because the amount never changed.

"We're almost at my mothers and I want you kids to behave yourself." Mama's voice was stern. She glared at Dad when she said it because she knew if he had his way he would encourage all of us to run through her flower beds and scatter the little white rocks around them.

He smiled and winked at Linda. "Ya hear that Injun, be good," he said playfully.

Linda laughed at him.

"Where in the hell is that turn?" Dad asked, searching street signs. While he got flustered, I turned up the music on my little radio; *Twist and Shout*. When he turned and gave me that *look,* I hurried to turn it down — loud music and loud kids were a bad combination when he was trying to concentrate.

"It's on the right. Couple more blocks," Mama said. She removed her red sweater — which really wasn't needed in this heat — and smoothed wrinkles from her stained cotton blouse and polyester pants. The cats had clawed a leg of her pants and it looked like fuzz was growing on her. Dad had warned us earlier to keep the cats in the back, or he'd make sure another one got a new home. The new dog got out, though, and Dad tied it to the bumper with a rope. Between the canvas water bag hanging on the front of the car and the U-Haul trailer with the dog tied to the back of it, we gave the neighborhood some color.

I looked down at my clothes. Pink shorts and a plaid cotton blouse — not clean, but cleaner than what I had worn for three days. None of us were *Grandma-worthy*, but none of us particularly cared.

California this time of year captivated me with its sunshine and fresh smells. As many times as we had moved in and out of this state, its splendor still amazed me.

Having flowers year-round was a real treat. Of course, parts of the city we had passed weren't as beautiful. That's when we saw the down-and-out road people.

Dad threw his lit cigarette out the window while letting Mama know this visit would be short. "We need to get a house so we can get this trailer back. It's gonna cost more as it is." He sounded tired and his face, puffy with black circles under his eyes, made him look old. He had a habit of driving all night so we didn't have to rent a motel. He said Gary and I could take over some of the driving when we got our licenses, which wouldn't be too long.

In some ways, I was excited to see my grandmother, mainly because it was nice getting out of the car for a while, and also to see if she had changed at all. I smoothed my ratted hair then spit on a blanket and washed my face with it. The last time I came here I looked like a poodle from the frightening perm Mama gave me.

Grandma hated kids. Dad told us one time, when Mama was young, her mother locked her in the closet so she wouldn't run off with boys. She made regular comments about sex and what a ghastly waste of time it was, and if Mama hooked up with a less than decent man, she was no longer welcome back.

Gary's stick-thin body looked like a pecan, all dark and shiny from being outside so much. When he pushed his sun-bleached hair from his eyes, I saw the mischief building up, playing unbridled in his mind. The narrow streets leading to her house were perfectly lined with shrubs and flowers. Most of the houses had a white picket fence in the front, and palm trees for shade.

There wasn't enough room to park the Hudson and the trailer in front of her house, so we pulled up in front of her neighbor's house. We saw the curtains flip open and eyes staring out as we parked. Then we all piled out, stretching and trying to brush crumbs and wrinkles from our clothes and tangles from our hair.

When we got to Grandma's house — one of the only houses with a tall wire fence stretched around the yard — Mama walked up to the door. We waited outside the metal fence. Mama looked so small and fragile while she knocked; like a little girl who just wanted the love of her mother. Her face looked serious and her eyes intent. Bobby pins poked out from her head like a voodoo doll — lots of them; her way of keeping her hair in order.

We didn't call ahead, so weren't even sure she was going to be home, but to

Dad's dismay, the door opened and a woman stepped out onto the small cement porch. She towered over Mama, a tall, thick English woman who wore the burden of life across her face. Her hair, cut short and straight across her forehead, was dark but sprinkled with gray. Her cold, brown eyes did not indicate a mood or an emotion as she looked from one of us to the other.

Mama looked up at her with pleading eyes, then said something we couldn't hear while she tilted her head toward us. She must have talked her mother into coming out to see us because Grandma began walking to the fence. Mama joined us on the outside of the fence where, as usual, our conversation would take place. We were never allowed to go inside her house because we were all heathens — or at least that's what Dad said.

Only once when I had to use the bathroom did she let me in.

"Hello, kids, Al, how are you?" When she said *Al*, she strung it out a little too long, making it sound dull, like *Owwwel*. Gary and I answered a few dry questions about school while Mama worked to get her mother's attention. Then Grandma went back in her house and came out with an oatmeal cookie for each of us. Dad refused his, but Mama munched away with all the excitement of a little girl. We sat on the lawn between the sidewalk and the road and ate our cookies while the three of them talked for another fifteen minutes. Grandma asked Dad where — or if — he thought we were going to settle. Gary and I hoped that Dad would lay into her just for the excitement, but he didn't.

"We'll settle where we settle," Dad said.

She batted more questions his way, drilling him about the low minimum wage, now just over a dollar, and haughtily asked how he was going to get a house and settle down with the kind of money he made. Gary and I were near enough to hear and could tell that she was trying her best to belittle our father. Gary wanted to jump up and give her his two cents, but I grabbed his sleeve and told him to sit down.

It was then that Dad yelled at us to get ready to go. "We better get going kids, before all of our money is gone and we're living on the street again." He said it louder than he needed to just to get our grandmother's goat.

She glared at Dad, then at the rest of us as we piled into the car. Then she waved, turned, walked back into her house, and shut the door without a backward glance.

Once inside the belly of our security, Dad shook his head, probably wondering how his mother-in-law could be so cold, but he didn't say anything, which was difficult for a man with an Irish temper like his.

When Mama climbed in the car after us, she bubbled with chatter and laughter.

Her mother was fine, she said — looked really good, too. "She said she thought you kids should be in school instead of the car, but I told her school was out. Oh well. I think it was a good visit."

Finally, Dad couldn't stand it. "She's just an old bitch, wouldn't even let her own grandkids in her house. Blood is blood, and these kids are her blood, damn it."

It didn't faze Mama, though, who aimed her giggling small talk at Linda.

It wasn't long before we moved to a little suburb of L.A. We stayed with an uncle and his kids, our cousins, who had just moved into a duplex in Pasadena. The cousins were older than us and took turns smacking us around, saying if we told anyone, they'd beat the shit out of us. They were tough kids and taught us how to make spider guns out of clothespins, and we were thankful for that.

Dad's job took him out of town for a week at a time, which meant misery for us most of the time. Mama wasn't good at living without him. In fact, sometimes I wondered what she would do if Dad was gone for good; and the way he was piling on the weight around his middle and having chest pains, it could be anytime.

After moving into our own place, we once again felt the gnawing hunger that came with every new house; that we would stay this time, start school, and have friends for more than a few months. We didn't believe it would happen and never put our hopes so high that it caused us emotional stress when it didn't.

Mama spent an hour or so each day cleaning the house. After that, she was lost, since coffee klatches were becoming less and less of a thing to do with spare time. If we didn't play games with her or go on long walks to town, she was miserable. She embroidered some when she had the supplies, but complained about the price of stenciled pillowcases, buying only when they went on sale. In the winter, she did paint by number pictures and tried to get me into it with her. I tired of it real soon.

Mama was beginning to get agitated more and more lately, especially when Dad was gone. As usual, she took it out on Linda. At first glance, Mama looked like a tiny waif with a cute ass and large brown eyes, but she was not to be reckoned with when it came to us. She screamed so loud neighbors came outside to see what was going on. If she saw them, she'd scream "fuck off."

Days in a new place without knowing anyone made us kids closer. We were our own friends. When Mama had money, we'd walk to a nearby pharmacy where the soda fountain had vanilla cokes and chocolate sodas. Then we'd head to the park and hang out while she sat and read her true romance magazines. We'd stay most of the day, sometimes taking sandwiches for lunch and sometimes going without.

After several visits to the park, Mama met a man named Ted. He had pimples sprinkled across his ruddy face and a permanent puppet smile. He had coarse hair that looked like wire, and he dressed as if he'd just walked off a page of a fashion magazine. Mama said he was her age and *just a friend*.

I'd never seen her giggle and flirt with any man the way she did with this man — not even with Ray, the polaroid photographer. The tired look she carried most of the time had faded, and when she laughed with him, her eyes lit up. We could only wish she was like that more often. But I guess it took a guy friend to bring it out of her.

"Kids, behave. This is Ted. He's going to take us roller skating someday if you're good."

Gary and I looked at each other. It was just like Mama to still think of us as her little kids. I could tell Gary didn't know whether to punch the guy or be happy about the possibility of getting to do something, even if it was just a bus ride to the skating rink.

Either way, we were a little confused.

After their first encounter, Mama began hanging out at the park almost every day — except weekends, when Dad was home. Some days, Gary and I stayed home and tried our hand at singing like Sonny and Cher, only we called ourselves Bucky Beaver and Judith Priest — Bucky Beaver because Gary's front teeth were large like a beaver's, and Judith Priest because that's what kids in school had started calling me. We'd sing loud, usually with me doing background vocals. Other days we tagged along with Mama, especially if Ted was going to take us on a bus to the inner city for lunch at a real restaurant.

Ted was friendly enough, but I could tell he liked us better when we took off and left them alone. Sometimes, he'd even give us money so we could walk the four blocks to the nearest store.

"What do you think they talk about all the time?" I asked Gary on our way to get a soda. Linda jumped in and said she liked him and it didn't matter what they talked about. She was still too young to know what we knew about sex and relationships. We always seemed to run with a crowd of kids who knew the ropes when it came to drinking, sex, and how to have fun. Plus, I'd read plenty of Mama's romance magazines.

"I don't know, I think it's kind of weird though. Bet if Dad knew, he wouldn't be happy," Gary said in a low voice so Linda wouldn't hear.

We didn't have the necessary experience to see at the time what was happening, but we were streetwise enough to be a little leery. You can't live on the road all your life and grow up like Pollyanna.

Gary and I both began to wonder what Dad would think if he knew about our new friend. Ted made Mama laugh and act like a kid, even more than usual. I could tell she had a crush on him because I knew how girls at school acted when they were around boys they liked. Mama let him touch her across her shoulders and move his hand down — until she saw us looking, when she moved it away. She rarely let Dad touch her, so it was unusual to see her allow this new man to have his way with her, and she even seemed to like it.

One day, Ted took all of us on a bus trip downtown to a matinee. When the lights were turned down and a cartoon splashed across the screen, I saw him put his hand on Mama's leg and she let him keep it there. I nudged Gary's arms, but he was so interested in the screen he didn't pay attention. Then, after the movie, she invited Ted over to our house. Not for dinner, because that might scare him away, but for a visit. They whispered a lot while we made bologna and white bread sandwiches with mayonnaise for dinner.

Because the days were long, we stayed out late at night with neighborhood kids.

Most of them were younger than us, but two pre-teens in the area appeared older. We didn't know what was going on inside the house; maybe we didn't want to know. But the next morning I heard Ted open Mama's bedroom door, whisper something, then tiptoe through the kitchen and leave through the backdoor. Gary must have heard him too.

While we poured cereal into our bowls, we looked at each other, and we both knew what the other was thinking.

"They're just friends," he said. "Don't tell Dad about him."

I zipped my lips with my thumb and index finger and that was it. Ted wouldn't be back anyhow. The day after he left, Mama must have felt guilty or nervous, because she somehow got a hold of Dad and we heard her crying on the phone (we actually had one this time) for him to come back. "I can't take it anymore." She was sobbing, trying to tell Dad how hard it was to "take care of these kids." I think she was saying she didn't know how to take care of *herself* and her need for attention.

Gary and I never mentioned Ted again, and when Dad got home at the end of the week, he gave us the news that his job was ending and we would be moving. All for the best this time, I decided.

Chapter 11

Dad hopped out of the car and made his way to a tiny log house with a *For Rent* sign out front. The heat was getting to him and he pulled up his t-shirt to wipe the sweat from his face. The neighborhood was quiet, with just a few dogs barking and a kid riding up and down the street on a tricycle. When Dad got back to the car, he had a smile on his face and was waving a sheet of paper back and forth. "It's the log cabin in the back, three bedrooms, no heat but an outhouse, better than nothin'. Oh, and we pump our own water. Come on, let's unload this thing."

It seemed the white-haired man he talked with knew some of the other members of the McAlpin family but rented to us anyway. Dad laughed when he told us that. Mama did the *tsst* thing she does with her tongue when something isn't to her liking, but Dad ignored her, not wanting to argue. Once again, we were back in Dillon, having dotted the land and towns across the west for a couple of years before returning.

Our family history, it seems, dates way back to Dillon. Dad's parents lived here on and off as far back as the mid-1800s. Of course, their last names were different, but they were our blood. How they all ended up here is a mystery to me, as they had first settled in Pennsylvania. Many of the older ones, including my great-grandparents, came from Germany and England and, before that, Scotland and Ireland.

The log cabin Dad rented was cozy and basic, but this time no one had to sleep on the couch. Linda and I shared a bedroom with one bed, which caused a lot of fighting, while Gary had his own room. The interior was dark, with unpainted wood and undersized windows. The tar-like smell of coal had permeated the walls and some of the window sills were coated in a black layer of dust. The outhouse was not a problem as long as the weather was good. My experience with outhouses in the winter was not pleasant — nothing worse than dragging your ass out of a warm bed to walk on a trail piled high with snow just so you could sit down on the ice-cold seat. It certainly wasn't the first time we'd had one and most likely not the last.

Once we settled in, we explored the rivers, creeks, and countryside nearby and tried to get reacquainted with old friends. We felt at home, at last. Cousins down the road came to help us settle in and a great uncle brought us venison and antelope for the dented freezer Dad bought at a second-hand store. A willow tree drooped over one side of the yard, giving us shade from the heat. Montana in the summer could be deadly hot.

Uncle Bob arrived a few days before us and said there would be work here for a long time, and both he and Dad were anxious to get at it. Their first job was framing a church and building an addition. Dad acted like a kid when he divulged this information one night at dinner.

"The framing alone should take all summer and part of the fall. Then with all the finish work, I'm pretty sure we'll be here for a good long time. We may even end up living here. Hell, there's nothing wrong with staying here." We'd heard that too many times to take it seriously. But regardless, we had something to look forward to — a permanent place and starting high school in the fall.

Not even forty yet, Dad was already talking about finding a job that would be easier on his body, which had been destroyed by all the roofs he'd climbed and fallen through, all the hammering he'd done, and all the suffering he'd through endured as a kid in the orphanage. He would be red-faced one minute and white as snow the next. I heard relatives talk about how he should go to Great Falls to see a real doctor.

Dad had tried his hand at several other ways to make money, once cleaning a bowling alley so we could get money for gas to get to Pismo Beach, California, and another time selling sandwiches from a deli truck. At least we ate well while he had that job.

Mama wanted to celebrate our good fortune. Dad had just sold some of his jade, the last from his mine in Pulga, California. He'd tried mining and rock-hounding as a full-time job, but each time he failed, unable to pay the bills. Mama convinced him to quit and go back to carpenter work where he belonged. She had such faith in him.

"We're eating right when Daddy gets home, so don't forget," she said.

We always ate right when Dad got home and had for years — or at least until lately. Now that we had aunts and cousins around, inviting us to eat with them — probably feeling sorry for us and our in-house chef — we spent more time away from home.

When we sat down to eat, Mama put the last of our celebratory dinner on the table. As she bent over the table, she set down a chipped porcelain platter loaded with a dark roast that had baked all day. It clattered from one side of the plate to the other, threatening to displace briquettes of onion and carrot. Another bowl cradled boiled potatoes with a dollop of butter melting on top and sprinkled with lots of pepper, and a small pan with canned asparagus dissolving in a puddle of tepid, greenish water. Yes, this dinner was celebratory all right.

My older cousins, Barbara and Grace, taught me how to wrap my long hair up into a "beehive," a popular 'do at the time. They ratted it with a comb and sprayed it until it was stiff and tall. They wanted me to look older — like the sluts Dad said they were. I loved that I could look more mature just by putting my hair up on top of my head. Boys whistled, too. I noticed guys looking at me more and more since blossoming into a teenager. My teeth weren't quite so large, but my legs and arms were still thin as green beans. I was also way too small. I had a fear boys would always think of me as a little girl, but they didn't.

119

When we lived in Newport Beach, while fishing off the pier, an older man in his twenties — and very good-looking — approached to watch me fish. I could cast my line as good as any guy and I could reel in the big ones, even if they were only spider crabs. I couldn't understand why he wanted to watch me. After asking me a million questions, he asked me on a date. I had never been on a date and couldn't imagine a man like this asking *me* out. My heart raced when I thought of a nice dinner and a movie, later knowing what he obviously wanted.

I felt I finally had some good, juicy news to write friends about, and I would have if Dad hadn't intervened. When I told him about my good fortune, Dad ran across the pier, grabbed the guy by the front of his t-shirt, and began shouting something we couldn't hear, waving his arms and showing his fists. Then the man left in a hurry.

Mama doubted my story because she was certain it was always *her* that guys whistled at, but I liked to think it was me. Mama was beautiful, though, in her special way. Her skin was smooth and light compared to ours. She was petite like a doll, but with the beginning of a bulging belly. Dad must have thought she was pretty hot too.

Sometimes when he got home from working out of town all week, he'd chase her around the house as soon as he got through the door, eventually grabbing her breasts — our cue to leave the room. She pretended to slap him away with her butterfly hands, but I was sure she liked the attention, especially when he grabbed her crotch. He'd whisper, "I'll see you later tonight." I could tell, even at my age, that he was far more sexual than her.

Although she liked the attention, I knew she hated sex. Most of the houses we lived in had thin walls, and sometimes we slept in the living room next to their bedroom. I could hear them; Dad trying to get her to give in and fuck him, and her clicking her tongue in disgust with that *tssst* sound. Sometimes an argument would break out and he'd give up, or sometimes she would give in, saying, "Hurry up. Make it fast." And as the bedsprings creaked, she continued with the disgusted clicking sound, occasionally telling him again to hurry up. Now that I was older, I felt sorry for Dad. Where was the romance? Where was the lust?

Lying on my back under the shade of our weeping willow tree, happy to be in our new house, I stared up through the branches and beyond, as far as I could see, imagining life on other planets, wondering if we would ever really know if there was any. I had taken on a new appetite for the unknown, reincarnation, the occult, and life on Mars, and read everything I could get my hands on. I got into Edgar Casey, Bridey Murphy, and others. My love of the fascinating world of spirits and ghosts stretched throughout adulthood.

Cottonwood limbs reached out across our yard, and the vastness of the sky and earth filled me with hope for tomorrow — not just for myself, but for everyone. A *dreamer,* Dad called me. I dreamed of helping people, like orphans and travelers, making sure everyone had food and shelter. One day, after listening to recruiters who came to our school, I even mentioned my interest in joining the Peace Corps when I graduated.

"Poor all your life and now you're going to go to another country and be poorer still?" Dad was flabbergasted that I wouldn't want to go to beauty school and do women's greasy hair for the rest of my life and have a steady income. He had such high hopes for me.

Chapter 12

As I have said, we were taught from a young age to be entrepreneurs, and the quickest way to get money together was to sell things. Since I was a little girl, going door to door hawking the things I found and collected — religious mottos, rummaged house items, material ordered from the back of comics — I knew I had the bug to buy, sell, or trade. Dad bestowed that gift on me, and it was what began to drive me at a young age.

At fifteen, I got a job at a carnival that had come to town. Gary heard they were hiring, so we went over to talk to them as soon as they began setting up. It was summer and we were told if we wanted to do anything this summer, we needed to make our own money. Gary and some of his friends got jobs running rides like the tilt-a-whirl. My job was taking care of three small kids in a carney's tiny trailer behind the *ball throw.* I had never babysat in my life but needed to earn money to hang out with my friends.

The trailer was small, with one bed in the living room, a kitchen the size of a bathroom, and nothing in between. The woman who raised the kids looked like a large, round elf, but her voice was like a truck driver's — too many cigarettes, I figured.

"Now the baby here, her name's Ruthie, needs to be put upside down and patted on the back. She's got the crud. If she starts to choke, put your finger down her throat and pull up any phlegm. O.K.? Gotta go. I'll check back soon. Fix what you can for dinner." Then she left in costume and didn't look back at me as I sat on the small cot with the kids and a deer-in-the-headlights look on my face.

That night was rugged, and I put it down as one of the worst jobs I'd ever had. The baby choked many times and I had to dig my tiny fingers down the kid's throat, almost making me puke right on the child. The two older kids got stir crazy in the small space, screaming that they wanted to go to the cotton candy stand. But because the baby was on the verge of death, I couldn't take them anywhere. I swore I would never babysit again. My life so far was a series of things I learned to hate, things I taught myself, and all kinds of ways to make money that didn't include babysitting.

When the carnival left town, it wasn't long after that we took off. Dad had the wanderlust for California and couldn't seem to get it out of his system.

All the California towns we lived in were filled with sunshine this time of year and, by the time school started, we were dark as berries, but I still had my blotchy orange-and-brown hair from a bad peroxide job. I was beginning to care what I looked like and having bleached hair, I thought, would make me fit right into this town. When I mentioned what I wanted to do to my hair, Dad refused at first, asking why I would want my hair blonde when I had such dark hair that matched my skin. But he agreed he would do the job for me with a bottle of peroxide. I had no idea what peroxide did, but the fact that he agreed kept me from asking questions.

My hair turned carrot orange and, rather than letting me dye it brown — which Dad said would only make it brittle — I had to stay that way until it grew out. Nothing like starting a new school with a dark brown crown, while the rest of my hair remained an unsightly orange.

Uncle Bob and his family rented the downstairs of an old, rambling two-story house in Escondido, and since the upstairs apartment was still vacant, we moved in the day after we arrived. When we pulled into their driveway, the fragrance of orange blossoms wafted through the car's windows, reminding me of the orchard behind, Grandpa Virgil's house and the fresh-squeezed juice he made for breakfast.

The rooms upstairs were large and bright, with windows that overlooked what once was an orchard — now being devoured by a sprawling new housing development that looked like little boxes thrown on a bright green floor. The house was an artifact of a vanishing era. Dad said pretty soon the entire earth would be covered and we'd be lucky to have grass someday.

Living in the duplex above Bob and Babe had its good points. Babe treated me like an adult now. She told me all kinds of juicy stuff I otherwise might not know. Her thick blonde hair, tied back in a ponytail, slapped her back while she told me stories about my father and my Uncle Bob that I wasn't sure I wanted to hear. She said when my ass got bigger like hers, I could move it around in a slow circular motion and attract men like flies. Her ass was large and round like a washtub, and she certainly knew how to move it when she walked. I didn't know what to think about all this; boys were just beginning to attract my attention, but the more they flirted with me, the more I learned to flirt with them.

One day, while I helped Babe bake cookies — or at least watch her kids while she made them — she told me about what it was like when she met Bob. "At first it was all about lust. When I met your uncle, we screwed like rabbits, every chance we got. Sometimes in the back of the car or out in the woods, where I once got a stick shoved into my ass." Her words drifted through the open windows and out across the lawn. It was a little too much information for me, so instead of saying anything, I pretended not to understand. Babe seemed to enjoy my embarrassment and giggled like a schoolgirl with a secret.

"You'll see. Cute little thing like you, the boys are gonna be all over you. You wait and see."

"Not with hair that's brown at the roots and orange on the ends they won't," I said, smoothing my long hair.

"When you start school, you'll see. Kids will love that you look different. This is California, hon!"

Different is right. Not only was I the new kid with mismatched clothes, but the new kid with orange and brown hair as well. Kids looked at me like I was a freak and asked more than once what happened to my hair. I couldn't help but tell them that it was the rage in most places.

Babe loved to tell stories, and didn't recognize the concept of "family secrets." If not for her, many of the juiciest parts of my family history would be a total mystery to me. Dad told me things — what I call the top layer of our lives — while Babe told me things about the deeper layers. One particular story she imparted to me while I helped her fold laundry was one I had only heard parts of before.

It seems Babe's mother, Chick, had married my Grandpa Art — the bad Grandpa who laughed at my school picture — before Babe had even met his son, Bob, Dad's brother. Babe was not only married when she met Bob — working on a divorce — but also pregnant with her second child. When she met Bob, she said she fell instantly in love with his black, wavy hair, perfect smile, and sexy body. I imagined them meeting on the sly, having hot sex in the backseat of the car, and hiding everything from her then- husband. I had read a lot of *True Romance* magazines and figured that's how the story should go. But when Babe went on to tell me about their first meeting, it brought back memories of what I had experienced that same day — because I was there.

It had been a stifling hot summer afternoon in Dillon years earlier, when we were still kids with scabbed knees and dirty elbows. Uncle Bob, single at the time, arranged a picnic reunion for the whole clan, or at least those who were in the area at the time — even Chick and my Grandpa Art, who we hadn't seen in a couple of years. Everyone brought food and drinks and spread them out across the kitchen counter. I was fascinated with all the shapes, sizes, and colors of the liquor bottles, something I hadn't seen much of before since my parents didn't drink.

Bob's house was a small, rickety log cabin on the edge of town, with not much more than a stick chair and kitchen table for furniture. But we all spent the day outside on blankets or makeshift chairs from boxes or sawhorses. We kids played and spied on people, pretending to be detectives. We saw things we shouldn't have seen, like men hitting on other men's wives, who enjoyed a little touching underneath their blouses.

People were drinking, men were flirting with women — even with Mama — and it was so chaotic even we couldn't keep up with what was going on. But when Babe's soon-to-be ex-husband, Bill, showed up, putting the makes on Mama, all hell broke loose. Dad told him to hit the road.

"Get the hell out of here, you're not wanted here," Dad said, looking a Bob and Babe sitting on the lawn, probably hoping they would just stay there.

"Are you asking me or telling me?" Bill said, slurring his words. He looked like he had just crawled out of bed, drank his breakfast, then heard about the party and decided to pay a visit.

"I'm telling you. Get the fuck out of here."

"If you were asking me, I might go. So, ya asking or telling me?"

We all listened intently — especially Babe, who probably wished her ex-husband would leave and never come back, regardless of her pregnant state.

By now all the kids had gathered to see what would happen. For me, it would be my first up-close, in-person fight. Dad, who I had never seen drink alcohol before, called Bill to the street, rolling up his sleeves as he headed toward the dirt road. We all followed, even most of the grownups went out to take a look, forming a circle around the two men like a boxing ring. Mama stood at the edge of the circle, screaming, "You knock it off. Both of you." No one paid any attention. By now a few neighbors had stopped by for a look or a drink or both.

It was loud and Gary couldn't contain his excitement. "Hit him, Dad. Hit him."

Bare-fisted with sweat dripping down their foreheads, the men gave the crowd quite a show. They put their fists up, dancing across the road like a couple of cocks ready to go at it. Bill struck the first blow, but Dad counterpunched, landing a solid right hook to the side of his face. Bill almost fell over, staggering around while trying to stay out of range and clear his head. Before he recovered, Dad hit him again with a straight right to the nose and he fell in a heap.

After a minute, Bill got up on his hands and knees and tried to tackle Dad, but missed him completely and ended up on his face in the street. When Bill got up, he ran toward Dad, then Dad struck him again.

"Ya gonna leave or do I have to hit you again?" Dad asked.

All of us kids sat together, a little fear and a lot of adrenaline flowing through our veins. We whispered to each other as though it was improper to talk aloud when people were watching a fight. There was laughter in the distance, shouting from some of the women, and cheers from the men.

"What do you think they're fighting about?" I asked, holding a red Popsicle that was melting and running down my arm.

"They're drunk," Gary said. "It just makes people fight."

"How do you know?" I asked sarcastically. He was ten then and thought he was an adult that knew everything.

He said, "I've been around plenty of friends' parents when they're drunk."

"Better not tell Dad, you'll get in trouble," I said. Dad didn't want us anywhere near people who drank; this was a rare exception.

Linda started to cry until we gathered her to us and let her know it was O.K., that's what people do at drunken parties. I don't think she believed me until I said, "Besides, Dad will win, look at his muscles." That gave her some hope and she shut up and watched as they capered around, jabbing tentatively and wiping sweat from their eyes. Blood trickled from Bill's nose and he wiped it with his hand and then, when Dad hit him again, stopped and walked off, unable to get another swing in because he was falling all over the place. I saw a trickle of blood running from his ear as he sauntered toward the house to gather his stuff.

When he came out he said, "You can all just go to hell. You too, Babe." He glared at her with a turned-up lip, a sprig of hair hanging over his right eye. He weaved his way down the street, stumbling a few times and rubbing his elbow, then turning back to see if anyone noticed. He was not quite as bold as when he arrived. Now he looked withered and shrunken as he made his way to his car and drove off.

I had never seen Dad fight and I had never seen him drunk, and the combination transformed him into a fierce and frightening stranger. Everyone clapped when it was over and the crowd dispersed. It wasn't long after that incident that Babe got a divorce, and Bob asked her to marry him. That, my aunt said, was her romantic story of love and finding the man of her dreams.

So now, my Aunt Babe was married to her stepbrother, Bob, and her stepdad was also her father-in-law. God, how do I keep up with all this? This is how I heard it, as confusing as it was. I may be wrong.

"I should send that story into one of them *True Romance* magazines because other women would love to read about my weird life," Babe said. "God knows I've had more than a few strange things happen to me. Who knows, we could make some money off that story. Hell, you're a good writer, Judy, why don't you write it?"

Since Babe knew we had already found out about Dougie being our brother, she wasn't afraid to let me know what she thought about that whole thing — or anything else, for that matter.

She liked to see the shock on our faces when she told us where babies came from and how sex hurts on the first try. Gary would leave the room and learned not to hang out with the women very often. In the weeks that followed I learned more about my family then I'd ever known before. Babe was a wealth of information, and as long as I promised not to tell my parents what she said, she'd keep on telling me her sordid little stories about all kinds of people I knew.

She told me that the reason Mama acted the way she did was because she fell off a cliff when she was little while vacationing with her family at Niagara Falls. "She had to have a steel plate put in her head. And don't ya know they didn't know how to do it very well back then. I think it's rusted or needs to be replaced, if you ask me. But don't you say anything — she doesn't want anyone to know. Mum's the word, girl."

I thought about it every time I combed Mama's hair; about how she winced when I pulled too hard. Then one day she said,

"Be careful on that side, that's where I was operated on when I was a little girl."

So Babe knew what she was talking about. Dad called it all gossip, but I liked all the stories she had wound up in her head.

We talked about Dougie. Even though I knew some of the details, I felt there were still secrets I'd never know unless she told me. Most of the secrets in our family spread like jelly on bread. Walls were thin and word got around. But I never felt I knew the whole story about Dougie. Then she "spilled the beans" more than she ever had before.

"Your dad did what he had to do. He couldn't take care of that new baby any more than your mama could. Your mama went off the deep end and ended up in the hospital right after that baby was born, after your Aunt Helen rescued the baby. He said your mama had a nervous breakdown. She ain't always the most stable person. Your Aunt Helen said for a while your mama didn't even realize she had a new baby to take care of. Just left him on the floor and rocked in her chair. How you guys came out so good is beyond me."

Babe's hair flowed to her waist and spilled over the large hump of her stomach.

Her hair shined a greasy glean in the afternoon sun. Babe said if it wasn't for Aunt Helen, Dougie would have probably ended up in a foster home or an orphanage.

"I know you miss him, hon. But don't. Be glad he's where he is." Her face took on a serious look when she said that, and I believed what she said. Her words always had a way of calming me down and her beautiful smile calmed me.

As she worked on lunch, she never stopped telling me what I longed to hear. Her words stunned me and made my heart sink because I had felt Doug wasn't wanted enough to stay in our family. I hadn't thought about it as a way to *lighten the load* and make Doug's life better at the same time. Why would someone give their kid away as easily as dumping a cat on the side of the road? I knew I was wrong to think that because it had to be hard on both parents.

"Your dad hired a man who came in every day to take care of you kids while he looked in on Alice at the hospital — just until some of the other family showed up." Babe poured us each a cup of coffee with two teaspoons of sugar, in each cup then stirred it while her eyes darted around and thinking as she munched on her sandwich. I was not yet a coffee drinker, but I didn't want her to quit talking, so I took the cup, added even more sugar, and drank it down like syrup. Although it was summer and hot as hell, Babe looked like a piece of chalk, as white as the bread she used to make sandwiches — a real contrast to our chocolate-skinned family. She and Bob were like salt and pepper.

"One thing I've always wondered," I said. "Why didn't they get rid of all of us? How come only Dougie?"

"I think they were already attached to you, hon, and Gary too. Hell, Dougie was new to the family. Your dad told Bob he did it for the boy's sake. I'm sure he did. Like I said, your mama was in no shape to take care of him. She could barely take care of you two."

When I gave it some thought, realizing that Linda was born just two years after Dougie had taken his exit from our family, I grappled with the idea that maybe this was why Linda was treated the way she was. Maybe Mama was O.K. with two kids and could even take care of us, but when Dougie and Linda rolled around, she had no strength or compassion left for them. Hell, maybe she didn't have enough love left in her for more kids.

Again I was told about Mama's "nervousness" and how kids made her crazy sometimes, putting her over the edge. Babe called her a Jewish Princess, saying the way she was raised didn't help matters any. She lived in an upper middle-class family with one sister in a good L.A. neighborhood near Hollywood. Her mom and dad, my grandparents, fought over everything, and as soon as Mama graduated from high school, her parents divorced.

So, it seems, everyone knew about Doug and everyone knew about Mama, and they all accepted it. One thing about our family, as much as the relatives fought, as much as we all took to the road, following each other like a pack of drifters, no one seemed to be judgmental. What was done was done. Life went on.

***

"Pretty soon you're going to be a better cook than your Mama," Dad said when I baked and decorated a cake one day. God help me if I wasn't at least that good already!

I knew then that I didn't want to be a Jewish Princess like Mama, hanging out all day waiting for my husband to get home. I wanted my claim to fame to be more than putting dinner on the table right at five o'clock and making special tomato soup cake. I wanted my life to be fuller than that, even though Mama's goal for me was to marry and get a house right down the street from her so we could have coffee together every morning. I think she forgot about what we would do when it came time to move, because I doubted very much that either of my parents would give that up.

After four months of learning all the family secrets from Babe, it was time for us to hit the road and scratch the itch on Dad's feet. Bob and his family helped us load the trailer, and what didn't fit, we left with them. Before we drove away, Babe came over and hugged me. She whispered in my ear, "You don't have a thing to worry about. Someday you'll grow up and become a beautiful butterfly. Right now you're in your cocoon, but you just wait." I hugged her back.

I wasn't so sure I would ever emerge from my cocoon from the looks of my too- skinny body, too-big teeth, and too-chiseled face. I didn't see a lot of hope of becoming a butterfly.

I waved until I could no longer see them; I knew it wouldn't be long before we all caught up with each other again. The road, although big and strung out in every direction, didn't keep any of the clan from finding each other — phones or not. I wondered if they had all been traveling so much they knew each other's patterns.

Chapter 13

With Mama, each day was different. We never knew whether she would be in a good mood or off on a tangent. We didn't know if she was going to act like a crazy woman and chase us around with Linda's wet underwear, thinking it was funny, watching us run and scatter and embarrassing Linda for her latent bedwetting — or if she was going to slam the door to her bedroom and not come out for hours. Sometimes the latter was the best. Then there were her habits of avoiding anything that resembled responsibility, and when we were younger we didn't know anything different.

When Mama heard the knock on the door, she peeked through the heavy curtain, then crouched down and wriggled her way along the floor until she reached us. She whispered, "Get in the closet." We followed her along the floor. The closet was dark and cluttered with boxes that never got unpacked, but it had room for all of us.

"What's wrong, Mama?" Linda asked nervously. "Just keep your mouth shut," she said.

Gary and I knew what was going on. Someone was banging on the door for money — a bill that never got paid. If the power went off suddenly, we'd know it was the electric company looking for payment. The last time that happened, Dad came home to see us sitting in the dark, burning a candle. It was a game to us, though, and sometimes while in the closet we'd get the giggles and couldn't stop until Mama shushed us. It was stuffy and smelled of mildew.

Finally, when Mama felt enough time had gone by, she partially opened the door. "Stay here," she said, still whispering, then hunched over and walked quietly to the window, where she ensured that the coast was clear. When she gave the *all clear* sign, we hobbled out.

"Those somabitches," she said, still unaware that the word she used was actually supposed to be four words. We didn't ask questions; it was just what we did when a strange man or woman banged on our door. At least this time it wasn't the principal. Last time it was. He had come looking for us because we hadn't been in school for a few days, and when we saw him from our side yard, we ran to a cluster of cottonwoods and scrub oak and stayed there until he left.

It felt like it was time to leave, and each day I anticipated the words that we would be moving. It's like learning about something before it happens — you just know. I don't think Doug would have liked the road. He wasn't the type that could sit in a car for days with crawling cats and an occasional drooling dog, waiting for a place to land and hoping for the best. He couldn't handle it.

Dad waited too long to get out of town and snow began to fall. By Thanksgiving, our little cabin had thick patches of ice growing on the inside of the windows like moss on a tree. The coal stove generally went out by morning and it took a few hours to heat the house again. Getting ready for school, we dressed by the stove, ate by the stove, and bathed by the stove. If we ran out of coal, Dad sent us to the tracks for more, at least enough for the night and following morning. Money was tight and Dad said buying coal right now wasn't an option. I learned early on that's what happens when you get stuck in the winter in Montana; no work means no money.

The path to the outhouse, not twenty yards from the back porch, might as well have been a mile away. Inside the wooden box that smelled of shit, the cold permeated my bones the minute I pulled my pants down. I involuntarily shuddered when my ass hit the icy, wooden surface.

The gray sky became one with the earth and its blanket of white. Naked trees extended their arms downward, touching the earth and playing with the snow at their bases. The cold clung to everything, pushing its way through the walls and the cracks under the doors. My uncles said it was one of the worst winters in years, with more below-zero days than usual, and Dad was going crazy for not getting out sooner. We were stuck, and as far as we were concerned, there was no way out.

Our black-and-white cat — one of the longer-lasting cats I might add — was found frozen on the path to the outhouse, its paws stuck straight up in the air like it was praying before it froze. Mama looked everywhere for it the night before, knowing it would surely freeze if left out. When we found it, all we could see were black dots in the snow — the four little feet, stiff as metal rods. Mama sobbed until Dad told her we could get another one to take its place.

Dad tried to be positive when the blankets piled on top of us weren't enough to keep the cold out. "Just lay still and you won't get cold. Ya wiggle around and you let the cold in." That sure didn't work. In the morning, ice was thick on the window sills next to the couch, which was also my bed. Getting out of bed with the bitter cold was nearly impossible, even with the coat that I wore to bed.

Relatives, once again, brought venison and elk meat for us that, along with a few boiled potatoes, made a good meal. Dad hustled up small jobs when he could and everyone — except the *settled folks* — had a bad time of it. Uncle Bob and his kids were living out of town in a trailer that had frozen pipes, and when the wind blew it shook so hard things flew off the walls.

Two of Dad's cousins lived in a shack out near the dump along the frozen river. They found a wood stove someone had discarded and put in in their house. It's a good thing, too, because winter storms were coming on fast. The colder it got, the more we knew that this time, we would most likely be stuck here for the winter.

Dad said we had it a lot better than some people. "People in China are starving," he liked to say. "And the bums from the bars are still sleeping on the depot lawn."

Examples like these also conjured up his days in the orphan-age. "Go for a couple of days on bread and water and see how you like that," he said one day when we were whining about eating yet another elk steak with little to go with it.

The lines in Mama's hands were embedded with coal once again; her lifelines and pores making a mosaic of swirls. Since the women didn't get together for coffee chats when it was this cold, Mama stayed home alone most days, which was not a good com-bination with the cold. Some days she just sat and stared, or read outdated movie star magazines. Other days she became nervous and agitated, and nothing we did would change that.

Christmases came and went but one stuck with me like sap on a tree. And in the far reaches of my mind, I clung to it.

One morning when I was about nine years old, I heard my parents talking in the kitchen — it was hard not to in a small cabin — and I could tell they were discussing Christmas. It was obvious they were worried about what they would do for presents this year since they didn't have any money. It didn't bother me, though. There were times we only got $5 for Christmas, but if we didn't expect it, we were O.K. Dad always said he'd make it up to us later. If we moved during the holidays, we had our Christmas later, sometimes in the summer. And Dad, true to his word, always made it up to us.

Most of their conversation I didn't hear, but within an hour Mama came out, grabbed her wallet, and told me to get my coat on — we were walking into town. She had an unyielding look on her face and a no-nonsense stride — she was on a mission. Gary grabbed his jacket and followed, but Linda was bathing in a tub of heated water near the stove, and so stayed home with Dad.

When we got outside, noise from the trains butting metal on metal across the street attacked my ears with the grinding, bump-ing metallic sounds, irritating all of us — especially Mama, who would scream "Fuck heads!" to anyone who could hear her over the harsh sounds. Loud and obnoxious clatter is what we called it. Men wrapped in heavy one-piece jumpsuits walked around the trains, waving their arms, clouds of white puffing out of their mouths.

Mama walked with fast, little steps. I had to skip to catch up with her. Her tiny body seemed to glide over the snow and along the streets. So far she hadn't said a word about what we were doing out in the sub-zero weather.

"Where are we going?" I asked. She didn't answer and I could tell she was deep in thought by the way she swung the arm that held her pocketbook, while her other hand grasped the top of her coat to keep it closed. Darning things was not in Mama's repertoire; you wore holey socks until they fell apart.

Within a few minutes, we were in the heart of town, where Christmas sparkle hung from street lights and storefronts, saddening me. No matter how you looked at it, Dillon was just Dillon. It's like taking a cowgirl and putting her in a dress and lipstick. In the end, she's still just a cowgirl.

Snow and ice pushed to the side of the roads were splattered with black, and the men hunched in front of the bars had hollow, frightened faces — eyes staring blankly into the icy skies. In the window of Skeet's Café, I saw where the usual depot sleepers had ended up — it looked like every seat was taken. Steam formed on the windows and the people inside were blurry images, sipping coffee and wrapping their hands around their cups for warmth. The owner of Skeet's had a soft spot for these homeless men, and when they came around the back door, he would give them food.

The white-and-blue *Hogue's Department Store* sign mounted on top of the building was bright against the ominous gray sky. We crossed the street, climbing the piles of snow, and headed toward the welcoming sign. Mama told us to follow her as she bolted through the doors. Gary looked at me and I knew that he was as curious as I was about what was going on. I knew we weren't going to rob the store since we didn't own a gun.

At first, Mama just looked around like a little mouse. Her head was covered with her favorite red bandana tied below her chin, her boots large over her boney legs, and the coat she wore had threads hanging from the bottom

"Mama, what . . ."

"Sshhh," she said, putting a finger to her lips, squinting in our direction. We followed her to the toy section and she told Gary and me to pick out what we wanted for Christmas, and not to forget Linda. After I filled my arms with a record player, a sweater, and some art supplies, and Gary had scooped up some boy things, we picked out a few toys we thought Linda would like. Mama chose for herself a stuffed cat to take the place of the cat that had frozen. She said she would put it right alongside her real cats so they wouldn't be lonely.

When we got to the counter we piled our booty on it, stacking it just so, then waited for a clerk. Mama was as serious as I had ever seen her. Her mouth was set, lips in a straight line, and her hand clutched her coin purse so tight it turned her knuckles white, a contrast with the blue veins that stuck out. The clerk greeted us, looking from one of us to the other before beginning the checkout process.

"I want to charge these," Mama said matter-of-factly as if she was asking where the bathroom was.

"Do you have a charge account with us?" The young woman had hands like a porcelain doll, her fingernails perfectly manicured — next to Mama's black hands, they looked pale. Her hair, ratted high, looked like cotton candy, and her lips were bright pink. She looked at Mama's hands, then turned away as if Mama had an incurable disease. Her eyes darted from one of us to the other, maybe trying to figure out which one of us was the most pathetic.

"No. I can open one, though," Mama said, looking the clerk straight in the eyes as my eyes bulged at her statement. When has anyone ever given us credit? The only time I could think of is when we lived in Alder, Montana and the little gas station store let Gary and I charge candy all day long. We even filled everyone's Easter basket and continued to charge stuff until Dad got word of it. But credit here, in a nice department store? I was embarrassed and yet proud that Mama dared to walk to the counter, look the girl in the eye, and tell her she wanted to open an account. For Mama, that was a big thing.

The woman put a sheet of paper on the counter and told Mama to fill it out and she would see what she could do. While Mama scribbled, Gary and I looked around to see what else we could add to the charge.

"Think we'll get it?" he asked.

"Hell, no!" I blurted, but rummaged through hats and purses just in case we did. When Mama was done, she handed over the paper.

"Just give me a minute to go over this. I'll be right back."

While the woman scrutinized the paperwork, we continued to look around. The store shined with everything from furniture to clothing. The walls were vanilla ice cream white and the dark wood trim glistened next to it. Women behind various counters stood tall and stiff like fashion models, with heavy jewelry matching their clothing. I wanted to be like these ladies and have a different outfit for each day — and not have to wear the same getup four or five days in a row.

Within minutes the clerk told us we wouldn't get credit.

"But why?" Mama seemed shocked as the porcelain lady tried to explain things to her. She was getting agitated, I could tell, and it might only be a matter of minutes before she told the young woman to fuck off. Somehow, she honestly thought they would give our family credit. In my mind, they would be more likely to give credit to aliens then they would for a family of travelers like us.

"You have to have a job to get credit. We get a lot of people in wanting to charge things this time of year, but we can't accommodate everyone, especially those without income." The clerk had a weak smile on her face and I felt she would have done something if she could.

Gary and I scooped up our plunder — or what we thought would be — then went to the toy section to put everything back. Gary shoved one of his toys under a counter with a *let's-see-how-long-it-takes-ya-to-find-this* attitude. Mama glared at the woman and mumbled something that sounded like "Screw you," but I couldn't be sure. Then we walked out, wishing we could have kept at least one thing. Fortunately, Gary and I hadn't expected anything, so weren't as upset as Mama, who seemed to think the lady behind the counter was going to give her anything she wanted.

When we got outside, Mama held the door open and yelled, "Bitch!" to anyone in the store who could hear her. Then she rushed off as if a team of retailers was about to mow her down.

For the next hour, she screamed like a fish wife. "Can you believe that woman would turn us down?"

If I had to say anything about it, it would be *YES*, in capital letters. Not just *yes*, but *fuck yes*. God, was Mama hoping I would agree so that she could form me to be like her? Worse yet, was I starting to pay attention?

On the long walk home, snow fell on our bare heads and thread-bare coats, whipping and swirling around our feet — which were barely covered in our holey tennis shoes. The canvas never lasted long.

"Bastards," Mama said. "Just wait until they want my money again. I'll never shop there!"

We tried to calm her down by saying we didn't care about that junk anyhow. "It's all just junk, Mama. Who needs it?"

Mama looked at me with her eyes narrowed.

"The stuff was made of plastic and probably poison," I added.

When we got home, she told Dad about what happened and he bitched and yelled, calling them a bunch of *dumb fuckers*. While she explained, pulling her snow-covered coat off and trying to get Dad to agree that it was no doubt the worst thing that could happen to them, Dad just grinned.

"What the hell you smiling about?" Mama demanded.

"To hell with them!" Dad yelled. "Go look in the front room." He motioned with his arm toward the living room, a smile spread across his ruddy face, his black Irish eyes sparkling. This was the height of his excitement level, I decided, because there was no way I had ever seen him more excited.

We walked through the doorway to find a tall, thick Christmas tree, freshly plucked, standing tall and proud like a warrior. Nearly reaching the ceiling, it stretched across the surrounding walls. All it needed was a few decorations and it would be Christmas at our house.

Chapter 14

As much as we wanted to stay in Dillon with the friends we had accumulated, it was not meant to be. We loaded up the car and hooked up the trailer in early spring before the snow had completely melted, only this time our trusted black Hudson didn't go with us. It had finally reached the end of the road and Dad traded it in for a 1949 two- tone green Buick Special. The man — a friend of Dad's, who often mined with him — got sent to jail for stabbing someone, so he sold Dad the car for $200. Dad worked when jobs were available and saved enough for the car. Winter, as usual, was hard and money was tight, but it is what it is.

Not quite as roomy as the Hudson, we all crammed inside the Buick, minus two of the cats that we had left with neighbors (although I'm not sure the neighbors knew that). Now that we were in high school, it wasn't easy leaving. We had established friendships and didn't want to leave them. It wasn't like we were still little kids who could easily be talked into anything. Gary and I argued our case and Linda agreed, but in the end, we still took to the road.

When we left Dillon this time, we didn't leave alone. Dad had met a family — a man, his wife, and two teenage boys. The boys were shy but good-looking, and I was glad to have some company traveling with us this time. It made leaving so much easier. They followed us in their rusted Pontiac and, like a pack of Gypsies, we caravanned south to sunny California.

"Why are they going with us, Dad?" I asked. We had met up with travelers along the way, many times, and often had relatives follow us, but never people who were practically strangers.

"Gotta make some money and California's the place to do it, Doodle. Besides, they've never been there. When I told them about the state and all the opportunities, hell, they were sold on it. He couldn't wait to tag along."

"What's wrong with his wife?" Gary asked.

Mama interrupted. "Somethin's wrong with her, that's for sure."

"She's crazy," Dad answered. "Got some kind of brain disorder that makes her forget things. Hell, everyone's got problems. She's fine, though, right hon?" Dad glanced at Mama briefly, but she didn't answer. She had joined Juanita — the mom — for coffee a few times and got to know her a little, but each time Mama came home she would tell us about the weird things she did. One time, Juanita got up to go to the bathroom and ended up outside in the alley, sitting down in the middle like she belonged there.

Mama looked at him and clicked her tongue. "Juanita's O.K., but she better not start getting crazy while she's with me. Last time I was with her, she started talking to an invisible person." Mama snickered. I think Mama liked people with odd problems and quirky habits; it made her feel better about her own peculiarities.

Dad turned the radio on as a signal to change the subject.

It was a time when people began talking about going to the moon. Dad said if God wanted people to go to outer space, he would have made it easier for them to get there — which was similar to what he said when I got my ears pierced. "If God wanted you to have holes in your ears, he would have made you like that." Why he wanted to emphasize God is beyond me.

"It's just an ego thing between us and the Soviets to see who can do what first. If you ask me, they're all just wasting money on something that probably will never do us any good. And probably never happen."

"But Dad, what if it did happen? Wouldn't you want to see what it's like?" I asked.

Dad blew out a mouthful of smoke before answering. "Wouldn't catch me going somewhere like that. Hell, we have enough trouble just getting around the United States."

The family traveling with us, the McVeighs, were as peculiar as we were, so we put on quite a show when all of us pulled into a gas station or café. Juanita had gotten worse throughout the trip, and wandered off if we didn't keep an eye on her. Sometimes she'd walk right out into the highway and stand there as though there wasn't a car in sight. Her two boys, Paul and Jim, were quiet and smart — and handsome like their father, Joe. I secretly had a crush on both of them, but never let them know since they considered me one of the guys.

When we stopped for lunch at roadsides along the way, even the other Travelers stared at us. Like a pack of Gypsies, we rolled out the oilcloth and made lunch right there on the side of the road. I was fascinated by the stories Dad and Joe told as if they were trying to outdo each other.

Joe talked about his past experiences while traveling the country looking for a job or a decent place to live. He said he'd been run out of some towns, and looked down on as lower than white trash in others. His stories were no more captivating than Dad's, but we'd heard most of his, so we were enjoying the new tales.

"We got in trouble in the last place because the kids weren't in school. I was trying to teach them myself," Joe said with a slight Irish accent. He went on to tell us how some people were so kind, they'd offer him small jobs or give his family food when they were down-and-out. He turned to look at Dad and asked if he'd had similar experiences. Dad sat on a large rock while we listened intently, eating cold hot dogs on white bread.

To me, it was a good story and I wanted to hear it. The boys, however, left uninterested. "We've been called a lot of things," Dad said. "But I find that people are just people. There are good and there are bad."

Joe started again. "When I went to look for a job, people looked at me as if I was a thief and would steal from them, so a lot of times they didn't hire me. They called us tinkers and thieves and accused Juanita of peddling herself around the neighborhood when we didn't have money for food. That's a bunch of bullshit." Joe's hair flamed red in the afternoon sun.

Juanita and Mama sat on a nearby fallen down picnic table, barely saying a word to each other.

Dad opened his thermos and filled his cup with coffee, then Joe's.

"It's not a wonder," Joe said. "The way the media treats us, it's worse than the Indians. They think we all steal and raise uneducated kids. I admit my kids miss a lot of school, but they're pretty smart. Hell, we aren't any different than anyone else." He reached into his burlap bag and brought out a folder, opened it, and pulled out a wrinkled newspaper article. "Here," Joe said, handing Dad the clipping and watching as he read. "This is how they talk about us. I saved this along with a bunch of other writings I picked up along the way. Don't know why."

I went around behind Dad so I could read it, too. The article was about some people in Oklahoma who insisted something had to be done with the Irish Travelers — Tinkers, they called them. They were spotted going from store to store looking for work and trying to sell things.

"Oh brother," I said, thinking, *that is just a bunch of bullshit.* We had not behaved like that on any of our travels. Dad did odd jobs when he had to, but he didn't steal from the people he worked for as it said in the article. I couldn't stand it — I had to laugh, and pretty soon we were all howling with laughter, even Mama and Juanita, who didn't have a clue what we were laughing at.

When we got to Costa Mesa in California, Dad decided it would be a good place to *settle down.* Boy, had we heard that one before. After the icy winter we had spent in Montana, the sunshine and flowers filled my heart. I breathed in the smell as if there was no other like it in the world, and felt the sun on my face, sucking away any troubles or bad thoughts. I could see the others doing the same thing; we were sun people. Flowers, green lawns, and people walking and playing on the sidewalks were sights to behold.

I wanted to jump out of the car and roll on one of the green, lush lawns. Instead, we waited while Dad searched for a place to live. Mama said she didn't want to share a house with the likes of our traveling partners, but Dad reminded her they had no money, and would she rather let them sleep on the street? She huffed, then turned to look out the window.

We found a cheap apartment complex that had one empty apartment and we all moved in, families, junk, and all. We emptied our trailer while the McVeighs emptied their sparsely-packed car. All nine of us squeezed into a three-bedroom apartment in a sprawling suburb. When Mama complained again, Dad told her it was just 'till Joe got his first paycheck.

It didn't take long before we began to see the true side of Juanita, which also brought out the true side of Mama. When Mama got irate with Juanita the way she did with Linda, she took it out on all of us, especially Paul and Jim. But they were so polite and shy that they took it without saying a word. I was embarrassed by the way she treated them.

Juanita was a mess and should have been locked up. Why she was allowed out in public was beyond me. She took off three times in the first week, each time being escorted home by a police officer. If we didn't watch her, she would be out the door and gone in a flash. One night, we all spread out looking for Juanita when she slipped out after dinner. We found her sitting on a park bench, babbling to the squirrels, trying to feed them little marshmallows she carried in her bag. When she saw us, she threw a handful to the squirrels and followed us home.

Mama began to have fits about this woman and, between her and Juanita, things were getting out of control.

"You crazy bitch!" Mama yelled one day when Juanita set a pan on fire. The boys rushed to their mother's rescue; as time went on, they were getting bolder, and I saw that they were very protective of their mother.

"Don't call my mom a bitch," Paul said.

"Then you keep her on a leash or something. She's going to burn the house down," Mama screamed, her lips stiff and her eyes squinting in Juanita's direction.

Luckily for all of us, the men were paid for their first two weeks of work and the McVeighs moved out. I missed the boys, but if it meant peace in our house — except for the fights between Mama and Linda, which still emerged almost daily — it was for the best. Dad said it was about time we got back to our normal life and they could get on with theirs, which is what we did when we moved a month later.

Chapter 15

We moved dozens of times while I was in high school. Between towns in California — like Morrow Bay, Atascadero, Dana Point, and Pismo Beach — and the Mojave Desert, we were always the short-time students. We traveled across Idaho and Montana, tramping the ground down like squatters, attending schools dotted along the way, a little cockier, and a lot more independent than the kids we came across. We were always looking for something that we never seemed to find.

I grew out of my shyness as I entered high school. At first, I felt like a speck on a window, feeling little, scrawny and unworthy. I wanted to be tall and slim like the popular girls; I wanted to have poise and grace. I was short and petite, but Aunt Babe said guys liked small women.

My confidence grew when I realized I was not the ugly duckling anymore. Of course, I always wanted someone to reiterate that fact to me, to tell me I was prettier than a damn duck. I became more confident with every wink of the eye, with every smile and sexual undertone, because I knew that I was not only a well-traveled girl but the kind the guys seemed to like — minus the sex.

I didn't drool over guys the way I did when I was younger. I realized there was time for me to shop around and be friends with boys, rather than take them to bed and fuck their brains out the way my friend Chris did. She would meet a guy and fuck him in the backseat of her father's car, then pass out while the other guys took turns on her. He was not in my normal group of friends, but she and Gary had hit it off and we all started hanging out together.

The teacher in my P.E. class, Miss Raison, with her ratted hair and systematic order, always told us that when we met a guy we were interested in, we should have fun with him, kiss him, and treat him like a friend, BUT NEVER HAVE SEX. There was always that potential of getting pregnant.

When I walked into a new school, I tossed my long hair over my shoulder and flashed my large brown eyes, not caring what the other students thought of me. Along the way, I read everything I could get my hands on, including books on the spiritual path to try to quiet my mind. I read about the occult, reincarnation, stories of people reborn into other families, spirits, and everything else. I figured I was a witch because I was a Scorpio and it was why I was here and who I was. Through intimidation and lots of gawking throughout the years, I learned not to take anything personally. Besides, I was no longer the ugly duckling; I and the girls I ran around with could get what we wanted with a blink of the eye. We were catching on.

Now we kids were bolder and more confident when we entered a new school.

Even Linda didn't use her finger telescope anymore. She was happy to be back in Hamilton with old friends. She was also glad that Mama had someone to hang out with — our cousin's new wife, who lived right down the street from us.

I knew the boys stared at me and I ate it up considering the ugly little girl I had been, the one whose grandfather laughed at in the school photo. Even though I was still *little*, I had grown out of my big-toothed, bony-armed look into somewhat of a butterfly.

I loved being in high school and getting all the attention from the older boys — I was the new girl from California with the short skirts, love beads, and hair to her waist.

And a new set of tits. Plenty of boys asked me out the first day I started school, but I didn't accept, knowing Dad would never allow me to date. Barely sixteen, I had never gotten so much attention. I was beginning to feel all grown up. I worked at attempting to dress better and even made short dresses out of bath towels sewn together and halter tops out of pieces of material that wrapped around my slender waist.

We knew we were more independent than most kids. We went where we wanted and did what we wanted, as long as we didn't get in trouble — or at least as long as Dad didn't find out about it. Things didn't bother us the way they did permanent kids, I guess because in the back of our minds we always knew, no matter how tough things got, we could always move on. These other kids feared change, even though some envied our lifestyle. They knew from their parents that we were raised like a pack of dogs, common Gypsies. Or so I thought.

As much as the other kids envied our traveling, we envied their stability; being able to finish high school in Hamilton, enrolling in the band and staying in it, or any other activity for that matter would suit us just fine.

It was usually the creative, funny, talented kids — and the kids looking for adventure, like Gary and me — who were already considered the *fucked* crowd: the most likely to get pregnant, smoke dope, and run the streets. They were the kids from the other side of the tracks; where I spent a good deal of my time.

I wanted adventure just like Dad's sister, my Aunt Ruthie, did when she was young — dancing across marble floors until the bottom of her feet pulsed and ached of overuse. When she wasn't yet my age, she tired of traveling with her family, so she ran off to California, planted herself in L.A., and began dancing professionally in a club.

Later, I heard she became a call girl. She wasted her freedom.

We walked the streets in the evening, the smell of lumber and cottonwoods greeting us on our way to a local diner to get five-cent cokes and hang out with all the other kids our age. Hamilton, a small town nestled in the Bitterroot Mountains in Western Montana, is where we landed after several pit stops along the way. In the middle of town was a '50s diner called *Ranger* where girls went to find guys who went to show off their big, fancy cars. The older girls took turns cruising the drag with the hunks in their hot cars, past the college and down Main Street, catching a slight sunset. I sat inside the diner, turning down any invitations for a spin. But it didn't take long for me to branch out.

When I did finally expand my horizons and take a ride with a bunch of kids, including a buff boy named Danny, I sat in the backseat, looking like a terrified baby bird. I didn't know if I should be excited or fear the inevitable consequences. Dad had drilled it into me that if I didn't watch it I would end up like *them,* the other McAlpins — meaning the ones who got pregnant or sent to jail. I tried to be good, but my hormones were reeling, and I now had a quest for fun. But my girlfriends and I hung together, never contemplating a night of sex. We had each other's backs.

One night, with six of us cruising in Danny's car, he stopped and pulled out a bottle. Since I wasn't familiar with alcohol, I wasn't sure what kind it was, but the excitement level rose when he held it out for everyone to look at. That is when I had my first drink of alcohol (other than an occasional sip of beer from Mama when her iron level was low). Vodka with a splash of orange juice — such an innocent-sounding drink — made me feel all grown up, but it also made me sick.

We sat in the crowded car, sipping like we knew what we were doing. Gary and two others in the front seat, and me and two friends in the back. Since my parents didn't drink, I wasn't sure what to expect. But then the nice orange drink hit me. I was confused, wanted to barf and pee at the same time, and wanted to go home, but was also scared to go home for fear that Dad would know I had been drinking. But the reality was that I still had to go home and face the music.

"I'm not going home," Gary announced when I said we needed to get going at almost eleven o'clock. Huddled together in a dark car, under a star-filled sky, surrounded by trees — a notorious make-out spot for couples — I felt my head spin. Everyone seemed to be having fun except me.

"You have to go home. You'll get grounded," I said, wishing I didn't have to go home either. Gary said he'd rather take whatever happened than to go home and weave around like one of the Boomers. His face was flushed and plastered with a ridiculous look. One of the other girls in the car was crawling all over him, trying to get his attention. I'd seen it a hundred times before. Gary had the looks and the charm.

I finally insisted that I go home, so Danny dropped me off a block from my house, just in case Dad was up. The streets were dark and not many people were still up. I saw a night light on in our house, but that wasn't unusual. At first, I thought Dad was in bed and I was a lucky girl. But no.

When I opened the door and tip-toed into the house, holding in my breath, an enormous shadow loomed on the wall. Dad was reaching into a cupboard and, because of the dim lighting, it made it look as if his arm spilled out across the kitchen like a mass of fog. He looked like a madman about to lower the axe. I couldn't breathe for a second and thoughts ran through my head like jam through a strainer; I figured it was the alcohol, blocking my ability to put words together and think of what to do at the same time.

Dad was waiting up for us. Gary was right, only now it was me who had to weave around in search of my bed. I should have followed suit. But I would have to go home sooner or later, so, either way, I was fucked.

"Where the hell you been? It's after eleven." Dad took something from the cupboard, then turned to look at me. "And where the hell is Gary?"

"I think he's staying overnight with Ricky or James," I muttered, carefully trying to work my way to the bedroom.

But Dad saw what I was doing. "I can tell you haven't been over at your friend's house playing records like you said."

I spun my head around to look at him when he mentioned my lie, spoken earlier in the evening. It took me a while to locate his face because things swam around in my eyes and I couldn't remember where he was. When my vision finally focused, I cleared my throat and stood straight, one hand clutching the door frame. I was *that* close to getting into my bedroom, which was a screened-in porch.

Dad knew I had been drinking, and since he didn't imbibe, I'm sure he recognized all my wobbly attempts at slithering across the floor. He looked at me with disgust, and I could tell by his voice that he thought I was only days away from being like my cousins.

"Go to bed," he blurted. I knew by the sound of his voice that he was livid, most likely thinking I was befouled and it would only be a matter of time before I dropped out of school, pregnant. The trouble with that statement was that I had never had sex. My friends Alice, Helen, and Dee, made a pact that whoever got screwed first had to tell the rest of us what it was like.

Gary didn't come home that night, and not until late the next afternoon. I'm sure he stayed with his two loser best friends, Jim and Carlos. They had a car, and even if it looked like they drove it right out of a wrecking yard, at least it ran. They were from a large family like ours — not travelers, but longtime Hamilton kids whose history of bad luck went back generations. In school, they had an even worse reputation than we did.

Their brothers robbed gas stations, the father was a drunk, and one brother shot himself right in front of the Moose bar when his girlfriend dumped him.

Dad hated that Gary was running with a pack of kids who were not only known for trouble but whose folks were also branded for the things they did when Dad was young. It was hard enough to be accepted into a group when you move around the way we did, though. It was even harder to get accepted into a *good* group.

We had lived in this town a few times before and were starting to know everyone our age. Gary and I both ended up befriending fun, creative kids who liked to dance and party, which meant everyone from cheerleaders to the town hoods. Linda went back to the friends she had known before; carrot-top girls who dated Job Corps guys at the age of thirteen. Hamilton became our *hometown* when people asked. It was a hell of a lot easier than giving them the lowdown about our life as drifters.

By the time Gary got home late in the afternoon, the day after our party, Dad had worked himself into a rage. I think he was more pissed off because he knew there was nothing he could do. We were not the kids anymore who sat in the backseat. He didn't know where to look for Gary, so he just had to wait until he returned on his own.

When I saw the car drive up — a rusted '57 Chevy with a dented side — it took a wide turn around in the middle of the road before turning into our driveway. There were four boys in the car and Gary was one of them. I couldn't tell who two of the boys were, but I recognized Carlos and James. They all sat in the car with the engine idling, as if they were waiting for a movie to start on the big screen.

When no one got out, Dad walked over, threw the passenger door open, and told Gary to get his ass out. I had never seen Dad's face so harsh, so cold. When Gary refused to get out, Dad grabbed his arm and pulled him out. Since there were three other boys in the car watching the scene unfold, there was no way Gary was about to let them see our Dad push him around. His pride would not allow that.

Gary threw his arms up and pushed Dad's hands away. When he walked toward the house, Dad kicked him in the ass, then the fight started.

Mama ran out of the house screaming to leave her boy alone. "You somabitch. You bastard," she said between sobs. "You leave him alone."

Linda cried and I just stood and watched the whole thing unfold, along with some neighbors who came out to see what was going on.

When Dad saw the kids in the car still in our driveway, he yelled at them to get the hell out of here, waving his arms like a wild man. "Go on, go on home you ratty-ass losers!" he hollered, giving them the finger as he turned to walk away. Then Dad followed Gary into the bedroom and shut the door. All you could hear after that were loud noises, things getting thrown around, and Dad calling Gary a dumb little bastard. It was obvious there was some slapping going on, too.

By the time it was all over, Mama was crying her eyes out, then left, heading down the tracks to her friend Georgia's house — leaving Linda, Dad, and me alone in the house, and Gary still in the bedroom. Dad was exhausted, and since he'd had a heart attack a few years earlier at the age of 39, I was afraid he might have another. He muttered under his breath and we were afraid to talk to him. Finally, he said, "I just don't want to see you kids end up in jail, or worse." Linda and I agreed by shaking our heads and, in my heart, I knew that Dad did what he did to protect Gary.

When Mama got home, I could hear Dad and her fighting in the bedroom. Then Mama came out with a bag and left, heading back to Georgia's. For the first time ever, I saw there was a chance of my folks splitting up. No matter how much our family struggled, no matter how much time we spent on the road, we had never been threatened with the fact that our parents could split up.

When Dad came out of the room, he brought two boxes and a suitcase with him. "Gonna have to leave for a while. Mama doesn't want me here anymore. Gotta take some tools so I can work. I'll send money. Don't you kids worry." He sorted through the boxes just like he did when we were ready to move some-where. But this time he didn't look at us or joke about what to take and what to leave.

"But where are you going to go?" I asked.

"Don't know just yet. When I find out, I'll let you know." He looked tired, his face was white, and I felt like any minute he could start crying, which is what it made me do.

I went outside and talked to my neighbor — a kid named Yancy who was Gary's age — on the porch of the duplex. Yancy asked what happened and I told him.

"He's just leaving for a while so Mama can cool off, I guess." But I didn't know for sure what was going on.

Dad left for two days and Mama came back after the first night. Gary felt bad that he had caused such disorder in our family. The first thing Mama did was to ask where Dad was. I could see the fear on her face that there was a chance he would not come back and she would be alone to take care of all of us.

"Don't know where he went," I said.

"Did he say he was coming back?" She looked about as bed-ridden as a woman could look. She had either been crying a lot or sleeping too much, I wasn't sure which, but she looked like a street person. Her hair was in knots and her clothes were dirty and wrinkled as if she had been sleeping in them. She twisted her hands, and when she saw Gary she looked away.

"Ahhh, he'll be back," Gary said. He didn't apologize, but I knew that was what his words intended.

Later that day, we heard the front door open and Dad walked in carrying a thermos of coffee. He uttered "Morning" and nothing else, acting as if nothing had happened. He looked like a little boy who had gotten himself in a bunch of trouble. After greeting him, we kids walked out to the porch so he and Mama could talk. We knew if they got back together, things would be normal again — or as normal as they could be for our family.

The air was crisp and cold. Leaves had turned a burnt orange and yellow and all the beautiful lilacs had turned brown. The trains clattered by and, in the distance, the courthouse bell struck eleven times. When we looked through the window, Mama and Dad were hugging. We crawled back on the porch ledge and smiled. Linda giggled. Everything was fine.

Chapter 16

D ad didn't let his poor health slow him down, even when it began to deteriorate in obvious and alarming ways. His belly spilled over his beltline, he smoked constantly, and he got winded by an increasing number of everyday tasks. Heart disease ran in his family and he knew the signs; he had already had one heart attack. We urged him to go to the doctor, but he ignored our pleas. No matter how sick he got, he didn't complain, and he refused to leave the road.

While moving from California to Arizona — and later to Idaho — we made many pit stops in a string of colorfully named towns along the way. Every high school we attended was a new experience. In some schools, we were accepted and treated like world travelers, while in others we were outcasts, newbies lobbed in with kids who had spent their whole lives together. More and more, we were beginning to realize that the way we lived was not the way others lived. We wanted to be back in Hamilton with our friends.

We had missed a lot of school that year, always moving soon after arriving in a town, and sometimes Dad decided it wasn't worth the hassle of enrolling us. When we did start school, we barely had a chance to meet new kids before it was time to move again. There were always those friends who wrote to us, but eventually, we lost touch.

Once again, the towns became transitory stopovers, often so short that we didn't even start school. Before moving back to

Montana, Dad got a letter from a cousin saying they were building a slew of new houses in the San Louis Obispo area. This time when we left school, we didn't even get our transcripts — just left without giving notice. At least we weren't hauled out in the middle of class — something that was beginning to embarrass me — nor in the middle of the night like we did in Great Falls, when I was in fourth grade and Dad had rented us a house that bordered a wrecking yard.

Broken-down cars scattered out for what seemed like miles. For kids like us, still too young to have fear, the wrecking yard became our playground and we couldn't wait to get out in it. We were so thrilled with our new location that Gary and I spent a good deal of time crawling in and out of the cars, looking for things and pretending we could drive. There must have been two hundred cars; some that still had things in the glove box we could scavenge, like pocket knives and postcards. Since we didn't start school right away, we had plenty of time to hunt for treasures.

"I have a great idea," Gary said in his then-squeaky voice. "Let's take all the keys outta the cars. It can be my collection." He was so excited that his eyes bugged out.

"Well, I ain't helping you if I can't have some of the keys," I said, walking away. "All right, all right, we'll divide them."

So for the next two weeks, we roamed the wrecking yard throughout the day while Dad was at work and Mama fielded calls from the school.

Eventually, we had a key from almost every car — a whole shoebox full. When the owner of the wrecking yard knocked on the door one night and talked to Dad, we could hear every word that was said as we froze with fear in the kitchen.

"They did what?" Dad asked the man.

"I know it was them. I been seeing 'em playing out there running in and out of the cars like a couple of little rats. I'm about ready to call the . . ."

"Hey, you watch who you're calling rats or you'll wish you'd never laid eyes on this family."

"I want those keys," the man yelled, his face as red as his shirt. We ran to the bedroom, got the box, and handed it to him, then ran back before we got in more trouble. "How the hell am I supposed to know which key goes to which car?" The man stormed off and Gary and I were convinced it was only a matter of time before the police showed up. Whether they would have or not, we weren't sure, because a few days later, we packed up and moved away when it was too dark to make sure we hadn't forgotten anything.

We were now spending way too much time in the car. Fights and arguments broke out regularly. Gary and I were too big for the backseat to be comfortable anymore — feet flying and long legs searching for room started fights and loud arguments in a heartbeat. We were sick of Linda and Mama's continual warfare in the front seat; instead of growing out of the fights, they only got more into them the older Linda got.

Mama became vicious toward Linda, and Linda wasn't about to back down.

Mama called Linda lazy and fat and made her life miserable when Dad wasn't around. Linda fought back, hardening herself to Mama's flailing arms and bitter words, often slapping Mama's hands away or calling her a wicked bitch. I took sides with Linda a lot of the time. She was bigger than me now and had a strong, round body, fit and solid.

Mama wouldn't have a chance if they really got into it.

I asked Mama why she didn't like Linda one evening as she lay in bed reading a *True Romance* magazine, but I always got the same answer: "I don't know what you're talking about."

"You fight with her all the time and act like you don't like her. Why?" I knew she would never admit that she was mean to Linda, just as she was with Dougie.

"I like her just fine. So don't ask me that again."

I quit asking, but I knew there had to be a reason. It was always Gary and me who got the extra treats. It was always me who got dance lessons or piano lessons — when we could afford them — and it was Gary who got a go-cart. Sometimes I cringed when I was given something and Linda wasn't. I would even give it to her if I could, regardless of the look I got from Mama. I had come to realize that the reason Linda was the way she was — tough, hardened, and deceptive — is because she had to be.

When Dad announced once again that we were moving so we could start school, we were ready for it. It wasn't right for teenagers to spend so much time with their parents, and I was getting pretty sick of it. So much so, in fact, that Gary and I threatened to leave the family and make our own way doing whatever we had to do. But now was not the time.

We settled in a small town called Baywood Park — or the Valley of Bears — in San Luis Obispo County. Just a dot of a village, it wrapped around the bay with sprawling neighborhoods and houses we called *proper.* The town was quaint and smelled of salty water and pine trees, just minutes from Morro Bay where we attended school. The sky stretched across the water, where seagulls landed on floating logs.

Once again, we were to start school late in the year. Kids stared at us like we were from Mars, and some called us the new little *Mexican* family that moved to town. I didn't like being called the *Mexican family down the street,* but it was better than some of the names we had been called. Dad told us to ignore the ignorant people because they didn't have brains in their heads.

Two teenage girls lived down the street from us, and when I met them at the bus stop, I knew we would be friends. Since they were also new to town, we struck up an instant friendship, especially once they learned that I could steal as good as they could, and I could cuss probably better than them.

Jennie and Laurie were audacious girls, and that's what I liked about them — they cussed, stole, flipped their noses at authority, and wore seductive clothing. The oldest girl, Jennie, had hair ratted about four inches above her head and looked like a model, with the bluest eyes I had ever seen. Her sister, Laurie, was shorter, with freckles on her nose, round blue eyes, and a doll-like face. Between them, they must have been the most beautiful girls in school. They stuck to themselves, though, and besides me, they didn't seem to hang around with anyone else.

They asked about things I had stolen and I laid it on thick, dishonest about some of it and exaggerating the rest. I even took the Soap Lake incident with the chocolate bar and blew it way out of proportion, telling them I stole a bag of food and walked right past the checker's nose.

"Wow," they said, marveling at my daring nature.

"Ah, it's nothing, you should see my brother steal," I bragged while we stood in line for the bus to take us to Morrow Bay. Gary got in with a group of boys and was seldom around.

"Your brother's cute," Laurie said.

"Yeah, that's what all the girls say."

"Does he have a girlfriend?" Laurie asked.

"Give it up, Laurie," Jenny said. They didn't move as much as us, and they certainly weren't Travelers, but they said it was no use getting attached to anyone they'd just end up leaving behind. Their parents seemed to be in bed screwing whenever I went to their house, so we started hanging out in town.

The construction in town wasn't quite what Dad had been told it would be. Once it slowed down, it was only a matter of time before we would move again; and this time I didn't want to leave my friends behind. Fortunately for us, though, Dad announced that instead of moving he was going to try his hand at a new career. Instead of being covered with the dirt and grime of his trade, he said he was going to wear a clean shirt every day and become a real estate agent.

"What are you talking about?" Mama asked, clicking her tongue and staring when he walked through the door with the news. "And why do you have that smirk on your face?"

"I have decided to become a real estate agent," Dad said, unable to control his wild grin. "Man who owns the house I've been working on said I had the gift of gab, well we all know that, and he said that I would make a good salesman." He even said he'd show Dad everything he needed to know. Dad was a quick learner, and, although not educated beyond tenth grade, he was intelligent and knew a little about almost everything.

Dad did have the gift of gab, that's for sure, and he also had the good looks that women loved — but a professional job?

"What?" Linda and I blurted at once, still a little confused about this new position Dad was taking. Mostly we didn't know what a real estate agent did. Dad explained what he would be doing and said he was going to start right away.

"Bullshit. You have to go to college for that. Even I know that," Mama said, followed by laughter. Dad assured her that he was asked to do it, and beyond a little prepping, there was no schooling needed — he would be learning all he needed to know while on the job.

Early the next morning, when Dad walked into the living room wearing the only black suit he owned — which was usually for funerals — with a white shirt and tie, we ran and got the camera. He stood proudly in front of our little red house, the customary cigarette in hand, while I snapped the picture. I was amazed our dad would dress like that and not be heading to a funeral. I don't know who was the most shocked. He was handsome and polished and looked like a model, although a little plump around the middle. His hair shined from a quick wipe of Brylcreem, and he smelled like Aqua Velva. He was ready to step into his new career.

Each day Mama ironed Dad a clean white shirt before he headed out the door and into our rickety, salmon pink Pontiac, ready to sell houses to rich people. At night when he came home, he was no longer limping or complaining about his back. Instead, he would sit and talk about the fantastic houses and the equally beautiful people who thought of purchasing them.

"Some of those people have more money than they know what to do with. Hell, you can't touch some of those houses for less than $70,000. Shit."

In the meantime, Gary and I were having way too much fun and getting in trouble. Laurie told me one day at school that she forgot her swimming suit so she couldn't attend swim class that day, which meant a bad grade. Well, I wasn't about to let her miss class; she was already on the verge of flunking out. So before class, when no one had yet arrived, I went into the locker room and *found* a suit for her to wear. She wore it for a few days until someone ratted that they had seen me take it from a locker.

The principal came knocking on our door a few days later, told Dad what I had done, and informed him that I would have to be suspended.

Dad stood face to face with the principal while I sat like a mouse, on the couch listening to what a thief I was and how my grades were going down because I didn't take anything seriously. My heart raced because I knew, in the end, I would be kicked out of school and stuck home all day with Mama and the cats.

"You must be mistaken," Dad said. "My daughter doesn't steal. She's a good kid and . . ."

"She was seen doing it and it's something we don't take lightly in this school," the principal said, interrupting Dad as he looked around the living room at the cats teetering on the back of the couch and on the window sills. For once, I was glad we had a nice house — and it was cleaned up for a change. "She'll be out a week."

The principal left without listening to what else Dad had to say, which probably wouldn't have been good.

By the time the principal left, Dad was livid. His face was red and sweat had beaded on his forehead. "You can just forget about going back to that school. Fuck 'em if that's the way they want to be. We'll get you into beauty school and you can start a new career. Shit." Dad went over to the coffee pot, cursing all the way, and poured himself a cup of coffee. "To hell with them."

I had heard all about my future as a beautician before but kept my mouth shut each time, knowing that it would be a cold day in hell before I fixed greasy hair for little old ladies. Gary quit going to school as well, and with the free time on our hands, we began visiting our older cousin, George, and his wife Natasha, who lived in a nearby town called Atascadero where we had lived for a short time.

Natasha was sixteen just like me. She was a little toad of a girl who thought being married to my twenty-one-year-old cousin would be better than finishing school. She got bored hanging out in the motel all day while George worked, so she would come to Baywood Park and pick us up so we could spend a few days with them. The motel was the same one we had stayed in when we first moved from Montana, a somewhat nice little place on the edge of town with a courtyard right in the middle. When George and Natasha moved into the same motel we were living in, it wasn't long before Dad started getting itchy feet.

We loved staying with our older cousin. George was immature, which is why he got along so well with us and his young wife. We loved going there, and eventually, we quit school altogether so we could hang out with them. No one seemed to mind that we put our education on hold. Dad was having such a good time with his new job that he didn't seem to notice.

Hanging out with George and Natasha was like hanging out with a couple of kids. They liked to have fun and, like us, they were filled with energy and mischief. The motel was small but had two bedrooms. I slept in the spare room while Gary slept on the couch. Minutes after I got in bed some nights, when George figured I was asleep, he would sneak into my room and crank up the electric blanket, laughing as if it was the funniest thing he had ever done. George was tall and thin like a stick of licorice. His laugh was high-pitched like Gary's, and his face was not much more than a sunken and hungry- looking bone, with large, thick glasses resting on the lower part of his nose.

Natasha was the opposite, short and round at the bottom, like a bowling ball, with long, greasy brown hair that hung below her large breasts. She liked to ask me personal questions so she could brag about what she knew on the subject.

"Have you ever had sex?" she asked, a smile on her tiny lips as if she knew it was something that I no doubt, didn't have a clue about. When I told her no she wanted to tell me all about it. Her eyes flashed with excitement and she looked like a kid with a secret.

"Aren't you just a little curious? Well, I can tell you, it hurts. Just be prepared for that," she said. That was way too much information for me because I still wasn't at the point where I wanted to try it, nor had I ever met anyone who interested me enough to want to give it a try.

"Well, if it hurts so much, why do people do it?"

"Because it can also be fun. You just wait, you'll see. Fucking is a way to be closer to your mate."

I began to think of myself as an adult, able to do anything I wanted while staying at the motel with George and Natasha. Mama was pissed every time George came to pick us up for a few days, but Dad told her to let us go. In his eyes, we were all grown up, independent the way he wanted us to be, and good kids. Little did he know that the older we got, the more we tried illegal, immoral, stupid things.

Natasha and I shopped or hung out on the lawn sipping ice tea during the day while George worked; sometimes Gary joined him. On weekends when George was home, he showed us all the things he had learned, and one day announced that we were going to go to a second-hand store he liked.

"Natasha needs stuff for the house so she can cook, we need a toaster, and I need some tools," he said. "I need you guys to go along with me so you can help. Can't tell me ya don't know how to steal, because I know you do." It sounded like a fun outing and we couldn't wait to go. We knew George was a pro at lifting things since he'd been in and out of reform school a few times.

"Well, what do we have to do?" Gary asked.

"Judy and Natasha have to keep the clerk busy. He's a slow guy so it shouldn't be too hard."

Gary asked, "Then what do we do?"

George looked at us like we were dumb as telephone poles, then told us to get in the car — a beat-up Ford station wagon with peeling paint — and he would tell us more when we got there.

When we got to the store, we pulled up in the back parking lot, where a large door led into the store. George said Natasha and I had to go in through the front door where the clerk was. He and Gary would hang out in the back by the small appliances and tools until he knew we were inside flashing our ivories and flirting with the owner.

"Judy, you need to show your sexy side," George said.

The clerk, a man with thick, matted hair, a flat nose, and a turned-up lip said, "How ya all doin' today? Ya want help, ya just holler."

We smiled and proceeded to look at the dishes and ask questions about the knick- knacks and where they came from. Sounds erupted from the rear of the store, but each time the noise caught the clerk's attention, I sidled up to him, smiled and bent over to show the tiny bit of cleavage I had. Then I would ask if he had any lead crystal. We must have looked at every piece of crystal, even stuff that obviously came from the five-and- dime store. He didn't know the difference, and neither did we.

We worked our way to the back of the store, and when we saw that the boys were in the car waiting for us, we hurried out and jumped in. I had to place my feet on top of a pile of toasters, auto parts, tools, and other kitchen items. The entire floorboard was covered and so was the back of the car. When Gary saw how wide my eyes were when I looked at it, he laughed. "Bettcha never saw a haul like that before!" He was proud of himself. George laughed the entire way out of the parking lot.

By the time we got back to the motel, George and Gary were whooping it up. I saw their excitement and was happy for George and Natasha getting things they needed, but like I told them, "Next time I get to be the one to take the stuff." I was a little pissed that they seemed to think guys knew how to steal better than women.

When we unloaded the car, Natasha's eyes grew wide with all the new things she had for her kitchen. George immediately began busying himself with his new tools and small appliances. Yes, spending time with them was fun and a real learning experience.

Chapter 17

On about our fourth visit to George and Natasha's motel room, I met a man named Bobby who lived there. His deep brown eyes drew me in and his dark hair, with curls spilling onto his forehead, made my heart flutter. He was George's age and had olive-colored skin. Between his sense of humor and good looks, I wanted to spend all my time with him, even though he was married and had a one-year-old child. Bobby began hanging out at George's more and more often because, as he told me, the constant fighting with his wife was getting out of control and he needed to stay away as much as he could.

"She's always mad about something. I'm better off here, believe me," he said one day while I sat with him on the couch.

Eventually, his wife kicked him out and that was much better for me since he ended up staying with George and Natasha — that is, until Natasha got tired of having so many people around and asked him to find another place to stay. So it was my idea to take him home with us to Baywood Park. Like Dad, I was becoming the one who brought home strays. Only this stray was a good kisser, and one who I thought — for the first time — I might even have sex with.

Dad liked Bobby right off the bat and told him he could stay with us, and even got him a job remodeling a house with Uncle Bob. I couldn't wait for him to come home from work each day, when we would take long evening walks through winding neighborhoods. I learned a lot about him during that time. When we kissed, it was as if I had never kissed anyone else — which, for the most part, I hadn't. On his days off, he went back to Atascadero to see his son and would be gone a few days at a time. I only hoped that there wouldn't come a time when he never came back.

Dad seemed to be enjoying his new life as a real estate agent, although he didn't seem to be making any money; he said it was just a matter of time, though. He called it an old-money town, and as long as people kept getting inheritances and having kids, there would always be houses to sell.

"Hell, this is as good a place as any to settle down. It's a safe town and someday maybe we'll buy a house and stay here."

Linda nearly jumped out of her skin, laughing and yelling, but Gary and I knew that if it happened, it happened, but we weren't about to hold our breath.

Gary and I were having so much fun with our new lives that we forgot all about Linda, who seemed to be getting lost in the shuffle. She was thirteen now and stuck to herself most of the time — maybe out of habit, or maybe to steer clear of Mama. I worried that Linda was suffering from spending so much time with Mama when Dad wasn't there.

I knew Linda was stealing candy from the little store in town because she always seemed to have some with her — as well as white lipstick and fingernail polish — but we were all doing that to some extent. We had gotten past the stage where banging on doors to sell stuff was out of our league; we felt we were a little advanced for that. I didn't know Linda's problems had grown out of proportion because I was so lost in myself, being a teenager and having a boyfriend. She no longer begged to hang out with us. She grew sullen and dark. When she fought with Mama, it was intense and hateful as her anger grew out of control. She didn't have tantrums like she used to; instead, she seemed to carry a deep sense of sorrow hidden in her dark eyes.

When I asked her one day if anything was wrong, she said everything was fine. Then she sat upright on the bed and said, "Why do we have to move so much? Haven't you ever wanted to just stay in one place? Why don't we move out of this place and find a better one? Like Dillon or Johannesburg? When we want to move, we can't!" Her voice quivered when she talked. I was surprised to hear she wanted to move after saying how much she hated traveling around.

"It's not that bad. Just remember I've done it a few years longer than you have. I want to stay in one place just like you do, but I also like it here and would just as soon we stay here." I was standing in front of the bedroom mirror and saw how grown up I was beginning to look, with bigger boobs — not much, but a little — and more curvature around my hips that dad said would one day attract the boys. He was right; I had attracted Bobby.

I only hoped that what I said to Linda would make her feel better. Just like her, I grew up wishing I could stay in one place, hang out with the same kids, and plant a garden we would get to see come to fruition. But after looking at her, I realized my words were not what she needed. Something was really wrong this time.

Linda looked at me, and I saw the sorrow on her face. Tears settled in the rims of her eyes and it looked as if she hadn't combed her hair in days. Her dress was wrinkled, the hem almost out, and she was barefoot with nearly-black toes. She had gained weight and it was as if she didn't care about herself anymore.

"But can't we just stay in one place and then go see the sites, like other people do? They call it a *vacation*." Her smirk turned to a smile as she made this last remark, and I was glad to see she at least had a sense of humor about it. We both laughed thinking about our family going on vacation. I looked across the small room at her. It was early evening and I had been out walking with Laurie and Jenny. I didn't have a clue what she did when we were gone.

"Because we're not other people," I said. "We're the McAlpins. That's what we do, move. We can do whatever we want when we grow up, we can live however we want," I told her. I had heard Dad and his sisters call us the McAlpin Travelers and as I got older, I knew we must be because we certainly weren't like most families, except for the circus and carnival people. There were too many places we had lived that Dad wanted to go back to and too many places he still wanted to see. But that didn't mean we had to follow in his path.

Sometimes when Gary and I got bored, we tried making a list of places we had lived. His memory was better than mine, and at one point we had covered both sides of a sheet of paper, but there were still too many places to remember. We were never sure if we should count towns we had lived in for just a few days; is there a certain amount of time it takes to live in a town before you can consider it your home? And what if you break down there and stay for a week or two? Does that count? Gary and I had long conversations on the subject. We both agreed that when we grew up we would never move around with our families, taking our kids from one school to another. But Dad told us he had said the same thing to his parents, and look where it got him. "The apple doesn't fall far from the tree," he said.

Linda said things were fine and she left the room. I knew she was lying, but I wasn't sure what — if anything — I should do. As kids, we had always been allowed to run in the streets, play in mines, or anything else we wanted to do, and this town was no exception. Linda spent more and more time away from home, or huddled in the backyard with one of the cats.

There was no reason for us to believe that anything bad could happen here. So the more Linda moped around, showing us her dark side, the more we thought it was just her pre-teens, like Mama told us. "Oh, she's fine. Just being a brat. She'll grow out of it."

Had Linda and Mama had a better relationship, maybe Linda would have told her about being raped while walking home from school one day in this *safe* little town. None of us knew what happened until years later when she felt enough time had passed that she could tell us about it without our family being in danger. She explained it to me as we sat having coffee one day, the chatter of birds all around us.

"I was walking home alone from school. A man grabbed me and pulled me off the side of the road," Linda said. Then he threw her behind a group of tall shrubs and raped her while seagulls drifted overhead. "He ripped my dress then stuck his hand over my mouth until I thought I would smother. Then he ripped my underwear off and when he stuck it in, I thought I was going to split and I could tell I was bleeding."

She said the man had hairy arms and stringy hair hanging in his face. "I didn't look, though." For once, her way of blanking out paid off.

Just a young girl, Linda had seen so much, hardening herself to life. She was never the same after that. She always seemed to be on the defense and ready to fight at any time. She watched every move people made, especially men, and it even took her a while before she would talk to Bobby.

When I asked her why she didn't tell me about it sooner, she said she had preferred not to say anything because the man told her if she did, he would kill all of us. If she had spoken up then, Dad most likely would have found the guy and killed him before he had a chance to get to us. And there would be no questions asked.

When Dad decided he was not cut out for wearing suits every day, trying to sell houses to rich people, he said it was time to find another place to work; in other words, it was time to move on. There was more work in Montana and if we got there soon, he would be busy for some time. George and Natasha had already moved back to Dillon, and Uncle Bob and Aunt Babe would be gone soon. It was just a matter of time before we left as well. I couldn't quit thinking about Bobby and how I was going to have to say good-bye. For the first time, I realized that if there was a way for me to stay where I was, I would.

But I worried needlessly because, right before we left, Dad asked Bobby if he had ever been to Montana. Bobby grew excited at the thought of leaving California for the wilds of Montana. "Nope, always wanted to see the mountains," he said.

"Well, you're welcome to go with us, there's always work there this time of year, but what about your baby?" Dad asked.

"Juanita's going back to Michigan to be with her parents. She won't be around much longer anyhow. She'll be fine." He looked over at me and I could read a thousand things in that look. Like little bubbles, I felt butterflies in my stomach. When I thought about spending more time with Bobby in Montana, those butterflies grew wings and tried to crawl out of my belly. Dad had not seen us kissing, so he had no idea that we were more than friends — otherwise, he may not have asked Bobby to go.

In less than a week, we loaded up the U-Haul and the car and took off, Bobby following along behind us.

Chapter 18

This move was different than others we had made throughout the years. There was no more jolly kid talk or singing songs like *California here we come.* Instead, we huddled near the doors as if trying to hide from our surroundings, Gary on one side and me on the other, where we now slept — no more floorboards stacked with blankets. I decided this must be how dogs in a cage feel.

When Gary and I made loud, obnoxious jokes or turned the radio up, Dad got angry, but at least he no longer threatened to stop and drop us off on the side of the road like he did when we were kids, because he knew we might take him up on that offer. We no longer kept it a secret that we hated our lifestyle and wanted to stay somewhere even if it meant not being with them. Gary and I would rather stay with strangers than continue our quest for something that we knew didn't even exist.

Dad knew how we felt about traveling, because he grew up that way, too, but he was addicted and there was nothing we could do or say to change his mind. We had to wait until we grew up. And then, we kids vowed we would settle down, have families, and live normal lives. *Sure.*

Linda still sat in the front seat, squished in between Mama and Dad like a damn hot dog between a bun. It was obvious she felt she was way too near Mama by the way Linda never looked her in the eye. As long as Dad was in the car it was fine, but the minute he stepped out to get gas or take a bathroom break, the two of them were all over each other. Just one little word and a fight broke out — a yelling, screaming, *I'll-hit-you* fight. Sometimes Gary and I joined in, mostly trying to get them to shut up, but things just grew worse; cats began screeching, we began cussing, and Mama neared the verge of one of her nervous attacks, throwing things around until the car looked like it had been hit by a crosswind from Kansas.

I could usually, but not always, tell when that was about to happen. The madder Mama got, the more her lips flattened into thin, hard lines. Then her lips puckered into a little asshole-looking circle. By the time Dad got back to the car, arms flailed and bitter words flew from mouths like cotton from trees.

Mama screamed that Linda was too big to be acting like that, her face red and her voice shaky. Dad would say, "You settle down, all of you. Jesus, leave you for a minute and look what happens." He looked at Linda. "Settle down, Injun, we'll be there soon." He used her nickname, which made her comfortable. We all settled back in and that was that. It was what families did — right?

No doubt about it, we were all a little stir crazy inside the belly of what was once our familial home. Except for the big black Hudson of yesterday, there wasn't a car big enough for all of us, and cars today were not meant to be lived in. Or maybe it was just that we were bigger now. Luckily, the boxes — once stowed on the backseat and covered with blankets for our makeshift bed — were no longer there and, although we still couldn't sprawl out, this time our heads didn't hit the roof of the car.

Gary and I took turns riding with Bobby, whose backseat was loaded with what little he owned. We fought over who could ride with him, then fought over how long we rode shotgun in his car. Anything was better than being in the Gypsy wagon, as I came to call it.

I could tell Bobby wasn't used to traveling; he *ooh*-ed and *aw*-ed as if he'd just seen a naked woman walking down the Las Vegas strip. Or maybe I was world-weary and had seen so much of this territory that I was sick of it, at least for the time being. What did I want? Where did I want to be? My hormones were buzzing, and I wasn't sure if I should meet some guy and fuck his brains out or settle with the fact that I was a virgin meant for Beauty School.

Rivers and creeks flowed the way they always had when we passed this area of the country. Little towns flashed by with a blink, barely making an impression. But even the little diners dotting the landscape along the way excited Bobby. I was beginning to wonder if maybe he was just a bit emotionally retarded. He was like a kid with a new toy, announcing every little thing that caught his eye, like the diner shaped like a giant cowboy hat called *Stetson Burger – All You Can Eat for $5*, which I thought was outrageous. He wanted to stop, but little did he know Dad didn't stop until he absolutely had to — when we moaned that we were hungry, when we were running out of gas, or when the car broke down. Then he would stop at the first diner with outdoor seating and let us order burgers or chicken-in-basket.

I was way past the stage of ogling over every little crappy diner and stupid billboard; I'd seen so many billboards in my life. I used to think they were artwork, especially when I was younger — big pieces of art that someone made and hung out for Travelers like us. I believed drive-in theaters were grand TVs for us road people, where we could drive in to sleep or watch the movie and occasionally hit up the concession stand.

It was stupid of me to think Bobby's obsession with diners was over-the-top because I also had that obsession once. I had to laugh at his enthusiasm and remembered that he was from Michigan. Although I had never been there (oddly enough), I figured they didn't have diners like we had in the west.

When Dad announced that he had decided to move back to Hamilton, it made the trip that much more enjoyable. It was as if we were going home — if there was such a thing for us. I couldn't wait to meet up with friends I had left behind and introduce them to my boyfriend.

Hamilton this time of year smelled of cottonwoods and fresh earth after rain, with pine trees dotting the nearby mountains. The glitter of spring rain shimmered and looked how I felt. Our family became happy again. I wasn't sure if Dad wanted to move there because he knew that's where we wanted to be and he wanted to make us happy, or if he had found some job opportunities among all the relatives. Either way, I felt a boulder had been lifted from my shoulders, mainly because the longer we were on the road, the more opportunity we had to hate each other. Our little squabbles could reach full-fledged battles in no time.

Pulling into Hamilton was like breathing in the sweet scent of lilacs. The spacious white house we rented was once an old folk's home, and sometimes I felt I could smell the old skin as if it had permeated the walls and floor. I knew the walls held stories, and since I was just getting into my spiritual side, devouring everything I could read on the subject, I felt they were speaking to me, and we were safe; they didn't want to hurt us. In fact, I think they liked us being there.

There was plenty of room for Bobby to stay with us until he got his own place.

We introduced him to countless cousins who came and went, helping us move in, which I could tell Mama hated. She said she was tired of people tramping in and out, especially the guys who spent hours talking about the road, their travels, the jobs they had worked, the road troubles, and the kids. She said she just wanted to have coffee with the women and didn't need a bunch of guys hanging around.

"Hey, glad you came along," George said to Bobby when he stopped by after we moved in.

"Never been to Montana, it's about time I did. It's beautiful here," Bobby said, looking over at me. My stomach flipped and I could feel all eyes on me. My face heated up and I'm sure it was red. Dad looked at me with questioning eyes, and I was sure he knew Bobby and I were more than just friends. I wasn't sure he liked the idea, either. He had bigger plans for me, like going to beauty school. I hadn't yet gone down the path of my *trampy* cousins, as Dad would say, because I had not had sex yet.

Right after we got to town, Dad organized a crew of carpenters that included most of the men in the family and Bobby. Even Gary was learning the trade and I envied the money he was making. More cousins moved into town, along with a half-brother named Danny — from Dad's marriage with June. Danny brought his wife and kids with him and settled into a tiny apartment next to our house, with only a small yard separating them from us, which Mama thought was just like sticking them in a closet with her. She was beside herself.

We were becoming a tribe once again, spilling across the town with the confidence that comes from being part of a band. Everyone lived within a four-block area and whether that was planned or not I don't know. There were evenings with long pinochle games and endless pots of coffee and iced tea. It seemed like the prerequisite to being a McAlpin was playing pinochle. From the time I was ten and they were short a player, I was called to sit in.

We scoured the town in search of our old friends and found them still living in the same homes as before. It was no surprise, though, since this town went back generations and not many of the people moved around. It was as if we had never been gone. Friends invited us to parties in the woods, where I took Bobby so everyone could see that I had a boyfriend; one I picked up along the way like some people pick up pets.

I had never gotten to know Dad's kids from his marriage to June, except for the small amount of time when we had lived with them. It seemed like the older they got the more they wanted to get to know what Dad was like. June had always bad-mouthed him, and they wanted to see for themselves what kind of a character he was. His daughter Joyce also came for a week-long visit to see if she wanted to live in Montana. Her jolly nature kept us laughing, and when she laughed, every pound of flesh on her rotund body shook. But since she didn't get along with Mama, she left before we could even get to know her. Tiny little Mama looked at Joyce like she'd never seen anyone so fat. Joyce's large frame and spare-tire middle made Mama cringe, and eventually, she began saying things to Joyce about her weight, just like she did to Dougie.

"You're going to end up big and fat just like your mom if you don't quit eating," Mama said.

"If you must know, I have a thyroid problem and that's why I'm having trouble losing weight," Joyce answered. Her round face had lost any sign of cheekbones or curves it may have once had, and her tall, ratted hairdo made her head look even larger, like a substantial honeydew melon. Joyce let most of Mama's remarks bounce right off her — I figured she must have let comments like those roll off her back plenty of times before. It was only a few days later when she packed up and went back to L.A.

Summer was turning out to be one long state of excitement. Days lingered into nights filled with Danny playing guitar and Bobby and I snuggling or taking walks, with an occasional kiss thrown in when no one was looking.

Danny was taller than Dad, but had the same wavy black hair, chiseled face, and large pillowy lips like Elvis. But as much as Mama liked Elvis (she stuck posters of him all over the house and owned every album he ever made), she could not get herself to accept Danny as her stepson. Danny handled Mama's ridiculing much better than Joyce, though, and when Mama found fault in him, he would give it right back to her — usually in regards to her cooking.

"I've never seen anyone make scalloped potatoes like that," Danny said one afternoon as Mama poured milk over sliced potatoes, dabbed them with chunks of butter, sprinkled them with salt and pepper, and popped them in the oven.

"Well, you just don't have to eat them. You eat here too often anyways," Mama said, glaring at him.

"Maybe I should have Donna show you how to make them," he said, referring to his wife, as he laughed the entire way out the door.

Mama never knew how to react to his sarcasm. Linda watched Mama's reaction when Danny stuck up for himself, waiting for Mama to explode or go off on him the way she did with her. But when she did, Danny would laugh like he'd heard a funny joke and that confused Mama to the point where she didn't know what to do. So instead, she would ignore him, and eventually rarely talked to him.

Gary and I bonded with all of our old friends once again. Our group consisted of Gary's friends and my friends, and like a gang, we all ran around together. We moved from the house we were living in, to a two-story house on Main Street that gave us all the privacy we needed upstairs. We could have friends sleepover, which was a rarity in most of the places we had lived. We felt settled. Summer days were hot and, if we weren't down at the river swimming, we were at the local teen club raising hell. Gary painted the walls with murals for the owner, and on Friday nights we danced, sometimes to the jukebox and sometimes to a live band.

Linda met up with girls she knew from before and at first seemed happier than I had seen her for a while. But as time went on, her fights with Mama once again grew out of control — now including hitting and slapping or, in Mama's case, throwing things.

Linda grew thick skin and didn't care what people thought of her. If she wanted to walk the streets with the Job Corps guys who came to town twice a week, she did — which then was considered trampy. Her self-esteem was shot, and doing things she wasn't supposed to do seemed to guide her. Taller now, with a thick mound of hair, darker skin, and a plump, solid body, she laughed with Bobby and me, but it was one of the only times I saw her so happy, except for when Dad joked with her and called her Injun.

Uncle Bob and Aunt Babe lived down the street from us, trying to convince us that this time they were going to settle down since the kids were all in school. *Yeah right,* I thought. I had heard that all too many times. Mama was a happy camper, walking down the street to have coffee with Babe and other ladies in the neighborhood. I no longer hung out with them because I had grown beyond listening to idle chatter and local gossip. I loved them both, but I didn't want to hang out with them.

One month after we moved to Hamilton, Dad caught Bobby and me kissing on the couch when he walked in the door unexpectedly, and that was the end of Bobby. Dad figured if we were "swapping spit" in the middle of the afternoon, we were most likely screwing in the evening as well. Little did he know we had never had sex. As much as I was attracted to Bobby, with his black hair and striking brown eyes, I wasn't attracted enough to end up like my *trashy cousins*. But for the most part, I think Dad didn't like the fact that Bobby was twenty-one and I was what they called *jail bait* back then.

The next morning when I got up, Bobby was gone. His room — a small converted porch — was empty. When I asked Dad where he went, he took a sip of coffee, put his buttered toast on the table, and answered, "He hit the road if he knows what's good for him. I gave him until noon today to get his ass out of town. If I catch him hanging around, I'll *kick* his ass out of town myself. Goddamn pervert."

I begged Dad to reconsider, as my heart was breaking in a way I never thought it could. Bobby was my first true love and I felt like my life was now over — there wasn't another guy who looked at me like Bobby did, who complimented me the way he did or would kiss me until my insides tingled. Dad had killed any chance of me having a future with the man I loved. He may as well have told me I was going to be a spinster and live with them for the rest of my life, a thought that made me cry daily.

"It's not the end of the world, Judy. You're good looking and won't have trouble getting a boyfriend your age," he said when he saw how distraught I was. For the first time, I felt Dad's actions were unjustified and I carried that anger with me for some time — at least until we moved and I found a new boyfriend.

Chapter 19

I was now in love with life. Each day was a new turn of events. My friends were like the skin I wore; they were the necessary ingredients that pulled the wild in me to the surface. My best friend, Helen, had a wild streak like I did, and between us, we came up with ways to enhance our summer days. We borrowed her mother's car and took ninety- mile-an-hour trips to Missoula to spend time with college guys who were more compatible with us. We hung out with them in their tie-dyed, incense-infused apartments near the university, smoking pot and listening to music.

When we got bored in Hamilton, we talked boys with cars into taking us to Connor Lake, letting us ride on the hood and hang onto the windshield wipers when we got far enough out of town. If we wanted a beer, we found older guys who would buy us a six-pack, then three or four of us would go hide to drink it. Eventually, we were able to talk Mama into buying beer for us, as long as she could have one for her *anemia*. Then we'd crawl out my bedroom window and sit on the roof drinking. Now that I considered myself grown-up at seventeen, she seemed to calm down about me hanging out with her all the time. Most of the time we enjoyed each other's company.

Life became a whirlwind. Dad came and went, working both in and out of town. Linda stayed out most of the time and Gary and I, since we ran with the same crowd, saw each other whenever he wasn't working. The money he made went to buying a beat-up '57 Ford station wagon, which he cherished even though it looked like some of the cars we'd seen in wrecking yards. When Gary was working out of town one week, Helen and a few other friends talked me into driving his car so we could cruise the drag. Mama had the keys, and since she was easily talked into anything, she handed them over.

I had gotten pink cat-eye glasses with rhinestones the year before when the teacher was finally able to convince Dad that I was half-blind. They were the kind Marilyn Monroe wore, and the only reason I chose those frames is that Dad thought they were classy. It didn't take long for me to quit wearing them all together, though, which is how I ended up smashing Gary's car into a telephone pole.

My friends laughed and screamed that it was the funniest thing they'd ever seen, while I sweated about what I would tell Gary when he got back to town.

"Just park it and pretend that someone else hit it," Helen said.

"That's a good idea," I answered, knowing that, since we lived on the main drag, something like that could easily happen.

As much as it sounded like a good plan, it didn't work. The minute Gary and Dad drove up Friday night, Gary saw his car and came screaming into the house. I pretended that I was busy and feigned shock at his words. I stuttered around like a maniac, hoping my preposterous attempt at innocence was working. It would have if Mama hadn't mentioned that she let me use the car so I could "practice driving" and take the driving test. For the first time that I could remember, Gary looked at me like he wanted to be rid of me, or maybe kill me — I wasn't sure which. I didn't care.

That night at the teen dance, with a small high school band squeaking out the words to a Jefferson Airplane song, Gary and his friends sat on one side of the dance floor and my friends and me on the other. He had told all of his friends what I did, and it seemed as if he was trying to plan an attack on us girls — at least until they wanted to dance. Then it was all over.

I needed to get a job. Most of my friends had one and if I wanted my own car, I would have to get one, too. A few years before while living here, my cousin's wife Natasha and I got a job babysitting for a single logger with three kids. He was a greasy, older guy named Ed and I figured he was way too old to have such young children.

When we got to the logger's house, we would first smoke at least three cigarettes, go back to bed, then get the kids up and send them on their way, and still have a full day to do what we wanted. The money was good, but since we had to split it, it wasn't as great as I thought it would be. Dad said he wouldn't let me do the job unless Natasha did it with me, and since she was a high school drop-out with little hope or expectations for a future, she was happy to share the job. It lasted almost a month. Still, the thought of becoming a beautician lingered in my mind and was looking better and better all the time.

I knew it wouldn't take me long to get a job this time. *Help Wanted* signs littered windows and the classified ads, and the school had a posting for low-income kids who wanted to work entry-level jobs. Between the thought of making my own money, teen dances, and meeting more and more good-looking guys, my life was a whirlwind of fun; surely my best summer yet. That is until Dad laid the nefarious bomb on us once again — we were moving.

Dad said his sister wrote from California, telling him about all the new building going on, and if he got there soon, he'd be busy for months, maybe even a year. When he told us the news, I felt my heart break.

"How could he do this to us?" I screamed, looking over at Gary, who sat motionless next to me on the porch. "I'm just not going!"

"I'm not going, either. I talked to Bob and Babe and they said I could stay with them. I think I'm going to do it, too, so I can still work." Gary had that defiant look on his face, and I knew he meant it. He was having too much fun and going out with different girls every few weeks, ever the popular, handsome new guy.

"I'll find someone to stay with, because this time I'm not going." I was so sure of myself, even though I knew that I may have to go.

My friend Alice, who lived with her elderly mother, said I could stay with them. She had a bedroom big enough for both of us. When Gary and I approached Dad with the idea, at first he blew up. "What? Too good to travel with the family now? You're almost eighteen and then you can do what you want, but for now, you're going with us." Dad looked from one of us to the other while I waited for Gary to say something.

"Dad, this time I'm not going," he said. "I'm going to stay with Bob and Babe and keep working." You could have heard a pin drop if it hadn't been for the decaying carpet on the floor. Gary brushed his hair from his eyes. It had grown below his collar and he had already been expelled from school once for the length.

I looked over and hoped he could see the pleading in my eyes. When he didn't, I blurted my own spiel: "I'm staying with Alice. Her mother said it was O.K. and I could help her out. She's really old." What the hell was I talking about? The words just popped out of my mouth. Maybe, I thought, if I said I was going to assist an old person Dad would think differently about the situation.

After arguing with Dad for the next two days, he came to realize we were no longer kids who would back down, so he agreed we could stay, but only after he talked with Alice's mother to make sure it was all right.

Mama and Dad went to Alice's house and introduced themselves — as usual, Dad did all the talking while Mama sat on the couch looking bored — and it was agreed that I could stay and Dad would send money every couple of weeks for food and whatever else I needed. He said he didn't know how long they would be gone, but we were to start school here. The minute we got in trouble, he said, we were on the next bus to sunny California. I couldn't believe my ears; we were going to be somewhat independent. Inside I was smiling, and when I looked at Alice, she was too.

But when I looked over at Mama, her face was stiff and it looked as if she was going to cry. Her once-pretty face was now lined and harsh, and she was as thin as a young cottonwood branch. If Mama had nothing else, she had her kids, but now two of them were going their own ways. Mama stared out across the living room that held only a TV, a small couch, one chair, and some clutter. I felt sorry for her, and when I saw her woeful face, it almost made me want to change my mind. Almost. As stubborn and sometimes mean as she was, she had a good side and loved Gary and me with all her heart.

As before, we all helped pack up the boxes, but this time Gary and I put our clothes in pillowcases and our other belongings in bags and set them aside. In all the years we'd traveled the roads together, something was happening that had never happened before — we were not going to be a family, and I wasn't sure how I felt about that. All of my emotions ran around in my head, tripping on each other. I knew we would always be family, of course, but for the first time, we would not be squished inside the car, piled on top of each other while the cats roamed freely — anywhere but the front seat, if they knew what was good for them. How would it feel to see the orange appendage drive away without us?

When the U-Haul was loaded and the three cats tossed in the backseat where Linda would sit, I walked over to Mama. I had become aware over the last few years that Mama lived through me, at least somewhat. She wanted us to grow up together and for me to be her neighbor when I got older and started having babies. All she ever wanted was a storybook life, and I couldn't blame her for that. But she still had Linda, and as much as I hated the idea of Linda being the only one there with Mama, at least she had someone.

"How ya doing, Mama?" I touched her shoulder and she turned to put her arms around me, something that she — or any of us — rarely did. She smelled of Vicks and the cheap cologne I had gotten her as a going-away present.

She pulled her arms away and looked at me. "I'll miss you, Juder," she said, using her pet name for me. "Don't forget to write. You gave me Alice's address, hope I didn't lose it. I'll write as soon as we get an address. That better be soon, too, I'm sick of that damn car. All it does is eat gas and it is expensive!" I could tell she was getting nervous.

"Of course I'll write. I'll even call if you get a phone."

Before they got in the car, Dad turned to Gary and me to say goodbye. "You kids be good. Just because we're not here doesn't mean you can run around like wild animals. Then he turned to me. "Judy, don't run the streets, and stay away from boys, you're too young. Gary, you watch out for your sister."

Luckily, Babe and Bob only lived five blocks from Alice's house, and that made Dad feel better. Gary had always been a good older brother. He had protected me when one of his friends tried to cut off my long braid, and was always there at parties when guys tried to put the moves on me.

Linda stood near the car biting her fingernails. I walked over to her. I hadn't realized the consequence of Gary and I staying, at least as far as Linda was concerned.

"Hey. Take care of yourself. Don't let Mama give you any shit. Bet she's nicer to you now that we won't be there," I said, wishing at once I hadn't.

"Oh, I'm not worried about that," she said in her husky voice half-laughing. I had not noticed how mature Linda had become. She had lost some of her baby fat, revealing high cheekbones and a defiant look. She was becoming a beautiful butterfly. I would miss her.

"You're getting beautiful, Linda; don't let the boys take advantage of you. Here's Alice's phone number," I said, handing her a slip of paper. "Call me if you get in trouble or something happens." We hugged and she got in the car. I waved until the infamous orange tail of the car was out of sight.

"Seems odd," Gary said as we began walking toward our respective houses in a shaking-the-head sort of way.

"It's like we're grownups now," I said, shifting my belongings from one shoulder to the other, feeling the weight of my transistor radio, clock, beads, and supplies in my fringed bag. My hair was parted in the middle, hanging in my eyes and straight down my back. When an older woman passed us, she looked at me and did the *tssst* thing with her tongue the way Mama did. I ignored it — it had happened before.

It didn't take long for Gary and me to get over our feeling of loss. While we walked, fumbling with our bags, we babbled, joked, and laughed about our new lives. The excitement was just beginning.

Riding in the Backseat with my Brother

✱✱✱

It took me no time to move in with Alice and her mom since I had so little. The house was incredibly small, but Alice and I stayed in the bedroom most of the time when we were home, which wasn't very often. Now that I had my freedom, we constantly hung out at friends' houses, meeting up with Gary and his friends at the dances or drive-in theater. Alice had no trouble keeping up with me since her mother wasn't aware of anything we did. Sometimes we would gather at Helen's house and listen to *Surrealistic Pillow* by Jefferson Airplane for hours, or at least until her mother got home and shooed us away.

We planned our remaining summer days with care since school would be starting in less than three weeks. The dog days of summer were upon us. Helen and I both had boyfriends — or, rather, boys that were our friends and wanted to be more. They liked both of us; and we could talk them into anything. We borrowed John's car one day and went on a debauched ride to the country, where we proceeded to knock on the door of a red farmhouse with a weather vane on the roof.

"Shhhh. Let's knock," Helen said while I looked through the window. No one was home, so we walked in through the kitchen door in the back of the house. Once inside, the sweet smells of fresh-baked cookies floated around the room. The oatmeal cookies sat in a jar on the counter and we filled our bag with them. The clock on the wall made a loud ticking sound, reminding me that we needed to hurry. This was only our second time doing this, and I still feared what would happen if we got caught.

Then we looked into the large chest freezer, where at least a half of beef was piled up in tidy white packages, each with the contents of the package written on the front. We took two packs marked *steaks*. Then we ran toward the car and tore out of the driveway, laughing as if we'd just robbed a bank and got away with it.

"What the fuck? Was that fun or what?" Helen screamed. I looked at the excitement on her face and felt the same way.

"Let's eat the cookies," I said, grabbing the bag and pulling two out. It was not our last hurrah for the summer, but it was our last big one before school started.

The week after school started we skipped class since it was only a half-day anyway. As Helen, Alice, and I sat around at Christine's house thinking up all kinds of ways to make the afternoon more exciting, it dawned on us that our science teacher, Mr. Koots, lived just doors away in this smart little neighborhood with sidewalks, grass lawns, and neighbors not ten feet apart.

It didn't take long before we talked each other into seeing what Mr. Koots had in his house. After all, he was our teacher, and Alice said we needed to know if he was a pervert. We went in for the thrill of it; for the big adrenaline rush. We knew he was at school and wouldn't be home until late afternoon, so we had time. We weren't planning on taking anything, but Christine found the liquor cabinet and that's all it took for us to indulge ourselves. Then we found the stack of records and — although most of it was boring, like Frank Sinatra and Hank Williams — we found some good ones that we took to Christine's. By the time we left, we were drunk and laughing so hard that we were rolling on the floor when we got back to Christine's house. We were all jazzed up and it took several minutes before we could contain ourselves.

I knew what we did was wrong, but I also knew I was no better than these girls; in fact, I may have been a little more rebellious. Seventeen years of moving from place to place had always given me an out when things didn't go well because I knew eventually we would move and leave behind the bad stuff. But this time was different; there were no parents to take me away and plunk me nice and neat in a new school where no one knew me.

Helen and I went along with almost anything and most often we were the instigators. The kids in school looked at us like we were mavericks. We not only dressed differently than most — having gotten into the whole hippie style — but we also did things that most of them wouldn't do. Even the stuck-up cheerleaders liked us because they thought we were fearless, if not a little dangerous. Dad would have been disappointed, though, and probably would've said I was turning into my cousins.

It was all in fun until the next day at school, when the four of us were called to the office over the loudspeakers. It seemed Mr. Koots's close neighbors saw us run — or, I should say, *stagger* — back to Christine's house. We walked individually down the narrow hall of the school and met each other outside of the principal's office, where we were told to sit on a bench without speaking. We waited for our turn to be called, then went in one by one, wishing we would at least have had time to get our stories straight.

When we walked out of the office, we each carried a slip of paper that we were to give to our parents to let them know we were expelled for two days. *Well, hell,* I thought — I didn't have anyone to give the note to, so it would be vacation days for me.

Chapter 20

During the second month living at Alice's house, Dad sent money to her mom and I got a letter telling me they would be coming back soon because there wasn't as much work as he thought there would be. They said they didn't like the idea of us staying through the winter, but we could talk about that when they got here.

Gary had become involved with a girl he was getting serious about. He didn't even party with his friends as much as he used to. When we got together for lunch in the cafeteria one day, we talked about the letters.

"Sure, I know what will happen. They'll get back here and force us to move again, but I'm not going," Gary said, sticking his chest out and blowing smoke from his mouth. I couldn't blame him. He had a steady girlfriend named Bonnie who lived in a nearby town and was two years older than him. She was pretty enough, but looked much older than him, with squinty eyes, glasses, and short hair. He would hitchhike to see her. To me, she was dull and simple-looking, like a librarian, but she was sweet. I think it was the first time Gary had ever been sexually active with anyone, and he acted like a dog in heat.

Two weeks after the letter arrived, a U-Haul pulled up in front of Alice's house and I knew right away it was them. I ran outside, happy to see them. I had never gone this long without them and I hadn't realized how much I missed them. Linda jumped out of the car, a smile as wide as her round face. She was tan and her hair had straightened out some. She even lost more weight and was beautiful. "I missed you, Juder," Mama said.

Linda looked good and, after hugging her, I told her I wanted to hear all about the trip, which she said was nothing I hadn't experienced before. She hugged me back and I could tell she was trembling with joy. She was back with her family.

They stayed with Bob and Babe while looking for a house, and I stayed with Alice. I had to tell my friends — and casual boyfriends — that I wouldn't be able to hang out with them late at night as I had before. High school boys bored me, anyhow. I was beginning to realize that they were immature and insipid — trying to put their hands down my blouse, or their tongues down my throat. If they thought I was frigid, I was. I was not about to give up my virginity to a pimple-faced boy. I learned that the young college guys in Missoula had a lot to say, and weren't as vulgar. If I was to give in, it would be with one of them. Someday.

Dad moved us into a two-story house on Main Street that gave us more room than we had had in years. It was pea green, with three bedrooms upstairs away from the squeaking springs in the bedroom downstairs where Mama and Dad slept, and close to downtown. It was as if they had never been gone. Things went back to the way they were — but I didn't. By now, my miniskirts were so short I thought Dad was going to have a heart attack every time I stepped out of the house.

When Dad worked out of town, I ran the streets with my friends looking for action or hitchhiked to Missoula, about thirty miles away, to dance with college guys, not getting home until three in the morning. It wasn't always easy to get a ride back after the dance ended. Sometimes, Helen and I, still on an adrenaline rush from dancing all night, would hitch a ride to a truck stop located between Hamilton and Missoula and hit truck drivers up for a ride home. But we were young, half-dressed girls with hair in our eyes and love beads wrapped around our necks. Not many wanted to take the chance of getting in trouble for picking up jail bait. It never dawned on us that we could easily have been killed or raped.

When we saw a truck driver cleaning up the last of his plate, we walked over and introduced ourselves, saying our car broke down, and if we didn't get home soon, we would get busted by our parents.

Although most of the drivers turned us down, this one was different.

"I'll take you girls home on one condition. You stay in the bunk, don't talk, and don't lift your head. You get me in trouble and I might have to kill you." We weren't sure if he was kidding or not, but we jumped in and rode home without saying a word, breathing in the sour, sweaty smell of his bed.

Bonnie, Gary's girlfriend, began staying overnight since her home was twenty miles away. It was obvious to my friends and me that she was promiscuous — much more so than Gary — and ate him up like a fresh apple pie, or in this case, a fresh piece of meat. I wasn't sure if Dad knew that when she slept over, she didn't sleep with me; since our rooms were upstairs, he wouldn't know — but he could hear. I was convinced Dad knew they were fucking like rabbits. How could he not? They spent the night rocking the bed and banging on the walls as if they were doing calisthenics. Dad seemed to think it was O.K. for a guy to indulge in sexual encounters at a young age, but not a girl like me.

Gary announced to all of us one day that Bonnie was pregnant. When they stood in front of Dad to tell him the news, I watched from a nearby room. She couldn't have been more than a few months along since her belly wasn't much bigger than it was before, barely bulging from her skin-and-bones body. Gary hung his head and Bonnie smiled as if she was happy to snag a good-looking guy like Gary, who was sought after by most of the girls in town.

"Well," Dad started, looking from Gary then to Bonnie. "What do you plan to do about it?"

They looked at each other as if they never thought about the matter. Bonnie spoke up first. She was much more mature than Gary, even though she was only a couple of years older.

"We didn't mean for this to happen . . ."

"Dad, we'll just get married. I can get a job here and work until the baby comes and . . ." I had to keep myself from snickering because the thought of Gary with a baby made a strange visual image in my mind.

"No, I have a better idea," Dad said. By now Mama had come into the room.

She'd heard everything and a smile spread across her face as if having a grandbaby was more important than worrying about the couple's life. "You can both come with us and we'll stop in Vegas and you can get married. Hell, that's where we got married and it's not that bad. Those wedding chapels are open all night."

Gary and Bonnie looked at each other and I could tell they liked the idea. After discussing specifics, it was decided that Bonnie would tell her family what was going on, and the two of them would ride in Gary's Corvair, following along behind us. We would head out in less than a week. Bonnie's face dripped with excitement, her grin spread across her face and her eyes like dark grapes, ready to explode. She had never lived anywhere else and the thought of the bright Vegas lights and living on top of a mountain thrilled her.

Whatever, I thought. Little did she know that life with the McAlpins wasn't always a joy ride.

As much as I wanted to revolt, I knew it was not a good time. I had to go along with the tribe, especially now that Gary and Bonnie were going. Dad said we needed to leave before it got cold and that we would make friends at the next place — blah, blah, blah. The usual. By now we were sick of Dad's promises and concerns about getting a job. We begged him to find work somewhere in the area so we could stay, but he insisted Montana was no place to be in the winter and we would return in the spring, which gave me hope.

Helen and Alice offered for me to stay with them, and Gary's friend David did the same, at least until the announcement of the pregnancy. Helen was a wild girl, built like a stick, with golden-red hair and a quest for adventure. She lived with her mother and two brothers and ruled the roost. We taught each other how to be bad, and the wilder and more dangerous things we did, the more excited we got. We fed off of each other, always looking for excitement.

Alice was tall, snorted when she laughed and snored at night. She was older than Helen and me but in the same grade, and the thirteenth child born to a worn-out woman who still washed dishes in the back of her son's restaurant. Alice went along with most of the things Helen and I did but drew the line when we asked if she wanted to break into farmhouses to steal food. It was mainly for fun and the rush, but it was also a good way to eat without having to go home. You learn when the farmers are away doing fieldwork, that was the best time for us to *dine out*.

Our friends were now integral parts of our lives. Making us leave them seemed so easy for Dad, who always assumed we would make new friends, just like we did when we were little. But we didn't care about that anymore; we wanted to stay with friends who meant something to us. The '60s were buzzing and we wanted to be a part of them. Now was not a time to be holed up somewhere while the hippie scene moved right past us.

We had decided that family didn't mean that much to us anymore if all they did was make our lives miserable by pulling us from our friends. As much as we hated to move, we did anyway, especially after Dad promised Gary part of the take from the mine. If nothing else, we could hit the road and come back to Hamilton if things didn't work out.

I knew we would be back, and if I had anything to say about it, it wouldn't be that long.

Chapter 21

The road seemed longer this time. Bonnie had morning sickness and we had to stop often. She complained a lot and reminded me of Mama; she didn't like sleeping in the car, she didn't like eating lunch on the side of the road, and she didn't like not taking a shower. She was what Dad called a *pansy-ass,* but what was normal for us wasn't exactly normal for other people.

After driving for two days, we reached Vegas around midnight. Linda and I were scrunched up in the backseat and Mama was slumped against the door. Dad pulled over, and when he did, I woke up to see the bright lights of Vegas in the distance. Gary pulled up behind us and got out of the car.

"This is it, Buddy. Ya ready?" Dad asked.

Gary rubbed his eyes, then walked back to the car to wake Bonnie. We drove the short distance to the first sign we saw: *Wedding Chapel, 24-hour service.* I had never seen a wedding chapel and grew excited at the thought of entering one and watching the ceremony take place.

We all climbed out of the car. Linda's hair was ratted and we all had wrinkled clothes. Mama wouldn't take her shredded sweater off, saying she would be cold even though it was plenty warm. I smoothed out my long hair with my hands, then straightened my mini skirt, which Dad said only tramps wore. Gary and Bonnie walked in first, looking like they had just crawled out of bed.

Inside, the lights were dim and an organ sat directly in front of us on a small platform. Pink and purple plastic flowers were scattered from one end of the room to the other. Pictures of other couples in various wedding attire were stapled to the walls, and I would bet right then that they would never put a picture of Gary and Bonnie on their walls. It seemed they only put pictures up of well-dressed couples.

Soft music played in the background and I felt like we were about to have a funeral, but then a man appeared and asked if he could help us. He looked from one of us to the other, noting our special attire and voguish hairdos.

"We want to get married," Gary said.

"All right. Let's just step over here and fill out some paperwork."

The man's wife appeared in a robe and sat down at the organ, beginning to play as though she could do it in her sleep. I looked at Gary, standing so stiff in front of the man, and had to keep from laughing. He seemed so serious and I could tell he was using every bit of effort to act grown up.

The ceremony lasted less than five minutes, then Dad paid the man and we were out the door, back in the car, and on the road. Bonnie was content they were married and Gary promised to buy her a ring when he could.

"Hell," Dad said, "we'll make her one out of jade." That made her happy.

Eventually, we ended up in Pulga, California, a blip of a town in the mountains above Oroville, where Dad's jade mine sat. Not only were we pulled away from friends, but we lived in a town with a population of fewer than 100 people and no high school. I thought Bonnie's eyes were going to pop out of her head when she saw the town, then tears flowed down her face as if she had never seen anything so frightening. If she was going to be married to a McAlpin, she'd better get used to it, I thought.

We had lived in Pulga before when we were in grade school, where we attended a one-room schoolhouse. It was fun helping Dad bag jade on weekends, walking up the side of the small mountain dragging heavy, scratchy gunny sacks behind, and stopping only for a drink of water from Dad's thermos and sometimes a picnic lunch.

Grade school days, at that time, weren't quite as exciting as the mountain. The school was surrounded by a dirt playground and a creek that ran alongside it, and inside was a dirty old teacher named Mr. Black, who had long, steely gray hairs growing from his nose and ears, and a loud, bellowing voice. I was easily embarrassed at that age, and Mr. Black embarrassed me daily, batting questions that I couldn't answer (maybe because I missed too much school) until one day when I couldn't take it anymore, I grabbed my sweater and walked out the door, down the windy dirt road home. Mama had briefly asked why I was home early and I'm not sure she even realized how traumatic it was for me to have a teacher like that. At that time, I was very shy and cried at the drop of a hat.

The place we had rented back then was one in a row of identical cabins. Two skinny, ratty-haired boys lived in the cabin across the narrow road from us, and for entertainment, we stole boxes of matches from our parents, lit them, and tossed them at each other until we got caught. The railroad tracks and the mine were our entertainment. Once again, I was attracted to the tracks like a bug to light.

Dad had made his claim to the mine — clear California Jade, or Californite as he called it. It sparkled in the sun like giant globs of apple jelly and when I held it up to the light, I saw the sky as an emerald field. We helped Dad with the mine as much as we could, considering our age, but when his new career didn't pan out money-wise, Dad left it behind, *"as an investment for later."*

Now that we were teenagers, this little town had lost its glow and charm. There was no school for us since the grade school we attended as kids only went to sixth grade. For us to go to school, it meant riding a bus some forty miles down the winding road to Oroville. We weren't too worried about it, since it was still early in the year and no doubt we wouldn't be living here that long anyhow. We could always catch up.

Days were crisp and the smell of pine trees lingered. A tiny gas station and store hugged the edge of the road and a post office sat across the street as though it had been picked up and plopped there. As lonely, small, and desolate as it was, this was our new town and would be for at least a few months. I could only hope for a shorter stay rather than a long one.

Living away from anything remotely resembling humanity was frightening as a teenager, and all I could do was live for the mail each day, hoping to hear from my friends to hear what real life was like. As we drove up the winding road from Oroville — flanked on one side by a mountain and on the other by a cliff — we hugged the side of the mountain, our trailer swinging with every hairpin curve in the road. Looking down the other side of the mountain, the cliff and beyond, scared Mama and she hid her head under her sweater when we got too close. Regardless of the heat, she still carried her sweater around, "just in case."

"Dad, why did they build this town up here on top of the mountain? It's so far away from everything. Why the hell did they?" I asked, making sure my voice inflected how I felt about living in such a remote place.

"They built it for a lot of reasons, I suspect. The railroad goes right through here. You remember when we lived here last time, you kids used to help me drag jade down the mountain. You guys remember it, don't you?' he asked, looking at us in the rearview mirror.

"Yeah, how could we forget?" I said. I was scrunched up in the corner, trying to find a place to put my legs since Linda was now riding in the backseat with me. "You made us carry gunny sacks bigger than us!" Of course, that was an exaggeration, but we did drag down some heavy bags. Dad made it fun for us, though. We would pack a lunch with a thermos full of cold lemonade or water, and when we were done eating he would pluck the jade from the side of the mountain while we loaded pieces into the sack. When we had filled it, we pulled it down the mountain and dumped it on the porch where Dad sorted through it.

"Bullshit! You kids loved it as much as we did. Right, hon?"

Mama looked at him and made that clicking sound with her tongue. "Maybe you did! Too dirty for me." When she said that, it dawned on me that she rarely had anything to do with the jade.

Her hands were no longer black from coal dust but had become skin and bone.

"This time we're gonna make some money on that damn mine. You kids help and you can make some, too," Dad said, lighting a cigarette with one hand and steering into a curve with another as I rolled my eyes. "First things first, though. We'll get settled, then we can work on getting rich." He chuckled at his comment, but I'm sure he believed every word of it.

It didn't take long for us to drive the length of the block-long town where Dad spotted a house for rent. We waited in the car — as we always did — while he talked some potential landlord's legs off.

While growing up, rocks were our toys. We helped Dad gather garnets, clean sapphires, and agates, and on one occasion, break fine-grained slate, which Dad said was a metamorphic rock derived from shale. We weren't asked to break the stones, but Gary and I had a competition to see who could do it. On the third try, I not only broke a large slab apart but also slit my wrist, from which deep-colored blood began spurting out in all directions.

"God! You have purple blood! You have purple blood!" Gary screamed as the blood began shooting out all over the floor. Linda rushed over to see what purple blood looked like and just stared with her mouth hanging open.

I screamed for Dad, who came running from the next room. "What the hell, Doodle? What did ya do to yourself?" He was out of breath from running and he had a panicky look on his face. When he looked at the gashing wound, his face went white and every-thing went silent. I felt I could hear the sounds of the crystal-cold Montana night, a crust of snow getting ambled on by a muskrat. Then Linda screamed, followed by Mama, who said I was going to lose all my blood if I didn't get help. But living where we did, in Alder, Montana, there was no doctor and no medical facilities.

Like other Montana hick towns we had lived in, there was rarely a doctor handy at nine o'clock at night. This time was no different. Dad wrapped a towel around my wound where the blood had soaked through, then we all hopped in the car and drove twenty miles to the next town over where the doctor lived. When we got to his house, from which he ran his practice, we ran to the door. Mama worried that we were waking him up, but Dad said he could give a shit and continued pounding the door until the doctor opened it.

Inside, the doctor cleaned the cut and stitched me up in a little room in the back of the house with shiny tools, remarking on how little my wrists were and how skinny I was.

"She's a tough little thing, though," Dad said, thanking the doctor and telling him he would send the money when he got paid. "If you're going to be a rock hound, you have to take the bruises, right?" He looked at me and winked, then we headed out the door.

Much like other times, Dad had picked up a stray along the way and invited him to come and help out in Pulga. Biff had stayed with us before marrying a woman who had five kids — combined with his own three, there were eight altogether, the youngest of which they called Superdynamic. We had only met the whole tribe a couple of times when our paths crossed, but this time Biff was alone, saying he was having some trouble with his black-haired beauty.

"Sometimes you just have to separate yourself from each other for a while, if ya know what I mean?" Then he winked and said, "Plus, you know how fun it is when ya make up?" He looked at Mama and laughed. He was a flirt and a joker and at least brought some entertainment into our lives.

I was a little more than surprised when Biff showed up in Pulga, since Dad hadn't mentioned him coming. He said he had come to help out with the mine — apparently Dad had contacted him telling him where we were and how much money he could make here. He was younger than Dad, with curly hair and spar-kling blue eyes. I think Mama had a crush on Biff, with the way she giggled and flirted when he was around; the way she acted like a little girl, trying everything she could to get his attention, even making silly faces at him.

Biff said when he got enough money together, he would move his family to Pulga. He was quite the flirt, winking and laughing at everything we said. Dad let him sleep on the floor in the back room with a heater and a sleeping bag, and I could tell he was accustomed to better than that, but he didn't complain. He was as sure as Dad was that this venture was going to make him some money. Like Dad, he chased rainbows.

After we moved into a pair of tiny log cabins — one for Gary and Bonnie, and one for the rest of us — Dad spent the next few weeks hauling rock down the mountainside. There wasn't much to do, so Gary, Bonnie, and I walked the railroad tracks. Eventually, Bonnie got bored and pouted in her room while Gary and I explored alone. Bonnie began crying that she had never been to a place like this and hated the fact that there wasn't anything to do. She began to get on my nerves, and when I told Gary, he said she was getting on his nerves too. Her stomach got larger each day and she demanded things she would never get hanging out with us.

We listened to music, played cards, and started stealing the heart pills the doctor had given Dad the last time he had heart trouble. We'd pop a pill and walk around in a daze, laughing like a couple of druggies. When Bonnie found out what we were doing, she threatened to tell Dad but never did.

Gary occasionally helped Dad at the mine, but it soon became obvious that he wasn't cut out for whacking the side of a mountain and loading large chunks of stone into bags, so he began staying home. Dad had turned dark as a walnut and hints of silver dusted his temples. On the few days that he wasn't working, he spent time with the man who lived two cabins over — a man named Tiny who had diabetes and lost his feet due to the disease. He was the only other renter in the row of cabins.

Tiny was wispy thin, with little tufts of hair sticking out on both sides of his head and a nose with a small hole in the side of it. We all tried not to look at it, but it was hard not to if you wanted to look him in the eye. His skin was flaky, his eyes were pushed into his head like raisins in soft dough, and when he talked, it was a long, slow drawl that stretched out like the cobwebs that surrounded him. Linda stared in amazement until we told her not to.

Tiny, Dad said, had lived there for years, wasting away alone, waiting for his death. The stumps where his feet should have been were always exposed. He said he couldn't keep them wrapped up due to the heat. Dad told me if I wanted to do something good for the man I should make him a blackberry pie, which I had never made before. So I hunted up enough new berries—it wasn't easy this time of year—to make the pie, and although juice ran in streams when we cut into it, the taste was fine, and Tiny appreciated it. Dad said it was doing things like this that would make me grow up to be a good person. I just hoped like hell I wouldn't end up in a nowhere town like this when I was older.

As fall grew closer, the weather began to change and nights were cold. Since there was no heat in the cabins other than a small heater Dad bought at the second-hand store, it was never warm enough at night. Bonnie threatened to go home daily. Mama got sick of it and told her, "You want to go home, go ahead, like to see you walk down the mountain." She was beginning to treat Bonnie the way she treated Linda, at least when Gary wasn't around.

Linda was perhaps the only one who still enjoyed living on the mountain. She found a few friends her age, the only two girls in this small town, and was gone a lot. I was happy she could amuse herself because we sure as hell weren't too amused.

Gunny sacks of jade began to line the front porch and the side of the house. "Need to start selling this stuff," Dad said one evening as we sat around the table playing pinochle. The inside of the cabin was stuffy and smelled of mold. There was one bedroom in the back and two couches in the living room where Linda and I slept. There wasn't much inside the cabin other than what we needed for cooking and a few pieces of furniture. Dad put most of our belongings in another cabin that the landlord said we could use for free.

While I shuffled the cards, Dad talked about what he needed to do. It seems he hadn't thought far enough ahead as to how he would sell all of this rock so we could become rich and leave this place behind.

"I either need to hit the road and try to sell this shit, or we need to leave so I can get a job. Money's running out. Plus Christmas is coming." He had sold some of the jade to a small rock shop down the mountain — enough to keep food on the table and a roof over our heads, but not much more.

When he came down the mountain after a cool afternoon of picking and bagging the rock, Dad looked both exhausted and bloated. His eyes that always smiled began to droop at the corners, and his legs and arms were thinner than before, but his stomach was still round and spilled over his belt. He rarely complained of the pains in his chest, but I could tell that he experienced them periodically by the way he winced when he thought no one was looking.

Dad thought I was smart, at least business-wise, and it didn't take him long to figure out that I could be the one to *market* his rock. "Hell, if you could write letters and send them out to rock shops and gem stores we could get rid of this shit and make some money," Dad said one day while we sat outside washing the stones and separating the good, clear ones from the inferior ones. "You might even like it, and eventually your secretarial skills will get so good you won't have to be a beautician." I guess he thought being a secretary was better than fixing greasy hair all day, but I wasn't too sure about that.

So it began. I was now the business end of this jade venture at the age of seventeen when I should have been in school or having fun with my friends. Tiny let me borrow his typewriter and I got a list of rock shops located throughout California and Nevada. I'd sit at the kitchen table and surround myself with typing paper and phone books. I'd pretend I was a great writer completing a novel while Mama burnt something on the stove that filled the room with smoke. My working environment left little to be desired, but I had something to do.

My typing was terrible and the first batch of letters I sent out was smothered with mistakes and cross-outs, but I mailed them anyhow. Soon, we began getting letters back stating someone would take a look at the jade whenever we passed through.

Jesus! No one seemed to think about what would happen if the owners actually wanted to see the rocks.

Chapter 22

It was decided that Biff, Gary, and I would hit the road with a trunk load of apple- green jade and visit all the rock shops and gem and mineral stores that had contacted me. At first, it was exciting to think I was old enough to be going on such a grown-up adventure. Being a *saleswoman* at such a young age made me realize I had grown up much faster than a lot of my friends. I was anxious to try anything.

When the owners of the rock shops wrote back, some of them put my letter in with theirs, and when I reread them, my typing errors stared me in the face like little eyes. How these people were able to decipher what I meant was beyond me; jade became *made* and rocks became *socks*. My career as a secretary was not looking too great.

"You take good care of my daughter," Dad told Biff as I threw my overnight bag in the backseat of Biff's beat-up rambler. "Get the kids back safe and in time for Christmas." I could tell that Dad was sorry to see us leave, but he hoped we could make enough money to make it worth our while. Mama cried, then wiped her eyes and said we should call sometime when we got a chance and we better be home for Christmas, her favorite time of year. I had all but forgotten that Christmas was just over a week away.

Where we lived, there was nothing to remind us.

"I will, Mama. We won't be gone that long anyhow. I'll bring back a bunch of money, O.K.? Then we can get out of this shit hole." I didn't really care about the money part of it, but I was going into the world as a sales lady and for the first time I was going without my parents. I was ready for my new career. I was ready for a trip on my own.

Dad wanted to go so bad that his feet were itching, he said. But his health was so bad he couldn't — plus someone had to stay and make sure the three women didn't kill each other.

Gary stood outside talking with Bonnie in the pouring rain, promising that he wouldn't be gone long, and I could tell they were arguing. Her beady eyes were large in her Coke-rim glasses. I heard something about Christmas and boredom. She didn't want him to go, and she surely didn't want to be left alone in a tiny cabin with nothing to do, and with people she barely knew. I couldn't blame her, but I was glad Gary was going along with Biff and me.

I saw things differently in the back of the car this time. Being able to stretch out my legs and have the whole seat to myself made all the difference. The roads were the same windy ropes I'd been over many times before, but the air seemed sweeter, the sky bluer, and I had a home to go back to — that was something I had never experienced, and I liked the feeling. This time there were no flying legs, no fighting in the front seat between Mama and Linda, and no cats or dogs crawling all over me.

Biff treated me somewhat as an adult. On the first night, the three of us slept scrunched up in the car somewhere out in the desert. Until we made a sale, there was no money for motels, but Gary and I had become accustomed to that. I chose the driver's seat because I was the smallest and could fit in better than the two of them. My head filled with visions of meeting handsome managers who would buy lots of rocks to fill the ego I was developing — at least when it came to my business venture.

Before falling asleep, I dreamed of going back to Hamilton, or to the Bitterroot Valley and the people I loved. I was trying to fall asleep, but all I could hear was Biff talking about his wife, their sex life, and how I must be so naïve I didn't know a thing he talked about. Well, I may have been naïve, but I talked to enough people about sex to know most of what there was to know. I'd had more than one guy reach down my blouse for a feel, then grab my hand

and try to get me to push it down his pants, usually at a drive-in theater with my girlfriends. When that happened I would jump out of the car, tell the guy to fuck off, then race away.

"I bet you don't even know what *eating out at the Y* means." Biff laughed while I lay there and wished he would go to sleep. I was beginning to see another side of him, and I wasn't sure I liked it. No wonder he had so damn many kids; he didn't know how to keep it in his pants, as Dad would say.

But he was right — I didn't know what *eating out at the Y* meant, but I had a good idea.

"You ever let a boy put his hands down your pants and tickle you a little? Bet you'd like that wouldn't you? I could show you what I'm talking about if you were interested."

I tried to close my eyes and wished I had earplugs.

Then he reached over the front seat and put his hand on my crotch, laughing the entire time. I flew up and smacked his hand as hard as I could.

"You got any boobies?" he asked, trying to reach down the front of my shirt.

I opened the door and jumped out. Gary was sleeping and no help at all. This pervert was going to get a rock over his head if he didn't watch out. Growing up with a big brother had its advantages when it came to being tough. I walked a little ways from the car, not wanting to walk too far since this *was* the desert and I knew tarantulas loved to walk around at night, just as they did in Johannesburg when we hunted them and put them in coffee cans. It was also as cold as hell.

I jumped back in the front seat, unable to slam the door the way I wanted to because Gary was sleeping. Biff was still sitting up in the backseat and I could swear he was drooling.

"You just wait till we get home and I tell Dad what you did. He'll beat the shit out of you." I was trying to sound tough, even though I felt like crying and running away. I had learned in my years that you should never cower, never let the other person know you're scared and never, ever, cry in front of them. The silent night echoed my words and — besides the coyotes yipping in the background and an occasional plane flying over — I suddenly realized I was all alone in the middle of nowhere with a potential rapist or murderer. After all, what did Dad really know about this man? Nothing except that he had a bundle of kids.

"Oh, don't get your panties in an uproar. I was just kidding. I wasn't really going to play with your clit; I'm going to leave that for some skinny high school boy who won't know a thing about what he's doing. You just wait, you'll want it someday. You'll beg for some man to stick his dick inside you."

He lay back down and turned over facing the back of the seat. I grabbed my thin blanket and nestled down again under the steering wheel, but it was hours before I went to sleep, not only because of the cold, but also because I wasn't sure if he was going to try to touch me again or talk about sex. If he did, this time I would wake Gary and between the two of us, we'd beat this skinny guy to a pulp. When I heard him snoring, I finally went to sleep.

We stopped at restaurants and played a couple of slot machines the next day, and Biff acted as if nothing had happened; like he hadn't humiliated me and made me think twice about going anywhere with him again. We watched while he played blackjack, but I was anxious to get on the road and find the rock shops. The addresses were listed on a piece of paper wadded up in my purse. When we did finally stop at a few shops, they either bought a small amount of jade or nothing at all. We went through towns lit up with Christmas lights, like Bakersfield and Lancaster, trying to peddle our wares. But the minute we got inside, Biff jumped in front of me and began his jabbering.

It didn't take long for me to realize that Biff had the gift of gab even more than Dad did. After introducing myself and letting the owners know that I was the one who wrote the letters they received, I was soon ignored. Biff filled the man in on everything from where the mine was located to the eight kids he had back home, standing in front of me as if I didn't exist.

Once again, I felt like a kid trying to play grownup, and the more I was around Biff the more those feelings grew. I wondered why I went. All I wanted to do was go home, which is what Gary did on the third day. He couldn't take it anymore. He missed Bonnie and he was sick of the boring adventure we were on.

"I'm hitch-hiking out of here. There's no money in this and I want to see how Bonnie is. She shouldn't be alone up there. I mean, what if she went into labor? It's not like Mama could help and . . ."

"Yeah. Well, you're right. I would go too, but I want to see if I can sell anything; that is if Biff ever gives me the chance. What do you think of him by now?" I had never told Gary about the car incident.

"He's O.K. But he is getting on my nerves with his stupid jokes and talk about sex all the time. Be careful of him, I don't trust him anymore." Gary pulled his bag from the trunk of the car and tossed it over his shoulder.

"Don't worry, he gives me any shit and he's getting it in the balls," I said, wishing Gary wouldn't leave me alone with Biff, but knowing why he did. Gary walked to the side of the road and put his thumb out, and within ten minutes he had a ride in a station wagon full of boxes. Gary waved, and I wanted to cry.

At the next shop, Biff gave his spiel and I was like a fly on the wall, watching as if I had nothing to do with the reason we were there. I left the shop and stood out by the car with my wrinkled clothes and dusty shoes, waiting and wishing I was back home again. The streets in the tired little desert town were covered with dirt, and the wind blew it around my feet, reminding me of our many stop-overs in places like Johannesburg.

Colored lights and a Christmas tree decorating the town reminded me of the time of year.

Tears welled up in my eyes and for the first time in my life, I felt like I didn't belong; I didn't belong to any town and I didn't belong to anyone. All of a sudden it dawned on me — I was getting homesick! It was Christmas, and I was homesick.

I hadn't been away from my parents for any great length of time, and after spending so much time in the car together, we actually had become close. We may be considered dysfunctional Gypsies with our moving habits, but you can't spend all your time holed up in a car and not become close to the people inside it. We were closer than many families I had come in contact with.

Leaning against the car with the sunshine on my back and the cold on my face, I felt the heat and the silence of the desert as if it had entered my soul, and I thought I would cry. I had never experienced homesickness before, and I wasn't sure how to deal with it. Our family was often all we had, and we all stuck together, even when we hated each other.

Biff walked out looking like a busted man. His kinky hair shined from hair oil and his perpetually smiling mouth was turned down. He'd grown frustrated with our trip and the small amount of money he was pulling in. Since I was no longer treated as the *sales rep*, I wasn't even sure how much money he was accumulating. I was left out of the loop completely, and if I could have walked home, I would have. My guts felt twisted and my head stuffed with visions of what was to be, and what wasn't. This trip was not turning out the way it should have. My first business venture was a flop.

"Just ain't much call for jade right now. Hell, I could have made more money than this staying home and helping the old lady make doll clothes. Could have had the money for Christmas for the kids, too." He had begun, once again, to get on my nerves. His flirting made me want to wring his skinny neck, and now his whining made me want to punch him.

I couldn't take it anymore. I marched right back into that store and confronted the man at the counter. "Hi, I'm Judy, I'm the one who wrote the letter. We drove all this way to bring you what you asked for. I may be young, but I know for sure that you could make money off of this. It's good quality, and when made up into jewelry, it's beautiful. If nothing else . . ."

The man laughed, but it was a forgiving laugh and made me feel like he liked what I had to say. "Well, little Miss Judy. I like your style — you have a lot of spunk. I wish you were older, I would hire you. Go out and get me a few big chunks of that and I'll pay you."

I ran to the car, my heart pounding. I had been able to confront someone I didn't know! Biff was standing near the car smoking a cigarette. "Open the trunk," I demanded. He opened it and, before he could say anything, I grabbed a half-full gunny sack and ran back into the store. The owner gave me $100. I thanked him and left. Biff saw the money in my hand and grabbed it instantly.

"You did good, girl. I'll give this to your dad."

When we left, I knew he wouldn't be trying anything with me again. He saw a side of me he had never seen. I felt the power now, and that would take me a long way in life.

Mama had warned me to watch out for men like that — but then again, she hated sex, and I knew it every time I listened to them in the bedroom. Dad would beg, promising her things, and she would give in. They didn't know I could hear everything, but hell, how could they not? We rarely had a house that provided much privacy.

While we ate lunch at a truck stop on the edge of Bakersfield, Biff told me that he wanted to take a drive to Tehachapi to visit his sister, which also happened to be near where his wife lived. *What a coincidence,* I thought.

"But why aren't we going home? You told Dad we would be home by Christmas and I just want to go home." I didn't want to whine, so I tried to act as grown up as I could as I shoved French fries into my mouth. The dirty men with fat cheeks and round bellies, sitting on barstools at the counter, stared in my direction, wiggling their eyebrows up and down. One of them winked. I felt their eyes on me and my mini skirt, and for the first time, I didn't want to be stared at. When Biff wasn't looking, I stuck my tongue out at one of them; see how they liked that action. If I could have, I might have given them the finger as well.

"See that," Biff nodded his head toward the smiling men. "The men like you, look at them stare. I bet someday you're gonna be a beauty. A real heartbreaker. Get it while you can, though. Women tend to get fat when they get older and let their looks go to pot."

"Yeah right, that really makes me feel good," I said, letting my frustration show as I finished everything on my plate.

"Too skinny, though. Men like a little meat on their women, something to grab onto, if ya know what I mean."

"Dad's gonna be pissed at you, ya know." I threw a French fry at him and it stuck to the front of his shirt. I watched it slide down and land on his lap.

"Whatdya do that for?"

"Fuck off," was all I could think of to say, and it made me feel better.

Chapter 23

Tehachapi was a filthy little desert town in California that looked like God had scraped the top of it with a metal rake, then shook out whatever didn't stick and let it fall to earth. The scattering of narrow streets, dust-covered buildings, railroad tracks, and fallen-down houses reminded me of many places I had lived, and the number of towns and houses in between. The only positive thing about this town was the few Christmas lights strung up, which had been whipped severely by the wind, making them look as if they had been thrown up there — that and the men on the corners ringing bells to raise money for the Salvation Army made me want to cry as we drove into town.

"Does your sister have a phone?" I asked, thinking I would call Dad and tell him what Biff was doing — sticking me with his sister while he took off and had fun with his wife.

"Hell no. She doesn't have anything but kids. She's nice, though, and will love having you here," Biff answered as he pulled my bag from the car and pointed toward the door of her house.

Biff's sister, Marilyn, and her family were poorer than we were. She was a string bean of a woman like her brother, with hair pulled back in a tight bun, tugging on the wrinkles that had formed around her eyes. She wore a simple dress with a torn hem and flip-flops. Her house sat near the tracks, and the house was covered in layers of dirt from the yard. The porch was collapsing on one corner and the paint had long since chipped off of the entire house.

The inside of her house was filled with wooden boxes for chairs and a wooden table scarred across the top with one leg held on with electrical tape. She was a single mom, living on welfare with her three children, and she was friendly — I think she was happy that I would be staying with her for a while. At first, I was shy around her family and just wanted to get the hell out of there. But eventually, she made me feel at home.

She was outgoing, joked a lot, and welcomed me right into her family. If nothing else, she made me forget about my homesickness.

Since I was the oldest, Marilyn let me help her out with her young kids, and each day she showed me new ways to feed a family with little food and no money. Of course, she was preaching to the choir when it came to that. There was one thing she did that I found amazing, and that was to stretch a can of tuna fish so far she could feed an army. Like making soup out of a stone, she produced enough each day for everyone. I was impressed, but still felt sorry for them — even wishing I could go into houses and steal food for her, as I did in Hamilton. I may have to introduce Mama to her tuna techniques.

"It's all about the mayonnaise. You add enough, you can get six sandwiches out of a can, maybe more," she said, laughing as we sat around the table on my third day there. And she did — every day and every night until I began to hate tuna fish sandwiches.

When Biff left — supposedly out to sell — she spent hours showing me photos and talking to me about womanly things, like my period, having babies, and getting a boyfriend. I told her I didn't think about boys much, while, in fact, I did. At night, the sound of the trains screeching to a halt and changing cars reminded me of Dillon.

When Christmas Eve rolled around with still no sign of Biff, I wanted to call home, but there was no phone in the house and I didn't have money for a payphone. I didn't know if Biff had called Dad like he said he would, or if anyone at home even knew where I was. I knew they would be frantic by now, especially Mama.

"Marilyn, when is Biff coming back? I was supposed to be home by now. Mama's favorite time of year is Christmas. She's childlike when it comes to that, I know, but I still want to be there." I didn't want to tell her how childlike Mama really was, or about her tantrums. I tried not to sound like I was complaining. Dad always said when you were at someone else's house you don't complain — you help them clean, and you do as they do. "I mean, I just wondered since my mom and dad wanted me to be back before Christmas."

Marilyn looked at me while spreading sheets of bread with a thin layer of tuna mayonnaise and said, "Well, all I can tell you is that Biff is a free spirit. He comes and goes and ain't none of us who know when he'll show up. How do they say that? Oh yeah, he's like a penny that just keeps showing up." She laughed until she saw that her attempt at a joke didn't stir me. "It's O.K., Judy, he'll be here soon, don't worry. And besides, you can help me get the turkey ready. Welfare gave me a bird and all the trimmings so we can make a good dinner tomorrow, and if he ain't here, the more for us." The only thing remotely Christmas like in her house was a little Charlie Brown tree that sat in the corner with a string of lights and some silver tinsel.

Biff showed up that night with a big bag of candy for the kids and a bottle of whiskey for him and his sister. When he sat down to pour himself a glass, I saw my chance to ask him a few questions.

"Where did you go and why aren't we heading home?" I gritted my teeth the way Mama did and locked my jaw while my eyes penetrated him. I wanted to keep my cool because I was afraid if I didn't, I would never get home.

"Aw, settle down little one. We'll leave after Christmas dinner tomorrow. I called your Dad; he's O.K. with it and says they'll wait for you to open presents."

"Did you tell them where I was?"

"I told him you were with my sister and it was better to be there than out hitting the streets with me." His eyes were beginning to float and I could tell the alcohol was kicking in.

"Did you sell all the jade?"

"No, I tried. I sold a little, but no one wants it right now. Money's tight." After he said that I went and looked in the car. and the trunk, and besides a few small pieces, there was no jade to be seen. I stormed back into the house and, when Marilyn left the room to put the kids to bed, I walked over to the table and sat down near Biff. I was at the point where I didn't care about my cool anymore. If I had to, I would hitch-hike home.

"You're a liar. There isn't any jade left." I could feel my eyes squinting and my Irish temper getting the best of me.

"Sure there is. I left it at a friend's house and will pick it up later. What are you, the jade police?" With that, he laughed until I wanted to reach over and smack him.

"You just wait until my Dad finds out. I hope he kicks your fucking ass," I whispered — so Marilyn couldn't hear how nasty my mouth could be.

Biff laughed, took another big gulp of whiskey, and winked at me.

The next morning, everyone awoke and gathered around the scrawny tree — after I had helped stuff the bird and pop it in the oven — to open presents. I saw how small and hopeful the kids were. They were like we used to be at Christmas. The oldest one, Mike, grabbed a present that Marilyn held out for him. He ripped it open and saw a tablet and pencils. Each kid got the same thing and it reminded me of some of the presents we got as kids. Usually pajamas.

I watched until they were almost done, then Marilyn handed me a tiny wrapped present, a toothbrush. "Merry Christmas, Judy. And thank you for all your help here." I sat there holding back tears while the family laughed and ate candy from their stockings. I had to go to the bathroom to wipe my eyes and hoped no one noticed me.

It was nice seeing the kids happy and laughing. That's what Christmas was all about in our world, and the thought of it made me feel grown up in some way. I was happy because these kids, although poor, were not gypsies; these kids had a home, as trashy as it was. They didn't spend Christmas on the road, and they didn't go without a Christmas.

When Biff and I finally edged our way up the mountain to Pulga, I felt a burden lifting from my shoulders. I was so happy to be home that I didn't tell Dad all the things I wanted to say about Biff. Mama was so excited she ran me over to the tree right away where Linda, Bonnie, and Gary sat, obviously anxious for me to open my presents, the only ones left. I tore the paper off and laughed at the stuffed animals. I didn't care what the presents were, I was just happy to be home. I heard Biff and Dad talking in the kitchen and it sounded like the beginning of an argument. The next Day Biff was gone.

Mama hated living in Pulga, which wasn't surprising since most of us did as well. She complained that there weren't any women to hang out with, there was no TV, and no shops to visit — not even a decent grocery store. The store was so small, not more than eight people could fit into it at once. The wood floor was splintered and the counters half- empty since supplies only came once a week. The lady who ran the store told me the town used to be hopping when the railroaders lived here. But right now, it was boring.

It would still be several months before Bonnie had her baby. She and Gary were already picking out names and Bonnie was even crocheting a tiny sweater in a neutral color since they didn't know the gender yet. I still had a hard time picturing Gary even holding a baby, let alone changing diapers or feeding one. He still had that gangly look, with a bush of hair down to his collar and a wild streak like many of our other family members. I remember the days not that long ago when Gary and I would pretend we were Sonny and Cher and sing together when Mama and Dad were gone. He was Bucky Beaver and I was Judith Priest, and we thought we would make it big in the world of entertainment.

Bonnie had only been to a clinic twice since we moved to Pulga. There was a free woman's clinic in Oroville where they said everything was fine and her baby was healthy. Dad said he wanted to get off the mountain soon so they could have the baby in a hospital. Maybe we would move back to Hamilton or Dillon in early spring, he said. I didn't care where it was, as long as it wasn't here.

When my friends from Montana wrote to me, their letters were filled with exciting stories about smoking pot and going to teen dances — and some kids, Helen said, had gone to Haight Ashbury to be a part of the whole hippie movement. All I could tell them about was my mind-numbing trip to sell rocks.

Dad and Linda still seemed infatuated with the mine and the surroundings. When it wasn't raining, they walked up the mountain, where Dad gave Linda his undivided attention. I was glad to see that they had become closer, but I could tell that it made Mama jealous.

While Dad, Linda, and I played cards one afternoon for lack of anything else to do, Dad still oozed that *chasing-a-rainbow* attitude. He said he wanted the mine to work out and still thought it would, come spring, even though we had all agreed it was a nowhere road.

"You're going to be a miner like your old, fat dad, aren't you, Injun?" Dad asked Linda while he shuffled the cards.

"No, I'm going to be a carpenter. I'm going to build us a house so we can stay in one place for a change."

I had to laugh at her dream. Linda was able to open up with Dad, and it was obvious they enjoyed each other. She was the happiest when she was near him. She never complained about the treatment she got from Mama, either — in fact, she rarely mentioned it. She still spent a lot of time alone entertaining herself, but the older she got, the more she opened up. When she got nervous, she no longer made the circle with her thumb and index finger, instead ignoring everything around her.

While the rain continued to pour down, making it impossible to walk the mountain, Dad said it was time to get the hell out of there. He was too sick to do anything anyhow. When his chest pains grew bad enough for him to complain about it, Mama said he needed to see a doctor.

"You're so damn stubborn. You might be having a heart attack. You need to get in there," Mama said. Her hair rested in pin curls stuck on top of her head with bobby pins, and her face and eyes were sunken. She had always had dark circles under eyes, like a raccoon, but they had never been this bad. She looked almost as sick as Dad and had let herself go. I wasn't sure how often she took a shower, but I knew it wasn't regularly. And since there was no place to wash clothes — unless you went into Oroville — most of ours were dirty.

"Can't afford it, you know that." Dad coughed and tried to change the subject by talking about what he was going to make for dinner, but Mama wouldn't give in this time. It made me proud that she was sticking to her convictions for a change.

"You don't need money if you go to the emergency room at the *hospital*. Besides, if you die, we'll be stuck on this damn mountain alone." Mama looked as if every bit of joy had been leached out of her. Besides playing an occasional game of cards, she just sat around waiting to move, counting the days as if that would make time go faster.

Dad's face turned a soft gray and the lines around his eyes and in the hollows of his cheeks formed deep crevices. He no longer had a sparkle in his eyes the way he usually did, and he had also stopped talking about where and when to move. The road left his mind and it was a little scary.

When Dad finally was too sick to worry about his pride or the cost of the doctor, he asked Gary and me to drive him down the mountain to the hospital in Oroville. We all piled in the car; Gary, Bonnie, and I in the front seat and Mama, Dad, and Linda in the back. The tides had turned, and now we were in the driver's seat. Gary jumped behind the wheel, since he was the only one besides Dad who had a license.

When Dad got in the car, I saw the exhausted look on his face and knew this was more serious than any of us had thought. I didn't allow myself to think about what would happen to the family if anything happened to him. Would we continue to travel like road Gypsies or would we settle somewhere? I couldn't imagine Mama being able to take care of herself. The thought of one of us living with her and taking care of her flitted through my mind until I brushed it away.

The drive was long, but the excitement of getting off the mountain made it all worth it, even though it was not a time for fun. We had gone into the city just a few times for supplies since moving to Pulga — mainly because money for gas was tight and the little store supplied enough of what we needed.

When we got to the hospital, we walked through the admissions area while everyone stared at us like we were aliens, and then they admitted Dad and put him in a simple room where he would get tests and medication. We sat in the waiting room except for Mama, who stayed in the room with him.

"Think he's going to die?" Linda asked with a shaky voice. All of a sudden she seemed so grown up. Her hair no longer hung in long, matted strings, but was smooth and shorter since Dad had cut and thinned it. Her skin was dark, and her face chiseled and beautiful. I saw the worry in her large brown eyes as tears crept into the corners.

"No," I said. "He's tough and nothing's going to happen to him. Right?" I looked at Gary to back me up.

"Oh, hell no. He's a tough old bastard. He's gonna outlive us all," Gary said.

Bonnie rolled her eyes and looked as if she was going to die of boredom. She had cut her hair and it looked the way mine used to look when Dad cut it; like he'd put a bowl around it before he started. I could tell she was fed up with our entire family lifestyle, and if we didn't get back to Montana soon, she might go crazy — or at least divorce Gary and move on.

Mama came out of the room an hour or so later with a haggard look on her face.

She had taken all the bobby pins out of her hair, and the curls bounced around on her head like they were alive. Her hair was getting so thin I could almost see her scalp. She said Dad would not get tests run until later in the afternoon. So, after going into the room to visit with Dad for a while, Gary, Bonnie, and I took off to explore Oroville. Linda preferred to stay and read a book near Dad, and Mama said she would stay and keep him company until the nurses came to take him for tests.

Since we didn't have any money, we mainly window-shopped. I stole some lipstick and thought Bonnie was going to jump out of her skin when we got back to the car and I pulled it out to paint my lips.

"Why do you do that?" she screamed. "You're going to get caught and end up in jail. Then we'll all go to jail." I couldn't believe how much she freaked out.

I looked at her the way I usually did; as if she and Mama were created from the same mold. "Cool your jets, Bonnie. It's not like we haven't done it before. Right, Gary?"

"That's right. Hey, let's see if we can pool our money and get something at that Dairy Queen over there." Gary rummaged through his pockets and I did the same with my small bag. Between the three of us, we had enough money to buy a banana split, which we savored in the afternoon sun.

When we got back to the hospital, they had already run a few tests on Dad. Although one of his arteries was slightly narrowed, there was nothing they could do except give him medication to reduce the pains and run more tests. Since he didn't have insurance, I'm sure that had a lot to do with the lack of treatment. This had been only the third time I could remember Dad being sick enough to seek medical care.

For the next two days, we drove up and down the mountain to visit him, selling a few small chunks of jade to a rock shop for gas money. At least my marketing skills were giving us enough money to live on.

On the third day when we arrived at the hospital, Dad was being released and the room was filled with nurses bustling about, making the beds and cleaning. Dad sat on the edge of the bed looking almost as white as the sheet. He smiled, but it was faint and I think he was trying to make us believe that he was all right and everything would be O.K.

"Your husband's too pigheaded," the nurse told Mama while we roamed the room to see if there was anything we could take home. "He needs to take better care of his heart. He should have come in a long time ago."

The smells floating into the room from the hallway were a combination of what could have been vegetable soup and sandwiches. Whatever it was, it made me hungry; we all hoped they would offer us something to eat, but they didn't.

"Oh, I know that. But getting him to go isn't easy," Mama said, gathering a few of Dad's things and stuffing them in a sack, then starting the paperwork a nurse had handed her. I helped her fill it out, knowing it would all be too confusing for her.

"Make sure he follows this diet, too."

We all agreed we'd help him stick to the diet that she highlighted on a sheet of paper. The diet consisted of salads, fruit, fish, and vegetables. *Yeah, right,* I thought, knowing ice cream, butter, and greasy fried foods were his favorite things in the world.

On the ride home, I stopped at the rock shop again and pulled out a few chunks of jade. Dad almost demanded he go inside with me, but I told him to stay in the car; he didn't need to be moving around so soon.

The shop owner reluctantly agreed to buy a few more chunks — but that was it, since he hadn't been able to sell the others yet. He asked, "What the hell do you do with this money little lady? I bet you buy all kinds of teenage things, huh?" I couldn't even answer such a stupid question. If he only knew.

We stopped for gas and got what we needed for Dad's new diet. I fixed salads for him every day with lots of veggies, dry cottage cheese, and tuna. In the morning I made oatmeal and whole-wheat toast, but within two weeks he was back to eating the way he always had.

"Hell, you only live once, may as well enjoy it. Right kids?" When he said it like that, it was hard for us to say no.

Chapter 24

Within a few months, as winter bowed out, Dad agreed we would move back to Montana. He figured the mine was no longer going to make him money, and it was time to let it go. He couldn't have said it soon enough, as Gary, Bonnie, and I had started making plans to get enough money together to take a bus back.

Dad sold the mine to one of Tiny's friends, a man named Bill who took a liking to Dad. He agreed to sell the mine for $1,000, which to us might as well have been a million. It was like a light from above had gone off and we were saved from the dismal, hopeless life on the mountain. We all screamed and cheered. Mama said it was about time, then went into her room, pulled boxes from the closet, and started packing. It didn't take long for all of us to do the same.

On the road back to Dillon, all I could think of were the friends I had left there. And it was close enough to Hamilton that we would be able to see our friends there, too.

The sky seemed to grow the closer we got. Soon the horizon spread out, dotted with wildflowers and little dollops of snow around the trees. Gary's baby was due in just a couple of months and that's all they talked about in the crowded car. It was almost impossible to talk about anything else, and the closeness was getting to me. Bonnie was happy but insisted on using the payphone every time we stopped to tell her mother about the ragged group of nomads who were bringing her back. I told myself it was about time one of the unwavering, settled folks saw how the other half lived.

The rains had subsided, and the pleasing smell of pine surrounded us when we stopped for dinner. I wrapped my hair on top of my head, went outside, lifted my hands toward the clouds, and felt the cool mist on my face. I felt grown up; it seemed like it happened overnight. Too many things had transpired that *made* me grow up fast.

Breaking away from friends was hard, but that was one of the challenges of change. Some of my friends accepted changes in their lives, but a lot of people never do. I think I accepted it more than anyone I knew, and that is something that would always stay with me.

Thank you, Great Spirit, I thought as I breathed in the hints of a better day. I was happy to get off the mountain but also happy that Dad's health seemed to be improving, regardless of his diet. He was back to eating bologna sandwiches on white bread spread thick with butter and mayonnaise.

Before we moved, I made a couple of trips alone to Oroville and outlying towns to sell rocks. I still didn't have my driver's license, but Dad said not to worry about it since I was such a good driver. I was getting good at selling now and was not about to go back to Montana broke, even though dad had plenty of money now. Since Gary went with me to sell, we split the money.

Dillon hadn't changed: same old people lying around the depot yard, same old "Boomers" lined up at the bars on Main Street, same old good friends. We spent the summer catching up with friends, barely spending time at home. I felt free and unrestricted, spreading my wings to a whole new world. I even got to see Helen and Alice occasionally when they would take Helen's mother's car and come to Dillon. They kept me informed of what I was missing, and I told them I would be there soon enough — I just needed to graduate first.

Dad's health seemed somewhat stable, but I could still tell he was sick. He was back to his old ways, pounding nails for money throughout the summer and into the fall. Gary worked with him, and I was envious since my rock selling days were over for the time being.

When autumn leaves scattered the ground and the small college in town opened up, I learned that hanging out with college kids was more fun than hanging out with high school students, and a whole new world opened up to me. Spending time around intellectuals revealed to me all the things I still had to learn. I never took school seriously with the way my family traveled, but now I was meeting people my age or older who were ambitious and lusted for knowledge, and I wanted to be one of them.

Since Gary and Bonnie had already given birth to a baby girl, I spent a good deal of time over at their house, not too far from our family home. The little girl, Casey, looked just like Gary.

"You look happy," I said to him while visiting on a lunch break. Rather than hanging out at the school cafeteria every day, I chose to go to Gary's for lunch or home to listen to Paul Harvey.

"It won't be that long, and you'll be married with a kid of your own. You'll love it . . ."

I had never seen Gary so "settled" or calm. He talked about giving up traveling and staying in one place. "I'm not raising this baby the way we were raised, Judy. I'm done. I want to give her what we never had — friends forever, a home where we stay until she's out of school.

"Then you should," I said. I watched the three of them, and I hoped Gary could find a way to settle down. But I knew traveling was in our blood.

Chapter 25

We stayed in Dillon longer than we had in most places. The sprawling autumn days seeped into winter when the snow flew. For once, we had good heat inside and it wasn't so bad. Dad was sick a lot and none of us knew what to do. He wouldn't quit smoking or working, and on his last job had fallen through the roof and pulled ligaments in his arms, but he continued working until he couldn't anymore. His body was giving out, he said.

My school days were more fun than I thought they would be. At a college dance one night, I met a guy a few years older than me, and we started dating. He was not my type, but he seemed to want to hang out with me. Maybe a little too much. I finally met a guitar player my age named George who was in a band. Occasionally I went to watch him practice. I liked him and knew that he liked me even though we had never had an official date. But every time I tried to do something with him, or anyone for that matter, including my friend Martha, the college guy I met from the dance, Jess, could not leave me alone and followed me around in his car. I was glad for the attention, but at the same time I felt overwhelmed by his presence and demanding ways. He was three years older and intimidated me. He tried to get in my pants from the minute I met him, but I was good at deflecting his advances. Dates were a struggle, but I was beginning to like him — or maybe he just intimidated me.

I filled my senior year with things like the Future Homemakers of America and the cheerleading squad. Since I had never had the chance to do these things before, I was happy to give them a try. With Dad being sick, I knew we were staying at least until I graduated.

"What have you been doing, Linda?" I asked one day since I hadn't seen her for a while. We sat on the back porch watching the last leaves fall from trees, where snow had already traced the limbs.

She looked at me with her big brown eyes, her smile never leaving her face. "Not much. I spend a lot of time with Gracie. Remember her? She was the one who got pregnant by a Job Corps guy. She had a boy and treats him like a king."

"I notice you and Mama don't fight a lot anymore. Why is that?"

"She's playing nurse and her role is important," Linda said, followed by laughter. "If I'd have known it was that easy to keep her off my back I would have asked one of you to get sick a long time ago so she could play house nurse." With that, Linda howled with laughter, and I couldn't help but follow suit. I hadn't seen her this happy for a while and it felt good.

"Do you think he's going to die?" Linda asked again. I heard her voice crack and knew she had been worrying about it for some time.

"He's pretty strong. Just hasn't been the same since he fell through the roof on his job. He's tough, though. I'm sure he'll pull through, but . . ."

"That's what everyone says. But when you have a few heart attacks, it's not good. He needs to go to the doctor. But he just complains about the money all the time." Linda said.

I watched the sun slide behind Pioneer Mountain and knew it must be getting close to five o'clock. "Hey, what time is it? I have to go to the FHA style show soon. I finished my dress at Martha's house. It's pretty, with kind of an Oriental look. I'll show it to you when I get home. Are you going to go to school, or will you be here?" I jumped up and started for the door.

"Not sure. I may go to Gracie's. Well, knock 'em dead anyhow."

I stopped and turned when Linda said that. She was the same little girl with telescope fingers, a tough stature, and unruly hair —

or at least she was to me. But I could see she was blossoming into a butterfly; no more a lost little girl, or so I thought. I walked back and put my arms around her, something neither of us was too familiar with. I hugged her and felt her heart; the heart that Dad knew was good and strong and resilient.

I dropped my arms and looked into her face. I could tell she was shocked but also happy for the hug.

"Don't ever let anyone tell you that you are not beautiful, because you are. Gotta go." I waved and saw the smile on her face before I turned.

I put on the Asian-style dress and looked in the mirror. The orange and brown floral pattern hugged me tight, with a small slit up the side exposing my leg and a little collar surrounding my neck. I pulled my hair to the side and tied it, thinking it gave me a more Asian look.

Before I left for school, I went into the living room to see how Dad was. Mom had just given him some cereal, but it looked like most of it was on the floor. She wiped his chin. His last accident on the roof, the doctor said, had caused a small stroke, but he said it would just be a matter of time before he returned to normal.

"I'm leaving, Mama."

"Where you going? And . . ."

"I'm going to be in the FHA style show. I told you that before. How is Dad doing?" I asked, looking over at him. He smiled when he saw me and waved me over; I could see that he wanted to say something to me. I bent down to listen.

"Don't forget about your stocks and bonds," he whispered.

I looked at Mama, puzzled. We had never had any stocks or bonds that I knew of. "Just go," she said. "He says all kinds of crazy things now. I'll see you when you get home." Somehow the role of nurse suited her. She had a soft, kindness about her now and didn't seem so harsh. I liked the new Mama.

The auditorium was about half-full, for which I was glad. A lot of the people in the audience were guys from high school, parents, and teachers. But there in the front sat Jess, making sure he didn't miss this big event. He waved at me as I went to the back of the stage.

The bright lights made me feel like I was back in Richmond, Idaho in the Christmas play that Dad almost made us miss. My, those memories.

When I walked across the stage, promenading the way the teacher told us to, I heard the yelp of the guys in the audience. It seems they had a crush on me, but never wanted to ask me out, which was fine with me since I thought high school boys were immature. I heard Jess's loud clapping in the front row.

Gary and Bonnie were in the audience, and I heard them cheering, too — as if it was a beauty pageant. I waved goodbye to them when the program was over and left.

Jess took me home so I could change my clothes. We planned to go to the A&W for a drink and then probably park somewhere, knowing him. I wasn't sure I wanted to do that, because I didn't feel the same about him as he did about me.

"I'll go change. I'll be quick," I said to him as I shut the car door. Since we lived in a two-story duplex, I had to pass the downstairs neighbor's door to go up the stairs to our apartment. As I was about to take a flying run up the stairs, the neighbor opened the door. She yelled my name and I stopped.

"Judy, Judy! Something has happened." She spoke broken English and it was hard to understand her. "The ambulance came and took your father away. I'm sorry. Your mom went with them. Can I help you . . ."

I didn't hear the rest. I darted up the stairs as fast as I could. Hoping for what? To see my dad where he was when I left him? There was no door on our apartment upstairs and when I walked in there wasn't anyone inside. The silence was deafening. I turned, not knowing what to do. Go to the hospital?

I ran from the room and down the stairs. The excitement of the night faded, and when I walked outside, snow was falling in big flakes. I put my face up to the sky and let the snow cover it as my tears flowed.

The dilapidated hospital in Dillon was close to our house. The exterior had long ago fallen apart. Jess dropped me off and I ran up to the receptionist, asking for the room number. She stared at me, gave me the number, and wanted me to sign in. I didn't wait for her to give me the paperwork to fill out. I ran up two flights of stairs before stopping.

The hospital was nearly empty — no doubt it was on its way out. I went to the third floor and ran down the hall, where I saw Mama sitting on a bench outside the door, rocking and crying.

"Mama, what's going on?" I hugged her around the shoulders. "What's happening? Where is Dad?"

"He's in that room. The doctors said they would be back, but they just left him there, said they'd be back in the morning. I don't know . . ." She was sobbing so hysterically I could barely understand her.

I looked at the closed door, with the sign that said *Do Not Enter*. I stormed through, wondering why Mama was sitting out there instead of in here. I walked over to the bed. Dad's face was white and he lay there, stiff, as if in a coffin. No expression, no color to him at all. I was young and had not been around dead people much. I knew that with no doctors or nurses around, he had died in the quiet room where they left him for the night. I touched his face — it was cold, but I wanted him to know I was there. I wanted him to feel my touch. I think he did, but maybe I was hopeful for no reason. I smoothed his hair and kissed him on the forehead.

I took Mama to stay with her friend Georgia, then called Gary. We met up and agreed there was nothing we could do for Mama. She was frantic, shaking, and making no sense. The doctor gave her pills to calm her down and I made sure she took one before I left. Georgia's house — sitting between two sets of railroad tracks, where her husband worked — reeked of old cigars and smoke from the coal stove.

I asked Gary to give me a ride home. He invited me to come and stay overnight with him, but I was worried about Linda and had to get back to tell her the news. My mind was in a state of dishevelment. I went right home, got in bed, and cried as I have never cried before. Linda was gone, and the house was silent. It seemed my whole world was falling apart. Dad, the leader of our pack, the man who gave us the life we had — left us. I curled into a ball and cried myself to sleep.

Chapter 26

Morning light crept through the window in the living room while we all ran around, frantically deciding what to wear and making sure we wouldn't be late. Mama came out wearing a floral shirt with plaid pants. She had combed her hair and placed barrettes to keep it in place, which I admit looked better than her bobby pins. I went over to her and touched her shoulder. She jumped. I looked into her face and felt sorry for her. Dad was her whole world, all that she knew.

"You O.K., Mama? Are you sure you want to wear that blouse with those pants? I mean, it's O.K   "

"Daddy never cared how I dressed. He wouldn't care what I wore to anything, especially his funeral." She stormed off.

"It's O.K., Mama, you wear what you want, but we have to hurry."

Mama, Linda, and I walked into the funeral home, where Gary and Bonnie were waiting. My Great Grandma Moore sat in the front with her sister, my Great Aunt Madie. Cousin George, Uncle Bud, and a few other relatives sat in silence. I recognized most of them. We sat down and I looked from one person to the other, asking myself why these people hadn't kept in touch with Dad when he was alive. Why did they come to his *funeral* when they could have known his laughter, his smile that went all the way around his face? And why did I feel disembodied, like I was above the small crowd, watching from the ceiling?

The preacher said a few words about Dad and what a great man he was, when in reality, he didn't even know him. I wanted to stand up and yell, but I didn't want to spoil the gathering. I would tell him on the way out, I decided.

After the services, we gathered at our landlady's house. She put out a spread for the people who came. I couldn't understand this custom. I wanted to yell and scream that Dad would not have wanted this. But what *would* he have wanted? I sat at the table, looking at the food and not wanting any of it. I wanted my father back — that's what I wanted.

A few months after the funeral, we all tried to get our lives back together.

When spring crocuses started to pop up, Mama decided it was a good time to start hitting the bars, going out with her friend Georgia, and staying out late. Since she had never consumed much alcohol in her life, it was like watching a teenage girl starting to date.

She didn't even wait four months for Dad to be gone. It was as if she had to find someone to take his place, no matter who it was she brought home — so far it had only been one, but something told me there would be more.

While sitting on the lawn on a crisp spring day, I told Gary about the Boomer Mama brought home with her the other night. Gary said he would stop by in the evening to make sure she didn't do it again. "If it's that scrawny guy with the guitar, I'll kick his ass," he said.

"It is. The same one who came over that afternoon to howl and play on the porch."

As I lay there, looking up at the solemn blue skies, feeling the grass on the back of my head, I wondered what our lives were going to be like now that Dad was gone. "Hey, you gonna graduate or what?" Gary asked. "Isn't it about that time?"

"Nope. Got called in last week. I don't have enough credits to graduate and would have to come back in the fall. Fuck that if they think I'm coming back."

"But Judy, you're smart. You need to get an education."

"You are too, Gary. Why don't you give it another try? I'm not giving up; I'm just giving up at the school."

"I can't. I have a kid, a family now and . . ."

"Never say never. You can do anything you want, Gary. Remember when Dad used to say that. Of course, he wanted me to be a beautician, but other than that . . ."

"What are you going to do, Judy?"

"I don't know, but I'm not going to travel around anymore, that's for sure. Are you?"

"No, I'm settled."

"Will we always be? Settled, I mean. Or are we going to get the wanderlust and chase rainbows, Gary?"

He gave me a puzzled look. "Not unless we want to."

I plucked a blade of grass, put it to my mouth, and blew on it. A screech came out, and soon we were both blowing and screeching and feeling like we were kids again. Then we sat up.

"You know how Grandpa Virgil lives in Escondido?" I asked. "Remember the oranges?"

"Yeah. I remember his place. He must be rich," Gary said, dusting his legs off. "I think I should take Mama there. Maybe she'd quit being a barfly. We're supposed to get Dad's Social Security check soon, that's what Mama says, and there will be enough for me to buy a car. Nothing great, just something that will get us to California. What do you think?"

"You mean you'd stay there? What about me and . . . ?"

"No, unload the U-Haul, get Mama and Linda settled in and all that, then head back here. Either that or I'm going to the dance school there, and it would be paid for and. . . "

"You can do it," Gary said. "Taking them, I mean. Just don't go making the road your lifestyle. Come back."

"I will," I said, making a face at him.

We agreed that once I got a car, I would take Mama and Linda to Escondido, thinking maybe Grandpa Virgil would take her under his wing. Gary said he would help me hook up the U-Haul.

A few days later, Helen and Alice came to spend the night and hang out before I left.

"You're not gonna get there and meet some hot guy and not come back, are you?" Helen asked as we sat at Skeet's Café having a Coke. They were both excited about graduation and let me know how sorry they were that I wouldn't be graduating. I assured them that I was fine and would find another way to get an education.

"Are you kidding? I've had enough of the road to last a lifetime. I'll be back as soon as I can." I knew these friends would always be in my life.

When the Social Security money came, I had enough to buy a beige Studebaker Lark station wagon. Gary and my cousin George checked it out, and I bought it. I had already talked to Linda and Mama about the trip, and I knew that Mama would agree to go — no matter where I told her we were going. Linda easily accepted our road trip, even without Dad this time. After all, why *wouldn't* we be heading out?

When Jess and I went out the night before I left, he tried to talk me out of leaving. "I thought you'd stay here. I'm almost done with school for the year."

"I can't. Not now. I told you why I have to leave. It could be a matter of life and death for my mom. I need to get her out of here. But I'll be back," I said as he reached his hand down my blouse.

His kisses were aggressive. And when I kissed him back, I felt he knew he could have his way with me tonight. And he did. When it was over, I was no longer a virgin, no longer a naïve kid — but rather one who could tell her friends what sex was like, as we all agreed we would. Maybe I just felt I owed it to him since I was leaving and he wasn't happy about it. Regardless, I left that night and told him I would write.

The next day, when early morning light covered the car, and the U-Haul was almost hooked up, it was time to go. Mama got her sweater — a different one this time (but still red) — and climbed into the front seat the way she had for many years. I bought her clothes before we left and she looked cute in her pedal pushers and t-shirt. Linda crawled in the back; this time there were only boxes on the floor covered with a blanket. She had the best seat in the house.

Our dog, Tramp, squeezed in the back with Linda, and Mama's only remaining cat sat in the front with her.

Chapter 27

I had never driven a car with a U-Haul trailer hooked up to it. But it was a smaller trailer than before, and because I had seen it done so many times, I took to it like a pig to mud.

At first, the thought of driving the entire way to California was daunting. I had a map but didn't need to use it since I had done this so many times before. When we got closer to Johannesburg, Mama said she wanted to stop and see the Robertson's, some family friends. I found myself kind of excited to see our old friends, and so we agreed we would spend two days there. Mama and her friend Mary tramped up and down the narrow streets in the little wasted town while Linda and I talked to our friends about our travels since we had last seen them. They already knew about Dad. I saw that Linda was happy — maybe the happiest I'd seen her in months. She acted like she was home again. And before we went to bed that night, she and her friend Louise begged the moms to let Linda stay and live there for a few weeks. Mary agreed right away.

"Oh come on, Alice, let her stay. Look how happy she is here. She's been through a lot and needs her friends." Mary had a way of talking Mama into almost anything. So it was decided: Linda would stay with them and take a bus home.

"I'm gonna miss you," I said to Linda as we gathered around the car to say goodbye. She looked at me with a smile on her face, and it was good to feel her happiness.

"I'll miss you too. Don't let Mama get to you. At least I won't be there to stir up trouble."

"You never stirred up trouble. Mama just liked to see how she could get to you. I won't be staying there that long, once we get there I mean. We'll get a place and once Mama's settled in, I'm heading back to Montana. Keep in touch and I'll let you know where I am so you can come there." We hugged and I felt the strength of her body and her power, then Mama walked over and hugged Linda. I could almost swear I saw a tear in her eyes.

"Take care of yourself, Linda. Stay out of trouble. You hear me? I love you."

"I will," she said, walking back to the house with her friends. I don't know about Linda, but I was both shocked and happy that Mama said what she did to Linda.

We all waved at each other, then Mama and I took off through the desert on our way to the Escondido area. Little did I know then that it would be years before I saw Linda again.

It was a much different trip with just the two of us, and it made me wonder what it would be like if it was just me. I sloughed off the thought, telling myself not to think about it because as soon as I got the chance I would be heading back to Montana to settle down.

We ended up in Oceanside, and it didn't take long to find a cottage close to the beach. I followed Dad's routine and walked up to a door with a *For Rent* sign. After paying the rent and getting the keys, we walked into the tiny three-room cottage and looked around.

"Well, we've lived in smaller," Mama said, putting down her sweater and bag. She made the clicking sound with her tongue, but I could tell she liked the idea of living here, especially after meeting the neighbor woman who had invited her for coffee in the morning.

Within a few weeks, Grandpa Virgil came and picked us up for lunch. I told him I wouldn't be staying around for more than a few weeks or month before heading back to Montana. Since he loved the thought of Montana, he said he couldn't blame me a bit. He said he would keep an eye on Mama after I left.

Before the month was out, before making plans to leave, the smell of food started making me sick. I could barely eat without becoming nauseous. I wasn't sure what was happening, and since Mama was rarely around — frequenting the bars almost every night — there was no one I could talk to. I wanted to take off, feeling the traveling bug growing inside of me. But the more I thought of it, the more I thought maybe something else was growing inside of me. I was not so ignorant that I didn't know what morning sickness was.

I longed to get on the road and go where my heart led me. The hot summer days were luring me outside and back to the place I loved, to Gary and my friends. I didn't want to miss the summer. As it was, I felt I had missed out on a lot in my youth. But then again, maybe I had actually grown from it. Maybe I wanted more in life because of it.

Who knows? I just knew I had to go.

Did that mean I was getting the bug? The bug that pulled our family in all directions across the country? I vowed I would not let that insect push my life in all directions. I longed to be in a house with big windows and a two-way door so I could come and go as I pleased. Not because I had to. I refused to believe I would let the road lead me and promised myself to be settled and travel for vacations only, as Linda had wanted.

Or would I? As long as I had anything to say about it, I would.

I left on a hot sunny day. Mama walked me to the car and I could see that my leaving was affecting her. Linda had not returned yet but she wrote us notes from Mary's house. She would come and help Mama and we would all get together soon, we said.

The road felt good under my wheels as the sun shone down on me through the car windows. For the first time, I alone was doing what I had done all my life; following the winding road. Feeling the stirring inside me. I was ready for what life handed me.

Whatever it may be.

I smelled the air change the closer I got to Montana. The scent of Big Sky Country filled my nose. And the smell of Home swelled my heart.

I was going home.

JUDI BLAZE

Judi Blaze is a novelist, former print and media journalist, editor, and screenwriter. She has published three novels, a book of short stories, a memoir, and many novels and screenplays in the works.

In her 40 years as a professional writer, she has garnered many awards for her short stories, which have appeared in several anthologies. Her books include:

- Riding on a Rainbow, On Indian Time, Beach People, Normal People are Those We Don't Know Well, and her award-winning memoir, Riding in the Backseat with My Brother. She has been an editor for almost 20 years and has ghostwritten eBooks for others.

- SQUID JIGGERS, a multi-award-winning short story, is now her feature-length screenplay based on the story. She has also written six short screenplays: Roommates, Sign on the Bloody Line, Baby's Gone, Stealing Sobriety, Your Secrets Will Get You High, and Nightmare in a Jar.

- Short story Awards:

Willamette Writers Kay Snow short story competition. First Place

American Writing Awards, Finalist, Riding in the Backseat with My Brother

Oregon Writer's Colony 2015. Short Story/script; Honorable mention, Stealing Sobriety.

New Millennium Writing Non-Fiction Finalist, Baby's Gone

Her novel Orchid Island (unpublished) was selected for the University of Southern Florida's anthology. An excerpt from the same novel was selected for the Chick Lit Review.

- Her awards in screenwriting include:

Squid Jiggers:

Screenplay Festival 2018. Honorable Mention, Finalist in the Women in Cinema competition

Semi-Finalist in the Nashville Screenwriters Competition: for her first feature, SQUID JIGGERS, based on her award-winning short story of the same name.

Write Movies Summer Competition: **Quarter Finalist:** Squid Jiggers

Screenplay Festival: Finalist, Squid Jiggers

- Short screenplays:

American Gem; a short screenplay, Sign on the Bloody Line.

2017: Selected to co-write 'Woodstock or Bust' for Big Kid Films, Portland, Oregon. It is a feature released in 2017.

Judi Blaze has been an editor and ghostwriter for the past 12 years, working with Elance and Upwork, where she is a top-rated editor. She has edited hundreds of books in all genres, including novels, non-fiction, short stories, poetry, and self-help books.

She lives in the Pacific Northwest with her dog, where she works on her writing.